Beyond Borders

Beyond Borders

*Stories of Yunnanese
Chinese Migrants of Burma*

Wen-Chin Chang

Cornell University Press
Ithaca and London

The publisher gratefully acknowledges the generous support of the Harvard-Yenching Institute. All royalties earned from sales of this book are donated to the Thabyay Education Foundation (Yangon, Burma) and the Aung Myin Monastery School (Namaw village, Shwe Bo township, Sagaing Region, Burma) to assist their education projects.

Copyright © 2014 by Cornell University

All rights reserved. Except for brief quotations in a review, this book, or parts thereof, must not be reproduced in any form without permission in writing from the publisher. For information, address Cornell University Press, Sage House, 512 East State Street, Ithaca, New York 14850.

First published 2014 by Cornell University Press
First printing, Cornell Paperbacks, 2014
Printed in the United States of America

Library of Congress Cataloging-in-Publication Data

Chang, Wen-Chin, 1964– author.
  Beyond borders : stories of Yunnanese Chinese migrants of Burma / Wen-Chin Chang.
      pages cm
  Includes bibliographical references and index.
  ISBN 978-0-8014-5331-1 (cloth : alk. paper) —
  ISBN 978-0-8014-7967-0 (pbk. : alk. paper)
  1. Burma—Emigration and immigration. 2. China—Emigration and immigration. 3. Thailand—Emigration and immigration. 4. Chinese—Migrations. 5. Chinese—Burma. 6. Muslims—Burma. I. Title.
  DS732. C439   2015
  305.895'10591—dc23   2014019460

Cornell University Press strives to use environmentally responsible suppliers and materials to the fullest extent possible in the publishing of its books. Such materials include vegetable-based, low-VOC inks and acid-free papers that are recycled, totally chlorine-free, or partly composed of nonwood fibers. For further information, visit our website at www.cornellpress.cornell.edu.

Cloth printing   10 9 8 7 6 5 4 3 2 1
Paperback printing   10 9 8 7 6 5 4 3 2 1

To my parents

Contents

Acknowledgments ix

Note on Fieldwork, Names, Transliteration, and Currency xiii

Introduction 1

Part I. Migration History 19

1. The Days in Burma: Zhang Dage 21

2. Entangled Love: Ae Maew 46

3. Pursuit of Ambition, Father and Son 80

4. Islamic Transnationalism: Yunnanese Muslims 114

Part II. (Transnational) Trade 147

5. Venturing into "Barbarous" Regions: Yunnanese Caravan Traders 149

6. Transcending Gendered Geographies:
   Yunnanese Women Traders					176

7. Circulations of the Jade Trade:
   The Duans and the Pengs					207

Epilogue: From Mules to Vehicles				237

Glossary									245

References									255

Index										271

Acknowledgments

I encountered my ethnographic field among migrant Yunnanese by chance while backpacking in northern Thailand during the summer of 1993. The launch of my fieldwork among a Yunnanese migrant community a year later was, however, followed by a series of grave challenges, primarily due to the sensitivity of the research, which almost compelled me to abandon it. Without numerous people's kindness and trust in me, I would not have been able to overcome the initial obstacles and persist on my quest to learn about Yunnanese migrants' history. Although challenges have never ceased, following my informants' networks of connection I have expanded my research field from Thailand to Burma and other places. I owe enormous debts to these informants, and my retelling of their stories in this book is my humble repayment. Unfortunately, I am not able to thank them individually, not only because the thank-you list is too long, but primarily in consideration for their security. In addition to my informants, many local people and scholars in Thailand and Burma have helped me enormously. Again, for safety concerns, I can name only a few here: the late

Bhansoon Ladavalya, Kosum Saichan, Seksin Srivatananukulkit, the late Wantana Yangcharoen, Kanjana Prakatwutthisan, the Chaidans, and the Duans. The unfailing friendship and support of all these people helped me along the way and were essential to my research.

My home institute, Academia Sinica, has funded my research over the last ten years, allowing me to conduct fieldwork every year for about two months. I am deeply grateful for its intellectual and financial backing. I am indebted to colleagues—anthropologists, historians, sociologists, political scientists, and psychologists—here in Taiwan, especially Chang Ying-Hwa, Hsiao Hsin-Huang, Lin Cheng-Yi, Chiang Bien, Ho Tsui-Ping, and Fung Heidi (all from Academia Sinica), and Hsieh Shih-Chung (National Taiwan University). The Center for Geographic Information Science, RCHSS, at Academia Sinica helped produce the maps; I especially wish to thank two cartography specialists at the center, Li Yu-Ting and Liao Hsiung-Ming. Lu Hsin-Chun (Institute of Ethnology, Academia Sinica) was vital in checking the transliteration of the Burmese words and providing the Burmese characters. Eric Tagliacozzo (Cornell University) unhesitatingly shares his ideas and suggestions whenever I seek help.

I began working on this book while I was a Visiting Scholar at the Harvard-Yenching Institute, Harvard University, during the school year of 2007–2008, a year of inspirations. I am grateful for the generosity and continuous support the institute offered under the directorship of Elizabeth J. Perry. Her faith in me and her ongoing encouragement have played a crucial role in this book's publication, facilitated by a publication grant from the institute. Moreover, I benefited enormously from many discussions with Hue-Tam Ho Tai (Harvard University) about my research and writing during the visiting year. She has always been a caring and supportive figure to junior academics. I also thank Michael Herzfeld (Harvard University), who always made himself available whenever I knocked on his door.

I presented some of these chapters at several AAS (Association for Asian Studies) Annual Conferences and at Asian Core Workshops (organized by the Center for Southeast Asian Studies, Kyoto University, and my center). I am grateful for the participants' questions and criticisms. Portions of chapter 5 were published as "Venturing into Barbarous Regions: Transborder Trade among Migrant Yunnanese between Thailand and Burma, 1960s–1980s," *Journal of Asian Studies* 68, no. 2 (2009): 543–72, copyright ©

2009 The Association for Asian Studies, Inc., adapted with the permission of Cambridge University Press. I would like to extend my special thanks to Jennifer Munger, the managing editor of *JAS*. Her interest in my work and concern for Burmese society was a factor in my decision to write this book. It was not an easy task to write in English, as it is not my mother tongue. Dianna Downing and Yumi Selden helped edit both the language and structure of the manuscript before its submission to the press. I am particularly grateful for Dianna's steadfast patience.

Hue-Tam Ho Tai, Glenn May (University of Oregon), Yoko Hayami (Kyoto University), Penny Edwards (University of California, Berkeley), C. Patterson Giersch (Wellesley College), and Wang Gungwu (National University of Singapore) helped read parts of the manuscript and provided constructive critiques. The meticulous review comments from the anonymous referees further led me to sharpen the central theme of the text and articulate theoretical interpretations alongside quoted narratives. Above all, Roger M. Haydon, executive editor at Cornell University Press, has guided each step of the book's reviewing, editing, and production processes. I also wish to thank Sara R. Ferguson, Susan C. Barnett and Glenn Novak at the press. Their patience and professionalism have realized this book's publication. I am greatly indebted to all these people. Any remaining errors are my responsibility.

Finally, I would like to thank my parents. This book is dedicated to them. They have nourished me with their bravery and wisdom, and their unconditional love is the main source of my work and life. Moreover, I owe a debt of gratitude to my eldest sister-in-law, Wu Ching-Ya, for all kinds of assistance she has given me over the years.

Note on Fieldwork, Names, Transliteration, and Currency

My research subjects include primarily Yunnanese Chinese migrants (hereafter Yunnanese migrants) who are residing in Burma (or Myanmar) and secondarily those who have moved from Burma to another country, especially Thailand. The population is composed of both Han Chinese and Muslims. On account of their continuous mobility (in terms of both internal and external migrations), I often use "migrant Yunnanese" in this book. Sometimes I also specify "Yunnanese in Burma," "Yunnanese in Thailand," and so on, depending on the context. Throughout history the Yunnanese have basically undertaken migration from Yunnan in southwestern China to upland Southeast Asia by land; the Yunnanese migrants in the region are thus also referred to as "overland Yunnanese" (Chang 2006; Forbes 1987, 1–2; Hill 1983; Sun 2000, 10). The term is in contrast to "overseas/maritime Chinese." The latter are derived from the coastal provinces of southeastern China, primarily the Hokkien/Fujianese, the Cantonese, and the Hakka, who set off for host countries by sea.

I started my anthropological research among the Yunnanese migrants in northern Thailand in late 1994. According to the Yunnanese Association in Chiang Mai, the estimates of the total population of Yunnanese migrants in Thailand are between 100,000 and 150,000. Most of them are located along the borders of Chiang Rai, Chiang Mai, and Mae Hongson Provinces. Many in the younger generation have relocated to Chiang Mai and Bangkok. In 2000, I extended my fieldwork to Burma (now Myanmar), where a much larger Yunnanese population resides. No accurate population figure is available there, either, but estimates given by informants range from half a million to one million.[1] These estimates also include the Kokang Yunnanese, largely residing in Shan State. My field sites in Burma cover major cities, towns, and villages where Yunnanese migrants are concentrated, primarily in upper Burma. Because of practical constraints, I have however not been able to travel as widely as I wished for field research in the country. Apart from Thailand and Burma, I have also conducted research among Yunnanese who have migrated to Taiwan from Thailand and Burma and returnees to China (many of them investors in Yunnan, Guangzhou, and Hong Kong). The primary field data in this book are collected up to 2010, but later developments in Burma have also been integrated.[2] For data collecting I sometimes took notes, while at other times I used a tape recorder or, in later days, an MP3 recorder, depending on the situation.

Yunnanese in Burma and Thailand normally address each other with affiliated terms based on the kinship principle. Terms such as "Mr." and "Mrs." are used formally for people with some social status. Learning to address people correctly was the first step in my fieldwork. In this book, I refer to the narrators in the way I addressed them in the field. However, out of respect to teachers in Chinese society, most of my informants address me as "Teacher Chang."

All the informants' names given in this book are pseudonyms. Sometimes I have had to change the narrators' residential locations or professions in order to disguise their identification. Interview dates are indicated only when they will not compromise the interviewees' safety. I use the pinyin Romanization for transliteration of Chinese characters.

---

1. The estimate of the total population of the ethnic Chinese in Burma (including both overland Yunnanese and maritime Chinese) given by the CIA is about 1.65 million, accounting for 3 percent of the whole nation's population; see https://www.cia.gov/library/publications/the-world-factbook/geos/bm.html (last access date October 2, 2013).

2. The accumulated time on fieldwork from 1994 to 2010 is thirty-six months.

There are no standard transliterations for names of places in Burma. Some places changed names after 1988. I use new names in this book but add old names in brackets when they appear the first time. Some places share the same name, or the same place has different names. For example, "Panglong" is the name for the famous Shan town where the "Panglong Agreement" was signed in 1947. It is also the name for an important place that Yunnanese Muslims resettled after fleeing from Yunnan in the wake of the Muslim Rebellion (1856–1873 CE). As the first "Panglong" is also called "Pinlong," I use the latter name in order to distinguish it from the Yunnanese Muslims' "Panglong."

Kyat is Burmese currency. Its exchange rate with US dollars is 780 kyat to one dollar in June 2011. (It was around 1,000 kyat to one dollar two years earlier.) Baht is Thai currency. Its exchange rate with US dollars is 30.4 baht to one dollar in June 2011. NT (new Taiwan dollar) is the Taiwanese currency. Its exchange rate with US dollars is 28.7 NT to one dollar in June 2011. RMB (renminbi) is Chinese currency. Its exchange rate with US dollars is 6.39 RMB to one dollar in August 2011.

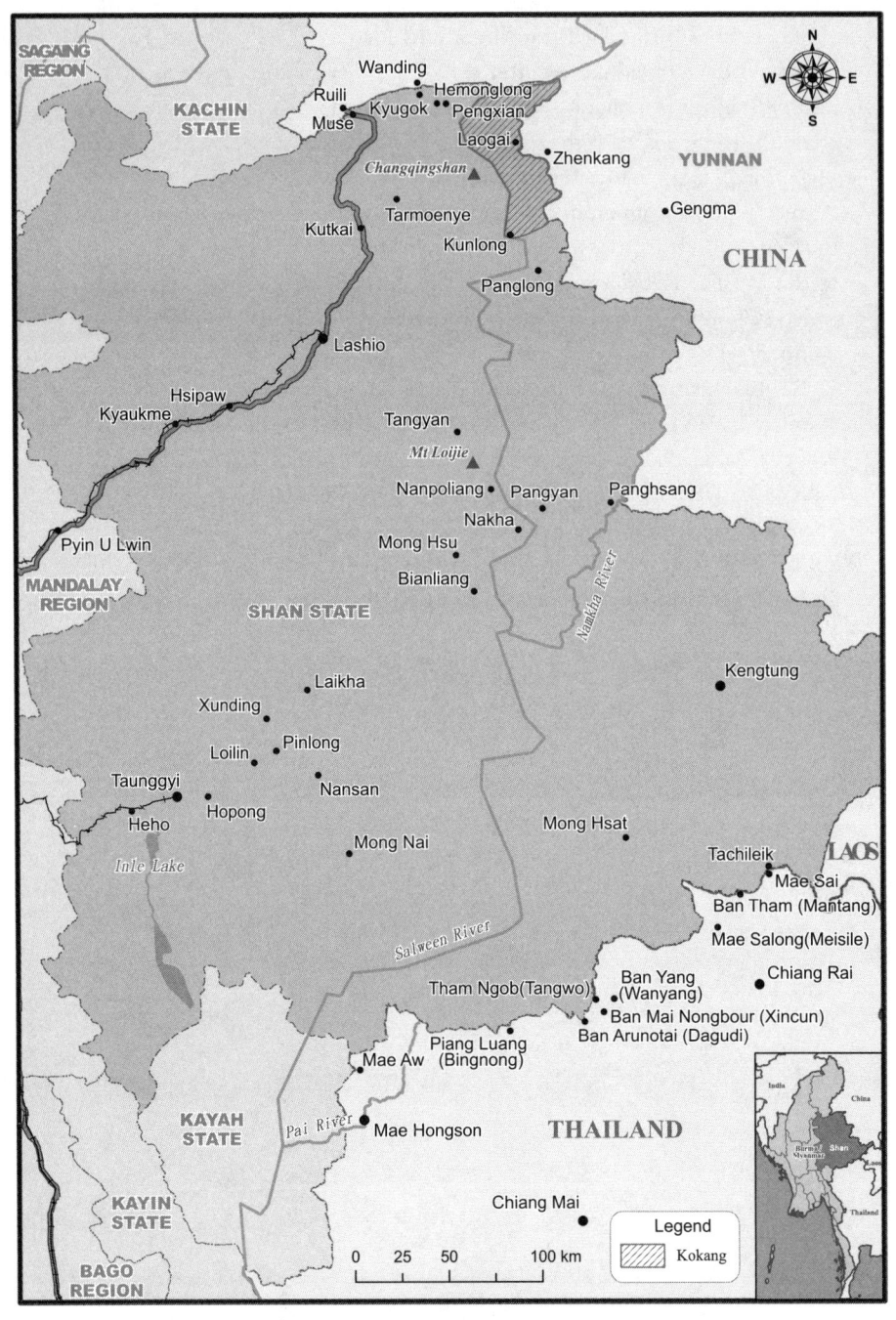

Map 1. Shan State of Burma and northern Thailand

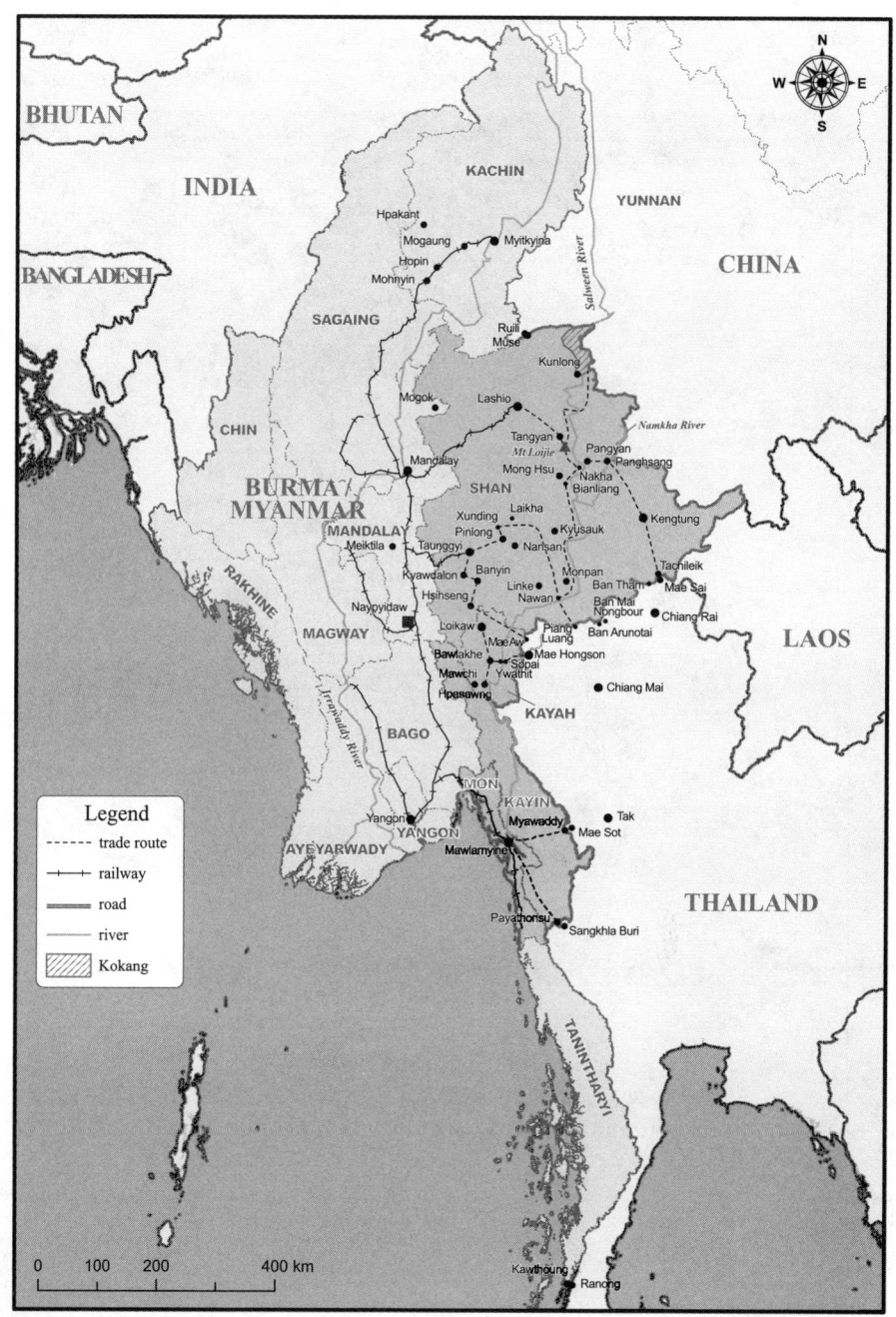

Map 2. Major underground trading routes between Burma and Thailand

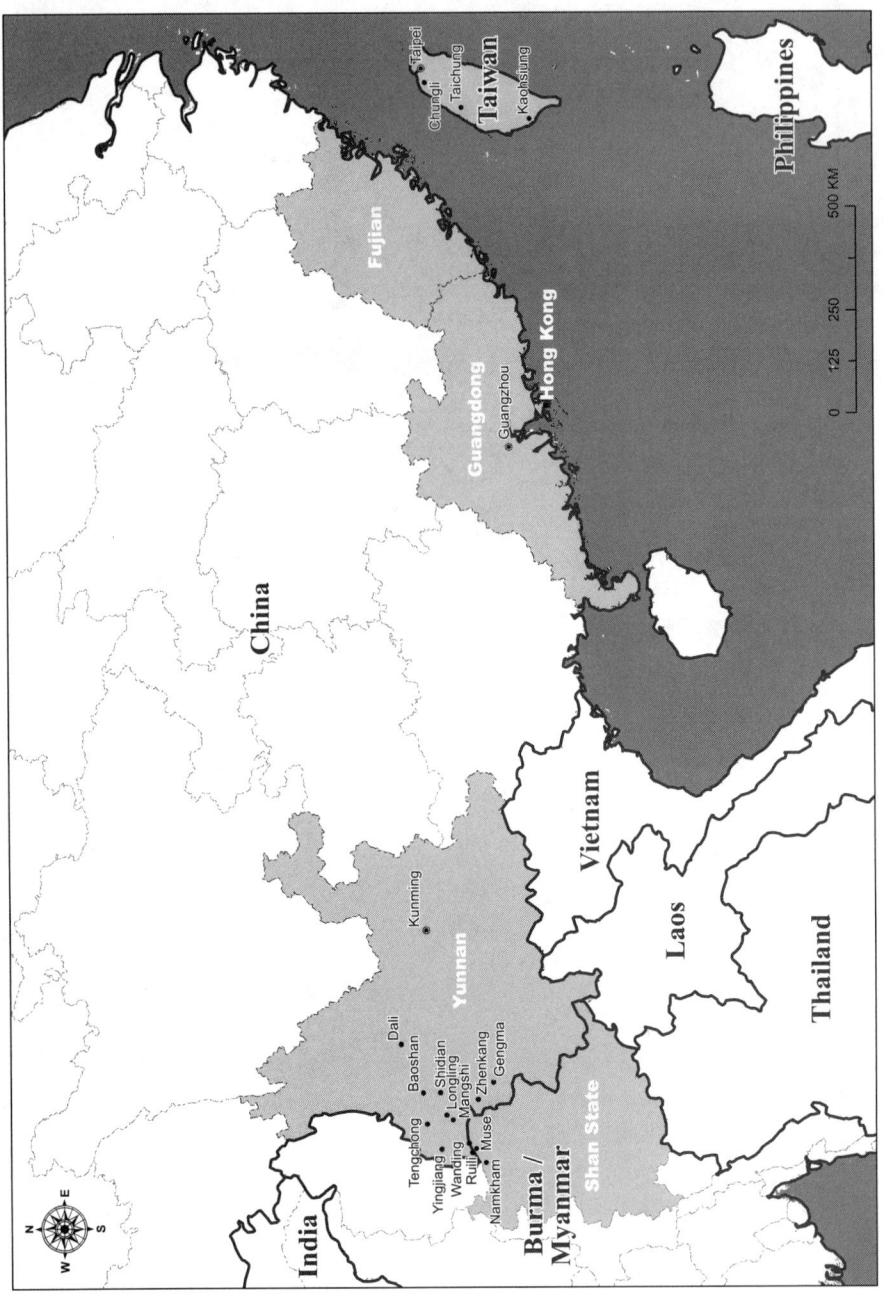

Map 3. Map of Shan State, Yunnan, Guangdong, Fujian, Hong Kong, and Taiwan

Introduction

"Three days and three nights would not exhaust my story" (wode gushi santian sanye ye shuo buwan). "Even three books would not be enough to record my story" (wode gushi sanbenshu ye xiebuwan). Over the years my informants, Yunnanese migrants of Burma/Myanmar, have frequently prefaced answers to my questions with such words. I was intrigued by these recurring phrases at the beginning. Their literal meaning must refer to many severe hardships in the experience of migration. But because only a few speakers then recounted what they considered important or appropriate for my data collecting, these phrases seemed to indicate reticence—perhaps a gentle refusal—regarding my inquiries. In-depth sharing of life stories came later, only after the relationship between us took shape. Such sharing often resulted from my informants' recognition of my repeated visits over several years and of my increased knowledge of their lives. Sometimes their agreement to talk was triggered by a particular moment—my presence or involvement in a tense family affair or my good appetite for Yunnanese food. As I accumulated life stories, little by little, I came to comprehend their lives' many dramatic disruptions, caused by political turmoil, ethnic conflicts, and economic constraints, and also realized their profound wish to tell how their biographies interplay with the region's geopolitics. The more we got to know each other, the more they told their histories, characterizing themselves in remarkable detail. Not only were many of them good storytellers, but they actively wanted to have their stories recorded in written form (and they would check with me from time to time about the progress of my writing).[1] Initial rhetorical declinations were gradually transformed into invitations to record their migratory lives.

In this book I retell many of these Yunnanese migrants' stories, illustrating not only their lived experiences but also what they expressed of their thinking, feeling, intimacies, courage, ambition, and despair. These experiences, thoughts, and emotions, which involve their inner selves and their relationships with other people and external environments, highlight their agency and individuality. At the same time they reflect a complex history of contemporary Yunnanese migration, first from Yunnan, in southwestern China, to Burma, and then, for some, from Burma to other places. These movements coincided with multiple national politics during the Cold War period, involving China, Burma, Thailand, Taiwan, and the United States (Chang 1999; Ministry of Information, the Union of Burma 1953; Qin 2009; Young 1970; Zeng 1964).

I focus on migrant Yunnanese mobility and (transnational) economic ventures, the most prominent themes in their narrative accounts. In *Merchants and Migrants: Ethnicity and Trade among Yunnanese Chinese in Southeast Asia*, Ann Maxwell Hill (1998) delineates the significance of Yunnanese migration and mercantile talents. She points out their "penchant for commerce," characterized by their knowledge of markets, credit arrangements, and adaptation to local political structures, as well as their risk-taking nature. Hill's interpretation of the interplay between trade and politics illustrates an interaction between mobile Yunnanese identities and the changing circumstances of the larger social world. However, while I share Hill's focus on migration and economic ventures, I go beyond the limitations of her fieldwork, which basically took place in Chiang Mai

---

1. When my informants saw me the next time I returned, many of them raised the question: "Teacher Chang, you must have written several books, right?" Also, when they introduced other informants to me, they often said to them: "Tell your story; Teacher Chang will write it into a book."

(Thailand) (ibid., 13, 27, 95–120). I have conducted long-term research at multiple sites in several countries (as referred to in the Note on Fieldwork), and I tackle a central issue that, at the time of her fieldwork, Hill could not: the complex connection between the repeated displacements of the contemporary migrant Yunnanese and their long-distance trade involvement with a range of armed ethnic groups and official agencies.[2] Moreover, I use a different method—an individual-centered ethnography primarily based on informants' narratives—which I believe is the best way to probe the complexities of individual experiences and to challenge the usual generalizations attributed to ethnic Chinese in host societies. Informants' accounts and my own observations suggest that travel is essential to opportunities and success for migrant Yunnanese, and in the process they traverse multiple borders, including social status, class, gender, corporal, and geographical borders.

Overland Yunnanese Movement in History

For more than two thousand years, mule caravans traveled between Yunnan and upper mainland Southeast Asia.[3] However, the trading connection was only officially noted for the first time in 128 BCE by Zhang Qian, a Han envoy visiting Daxia (in present-day Afghanistan) (Sima Qian 1988), and incorporation of Yunnan into the Chinese empire as a province did not take place until the Yuan dynasty (1277–1367 CE), a period of Mongol rule. Following its conquest of Yunnan, the Yuan brought in a large number of Muslim troops and civilians from central Asia and stationed them in Yunnan. Besides these Muslims, there were Han Chinese immigrants too, but on a relatively small scale (Forbes and Henley 1997, 27–57; Hao 1998, 28; You 1994, 284–86).

---

2. Hill's limitation is largely due to the timing of her research, when it was difficult for researchers to gain access to the borderlands of northern Thailand and Burma. Nevertheless, her pioneering study laid a good foundation for further exploration.

3. Several Chinese and Western historians have devoted themselves to the study of Yunnanese history focusing on its politics, culture, or economy (e.g., Atwill 2006; Chen 1992; Fang 1982; Fang and Fang 1997; FitzGerald 1972; Giersch 2006; Hao 1998; Kuo 1941; Liu 1991; Lu 2001; Shen 1994; Stargardt 1971; Sun 2000; Wang 1997; Wang and Zhang 1993; Wiens 1954; Wu 2002; Yang 2008; You 1994).

After the Yuan conquest, Yunnanese history entered a significant chapter in terms of Han Chinese immigration. The imperial court of the Ming dynasty (1368–1644 CE) carried out massive Chinese resettlement in this borderland to consolidate its rule. The recruited immigrants included troops (*juntun*), civilians (*mintun*), merchants (*shangtun*), and exiles (*zuixiyimin*). By the end of the dynasty the Han Chinese had become the majority ethnic group in terms of both size and political power. The Ming court also launched both military and economic explorations in upland Southeast Asia and what is now northeastern India. In a mountainous environment, courier stations and trading routes extended to different parts of the region and sustained the flow of goods through long-distance caravan trade. Because of its physical contiguity with Yunnan, Burma served as the major country for Yunnanese economic adventurism in ordinary times and for asylum in times of political unrest (Chen 1966; FitzGerald 1972; Jiang 1944; Kuo 1941; Lu 2001; Sun 2000; Wiens 1954; Yang 2008; You 1994).

The Qing (1644–1911 CE) further developed the province and by and large followed the policies of the Ming. Relocation of Han Chinese immigrants continued, and Chinese acculturation was reinforced among native ethnic groups, especially those adjacent to the Chinese (Wiens 1954; FitzGerald 1972; You 1994). Nevertheless, different ethnic forces continued to coexist in competition (Giersch 2006).

Transborder commerce continued to expand. Yunnanese Han and Muslims have been particularly active in economic exploration for long-distance trade and mining since the sixteenth century (Sun 2000, 138–55; Giersch 2006, 160). Both groups migrated to Burma, and the eventual penetration of the British and French colonial powers in upland Southeast Asia in the nineteenth century further intensified overland economic interactions. Flows of goods and of people were escalating (Kuo 1941, 30–31).

Transborder commerce depended on mules and horses, and long-distance trade required the organization of caravans. The trade also needed a large number of muleteers, a job that attracted many peasants eager to earn extra cash during the dry season. Participation in the caravan trade was thus a prominent economic activity among the Yunnanese.[4] This phenomenon was reflected in a common Yunnanese saying: qiong zou yifang ji zou

---

4. Among Yunnanese traders, the Han Chinese constitute the primary group. Other major groups include the Muslims, Yi, Bai, Naxi, Shan, and Pumi (Chiranan 1990; FitzGerald 1972; Hill 1998; Lu 2001; Wang and Zhang 1993).

chang—which means that when one was in need of money, one joined the caravan trade and traveled to places inhabited by "barbarians" (other ethnic groups), or one hoped to get lucky in the jade or mineral mines in Burma (Ma 1985; Wang 1993; Wang and Zhang 1993). To undertake trade in ethnically diversified areas, traders had to adopt the local politics of hill chiefs, just as the chiefs adopted the techniques of border feudalism institutionalized by the Chinese court (Hill 1998, 53). Many of the chiefs were said to be highly Sinicized, making use of Han cultural traits to legitimize their collection of tolls paid by traders for safe passage (Giersch 2006, 159–86; Hill 1998, 58).

Caravan trade between Yunnan and Burma continued through the two world wars.[5] After the Second World War, the region underwent political upheaval, and the Communist takeover of China in 1949 saw the flight of Yunnanese into Burma on an unprecedented scale. Because Yunnanese refugees did not have permission from the Burmese government to reside in the country, they initially moved into the mountain areas of Shan and Kachin States.

Among these refugees, a group of stragglers from the Nationalist army (the Kuomintang or KMT) and local self-defense guards from Yunnan organized themselves into guerrilla forces in 1950 under the leadership of General Li Mi. These troops received supplies from the Nationalist government in Taiwan and also the United States (Chang 1999; Ministry of Information, the Union of Burma 1953; Qin 2009; Young 1970; Zeng 1964).[6] Numerous civilian refugees gathered around the bases set up by the KMT to protect themselves from harassment by the Burmese army and other ethnic forces. However, the KMT guerrillas were disbanded in 1961 under international pressure.[7] The sole survivors of the disbandment were

---

5. During the Muslim Rebellion of 1856–1873, caravan trade was partially interrupted between Bhamo (in northern Burma) and Tengyue (present-day Tengchong in western Yunnan) (Huang 1976; Yegar 1966). But the overall trade between the two countries continued to flourish, especially in cotton and opium (Chiranan 1990; Dawson 1912).

6. The initial number of KMT stragglers in early 1950 was around 2,900 (Zeng 1964, 10, 11, 18). The forces expanded to 16,068 soldiers before the first evacuation to Taiwan in 1953 (ibid., illustration 6).

7. Compelled by a resolution from the United Nations in 1953, the KMT government disbanded the KMT forces in Burma in 1953–1954 and evacuated 6,568 people back to Taiwan (Qin 2009, 168). However, KMT guerrillas soon reorganized in Shan State. In June 1960, the number of troops increased to 9,718 (Zeng 1964, 91, 97, 229). After being defeated by the Burma army (in collaboration with troops from the People's Republic of China), the KMT forces had to conduct a second disbandment in 1961, and 4,409 people were evacuated to Taiwan (Qin 2009, 269). A portion of those evacuated in 1953–1954 and 1961 were civilians.

the Third and Fifth Armies, totaling about forty-seven hundred troops (Qin 2009, 276). The main part of these two remnant KMT armies entered northern Thailand in the early 1960s with the tacit approval of the Thai government. Their encampment along the border together with several other rebellious ethnic minorities from Burma was perceived as a buffer against the possible penetration of Thai territory by Burmese Communists (Nations 1977; Taylor 1973, 33–35).[8]

Burma did not resolve its internal division and violence in the wake of independence in 1948 (Callahan 2003; Charney 2009; Thant Myint-U 2006). Resistance against the central state by different ethnic communities succeeded the confrontation between local powers and the British colonial government and later Japanese rule. In 1962, General Ne Win ended parliamentary government (1948–1962) through a military coup. In his bid to guide the country under the ideology of the "Burmese Way to Socialism," he nationalized trade and industry. However, gross mismanagement, infrastructural weaknesses, and policy errors led to disastrous consequences: economic recession and the scarcity of essential goods. Moreover, the problems of an impoverished economy were aggravated by deep ethnic rifts.

Socioeconomic instability compelled many civilian Yunnanese refugees to follow the two remnant KMT armies into northern Thailand (though a larger number stayed behind). The troops helped their fellow refugees rehabilitate themselves in border villages that emerged as havens for later Yunnanese migrants throughout the 1970s and 1980s (Chang 2002, 2006a). Meanwhile, the KMT forces carried out transborder trade between Thailand and Burma. "The troops were caravan traders and the caravan traders were troops. Both were combined as a unit," a former KMT official wrote in his autobiography (Hu 1974, 195). Mule caravans were a major means for transporting smuggled merchandise. This particular mode of conveyance persisted into the mid-1980s, when cars primarily replaced mules. The KMT dominated the trade through the 1960s and 1970s (Chang 2002; Chao Tzang Yawnghwe 1990; Lintner 1994). They were not disbanded until the end of the 1980s. Their existence by and large coincided with that of the Ne Win regime.

---

8. I have treated the organization and leadership of the KMT guerrillas (Chang 2001, 2002) and trauma of the flight experiences among the first-generation migrants (Chang 2005, 2006b) elsewhere.

In 1988, the Burmese socialist regime collapsed as a result of a series of nationwide revolts. The succeeding military junta adopted a market-oriented economic policy and announced that the country was open for foreign investment. Many Yunnanese have moved to Yangon (Rangoon) for new economic opportunities since the mid-1990s. Taking advantage of politico-economic changes and applying their mercantile dynamism, Yunnanese in Burma engage in opportunities ranging from small trade to grand enterprises. Many of their ventures connect with transborder and transnational trade, both legal and illegal. One result of the economic success of these Yunnanese merchants has, however, been a xenophobic backlash, especially from the Burmans (the major ethnic group) who perceive the Yunnanese as opportunists and imply that their wealth has been accumulated via illicit or immoral means—collaboration with ethnic insurgents during the socialist period and with the corrupt state agents after 1988. Anti-Chinese/Yunnanese feeling has been growing; stark criticism of the group appears in the media as well as in academic writings.[9] In contrast, many Yunnanese informants tend to portray the Burmans, whom they call *laomian* (old Burmans), as lazy and untrustworthy and stress that they would not allow their children to marry them. A large number from both groups despise each other, and the gap that separates them is widening. Similar confrontations between Burmans and other ethnic minorities also exist.

In November 2010, the Burmese military junta organized a national election, which consequently transformed the junta into a semi-parliamentary government. Political and economic reforms have taken place since, including the release of hundreds of political prisoners; relaxation of media control; dialogues with the main opposition party, the National League for Democracy, and several ethnic armed groups; and changes to the exchange rate and foreign investment rules. Nevertheless, decades of ethnic conflict cannot be ended in a short time. The country still suffers from ongoing humanitarian crises, absence of the rule of law, and an institutional incapacity to cope with development.

---

9. For example, Mya Maung, a well-known Burmese scholar, strongly denounced what he called the "Chinese colonization of Mandalay" (1994, 455), characterized the "massive Chinese onslaught" (p. 458) as an "imminent threat" (p. 459), and blamed Chinese/Yunnanese traders for the "cultural decline and moral decay in Mandalay" (p. 457). Min Zin's review (2012) of cultural and media works published in Burma, especially after 1988, highlights the increasing anti-China and anti-Chinese sentiment.

According to my informants, over 80 percent of the Yunnanese in Burma today are descended from the refugees who fled Yunnan after 1949. They are second-, third-, and fourth-generation migrants.[10] The rest are offspring of earlier arrivals; some of their ancestors came to Burma many generations ago. So far, there has been very little research on the overland Yunnanese (or the overseas/maritime Chinese) in Burma.[11] The paucity of literature contrasts with the extensive studies of ethnic Chinese in other parts of Southeast Asia and the rest of the world, overwhelmingly focusing on the overseas/maritime Chinese (e.g., Bao 2005; Ma 2003; McKeown 2001; Kuhn 2008; Ong 1999; Reid 1996; Skinner 1957; Tan 1988; Wang 1991, 2001; Suryadinata 2006). The latter studies uniformly depict the overseas Chinese as trading and laboring diasporas. The contemporary Yunnanese experience is more complicated: as refugees, merchants, muleteers, miners, and soldiers, the overland Yunnanese have experienced victim, trade, labor, and military diasporas (Cohen 1997). Those who fled from Yunnan to Burma after 1949 have lived through these various modes and have continually extended their migration routes from upper mainland Southeast Asia to overseas domains (e.g., Taiwan, Hong Kong, Guangzhou, Japan, Malaysia, Singapore).

---

10. The refugee influxes went on through the 1970s. Since the mid-1990s, the Sino-Burmese trade has been accelerating, resulting in new waves of overland Chinese immigration. A large number of new immigrants are concentrated in northern Shan and Kachin States, and they move back and forth between China and Burma (Thant Myint-U 2011; Woods 2011). This ethnography does not discuss these newcomers.

11. There have only been a few essay publications. Mya Than (1997) presents a brief history of ethnic Chinese and their identity in Burma, largely based on old materials. Hsin-Chun Lu (2011) examines the public musical performances of Yangon's ethnic Chinese from 1949 to 1988. Hongwei Fan (2012) researches the 1967 anti-Chinese riots in Burma and argues that the Beijing government's export of the Cultural Revolution was the primary cause of the event. In addition, there have been a few doctoral dissertations. Chai Chen-hsiao (2006) investigates the ethnic Chinese living in Yangon and those who migrated from Burma to Taipei in the 1960s and to Toronto in the 1970s. Chai discusses how Burmese-Chinese in these three cities shape their identity through cultural performance and transnational connections. Duan Ying (2009) studies Chinese migrants' ethnicity and cultural citizenship in Burma. Jayde Lin Roberts (2011) explores what she calls "the ethos" of the Sino-Burmese in Yangon using four aspects: place and kinship, commerce, native languages, and Chinese New Year. Yi Li (2011) deals with the formation and representation of Chinese communities in colonial Burma.

Applying the Personal Narrative Approach

How does one present the life-worlds of migrant Yunnanese in Burma? Although having often been touched or excited by informants' narratives, I hesitated to write a book based on their personal stories. I was worried about vulnerability—my informants' security after revealing their intimate feelings, and my own academic neutrality and future access to Burma. I thought that perhaps in some late stage of my academic career many things would have changed and then it would be the appropriate time to write such a book.

The tragic Saffron Revolution in September 2007 compelled me to rethink this plan. Thousands of anonymous monks took to the streets in many cities across Burma, demanding political and economic reforms. Monks are highly respected in this primarily Buddhist country, and their protest against the military junta quickly encouraged many civilians to join them. Their concerted action was motivated by a hope for change, but it provoked a brutal crackdown by the military regime. The demonstrators' bravery contrasted with my timidity and reminded me of the urgency of telling the outside world about the lives of the people in Burma—at least those of the people I had been working with for years. In the spring of 2008, I started writing the story of Zhang Dage (chapter 1), a good friend. On May 2, 2008, Cyclone Nargis hit Burma and took nearly 140,000 lives. This sudden devastation compounded the hardships borne by the country's already destitute population.[12] It further determined my writing plan, and stories of other Yunnanese informants followed over the next several years.

Through writing, I recognized the seed of the narrative approach that had been planted by my informants. Once they got to know and trust me, wasn't their urge to tell me their stories similar to my own urge to tell those stories to the outside world? For them, I represented the outside world, a chance to transcend their sociopolitical marginality. Moreover, I am someone who writes. From time to time, I stressed to them that there had been very little written history on the migrant Yunnanese, and that I was interested in reconstructing it. But the unavoidable question arises: Am I appropriating their narrativity, or are they appropriating my academic position?

---

12. More than 2.4 million people were affected by the disaster (Yeni 2009).

Perhaps it is a mutual appropriation. Notwithstanding the answer, what is meaningful for inquiry hinges on the issue of intersubjectivity—how I relate to my informants and vice versa, and how my informants themselves relate to other people and entities in their narrations and practices. Digging into these questions helps disclose different facets of one's selfhood (whether mine or my informants') and one's multiple positions in relation to power.

Narration reveals fragments of realities or distortions of realities (Behar 1993; Bruner 1987; Cattell and Climo 2002; King 2000; Neisser and Fivush 1993; Nguyen 2009). All stories are unfinished and incomplete. Life goes on, and what the ethnographer has collected and written about projects only partial lives of the research subjects (Clifford and Marcus 1986; Denzin 1991, 68–69; Langness and Frank 1981; Ochs and Capps 1996, 21; Riessman 1993, 16; Waterson 2007, 24). In the field, I have repeatedly witnessed fragmentation, inconsistency, and contradiction in informants' accounts. I was often puzzled and sometimes impatient or even angry. Informants' narrations and my responses display our dialogic relationship (Portelli 1997; Waterson 2007, 17–20). I have integrated my interaction with the narrators when that integration helps illuminate the ethnographic situation for purposes of analysis. Still, the protagonists are my informants; I merely play a supporting role. Some stories may appear to end abruptly. It is, however, my intention to situate those moments of abruptness into the ethnographic setting.

During the course of fieldwork, my gender as a female has played a role. In terms of spatial movement, I had greater freedom when interacting with female informants. I could accompany them in both domestic and public spaces. We carried on our conversations in the kitchen, the courtyard, the bedroom, the living room, the market, the Guanyin temple, and so on. Moreover, I joined in their work, such as cooking, folding paper money, and cleaning, while conducting my interviews. In contrast, my meetings with male informants took place in formal sites, mostly in the living room and sometimes in shops, mosques, Chinese schools, and Yunnanese associations. I felt more able to ask women questions about private matters, such as family relationships. Although I come from a society very different from the women's and have different life experiences, a common identity based on womanhood exists between us, whereby I could probe their world of intimacy, especially in relation to their bodies and the other sex. In interactions with male informants, however, the gender boundary always exists, especially vis-à-vis senior male informants. While respecting that boundary by avoiding sensitive issues, I tried to obtain complementary information from other family members.

While listening to informants, I travel with them in my imagination and learn about how their traveling interacts with their livelihoods, family relationships, regional politics, religious networks (among the Yunnanese Muslims), local knowledge, gender, and space. Constantly, their narrations reveal a temporal consciousness that interweaves with their "inner life processes and affective states," or what we can term "subjectivity" (Biehl, Good, and Kleinman 2007, 6), which embodies both liminality and agency in an ongoing process of construction and change.[13] Resonating with many other anthropologists' findings, the informants' stories not only convey valuable data, I have found, but also shed light on the cultural meanings inherent in their commentaries (e.g., Marcus and Fischer 1986, 54, 58; Riessman 1993, 1; Thompson 1988; Waterson 2007, 10–12). An essential task of this ethnography is thus to enliven informants' narrative power and unpack the invested meanings (rather than factual accuracy) embedded in their narratives.

Along with oral accounts, I have also collected texts written by Yunnanese migrants—letters, essays, poems, records of family genealogy, and autobiographies. These oral and written sources help me reconstruct the trajectories of the migrant Yunnanese movement and economic participation. In writing, I have tried to preserve the "thickness" of narrators' stories by using first-person narratives as much as possible. Their personal accounts compose the main body of the ethnography.

Needless to say, the stories my informants tell are predicated on their particular viewpoints, with which other ethnic groups (or even other Yunnanese migrants) may not agree. However, these viewpoints speak to who these narrators are and also portray the entanglements between them and

---

13. This understanding of subjectivity, stressing its processual formation, is advocated by many researchers (e.g., Abu-Lughod 1993; Belsey 1991; Biehl, Good, and Kleinman 2007; Cohen 1997; Crapanzano 1980; Ellis and Flaherty 1992; Fischer 2003; Hall 2004; Herzfeld 1996; Hirschman 1995; Thompson 1998). Biehl, Good, and Kleinman propose an "ethnographic study of subjectivity," aiming to "investigate subjectivity in contemporary settings of economic crisis, state violence, exploited migrant communities, massive displacements, hegemonic gender politics, and postcolonial state" (2007, 15, 10).

a series of external contexts, ranging from near (and dear) to far (and unfamiliar) environments along their peripatetic movement. These entanglements parallel what Anna Tsing terms "frictions," a metaphor she uses to probe the disparities and unevenness in the development of global capitalism. She explores how seemingly isolated rain forest dwellers (the Meratus Dayaks) in Kalimantan, Indonesia, encounter national and global forces and are shaped and transformed in a process intriguingly characterized by embedded connections as well as conflicts and contradictions involving different layers of power structure (2005). With reference to the concept, I delve into Yunnanese migrants' persistent struggle against numerous external constraints. While Tsing focuses more on a structural dimension, I try to knit individuals' experiences with contextual elements to illuminate the intertwinement of their subjectivities and encountered frictions.

Shifting Focus from Central State to Borderland

While adopting a personal narrative approach, I take a transborder/transnational perspective for analysis. In light of the migrant Yunnanese's unrecognized refugee status during the initial stages of resettlement, their movement from a frontier province (Yunnan) to another frontier region (Shan and Kachin States of Burma and border areas of northern Thailand), and their participation in the underground cross-border trade, the migrant Yunnanese of Burma give us a remarkable opportunity to contribute to borderland studies.

The concept of "borderland" has by and large been associated with periphery, wasteland, backwardness, and lawlessness. It is in sharp contrast to the ideas of center, civilization, progress, and law and order. Such dualistic thinking results from the political ideology underlying state-building—the borderland is something to be tamed and controlled by the central state (Baud and van Schendel 1997; Chou 2005; Horstmann and Wadley 2006; Scott 2009; Walker 1999, 7). This top-down ideology stresses absolute national sovereignty and rules out notions of flexible or negotiable boundaries (Donnan and Wilson 1994, 1). It accepts national boundaries as a "given," and it subjugates borderlands; the subjectivity of borderlanders and trans-borderlanders is purposefully ignored. Likewise, those belonging to the categories of social borderland, such as women, ethnic minorities, the Green Party, and the laboring class, are often consciously or subconsciously considered inferior and perceived as needing governance by their "central" counterparts. The demarcation is based on differences in power position, drawing a strict line of inclusion and exclusion (Donnan and Wilson 1999; High 2009; Johnson and Michaelsen 1997, 20; Lugo 1997).

After the Second World War this sociopolitical mainstream of governance continued to dominate academia and the political arena. In the 1960s more social protest emerged, such as the civil rights movement, the New Left, and the feminist movement (see Freedman 2003; Mattson 2002; McAdam 1982; Tarrow 1998). Alternative voices called for recognition of social inequalities on the periphery and among the oppressed. Since then some subaltern communities have successfully challenged the orthodox hegemony and compelled the center to release resources to them; others have failed in their appeals. Whatever the result, their endeavors have inspired new directions in academic research that involve rethinking the traditional demarcation between the center and the periphery.

A burgeoning literature on liminal borderlands relating to gender, marginal people, culture, migration, environment, and underground trade has illuminated the dynamism of the peripheral and pointed out the fact of unidentified interstices in individual subjectivities and social categories (e.g., Anzaldúa 1987; Butler 1990; Chou 2010; Gilroy 1993; Hall and Du Gay 1996; Jonsson 2005; Ortner 1996; Scott 2009; Sturgeon 2005; Tagliacozzo 2005; Tsing 1993; van Schendel 2005; Warren 2007). It makes us look into the agency of borderlands embedded or hidden in our lives or marginal communities. Prevalent political discourse focusing solely on state-centeredness or mainstream social ideologies is being debated—it is from this angle that Renato Rosaldo, for example, probes the complexities of the life-world and suggests that instead of living in the "supposedly transparent cultural selves," our everyday practices are intersecting with "structure" and "agency" (1993, 104). Behind the façade of ascribed political or sociocultural identities, everyone embodies a part of the unidentified borderland that facilitates everyday life. This viewpoint reminds us of E. R. Leach's classic ethnography, *Political Systems of Highland Burma*, which set an example in the field of social organization more than half a century ago (1954). Leach's work illustrates the oscillating reality of the tribal identity and sociopolitical structures of Kachin societies as they interact with the Shans in the face of change.[14] "Every real society is a process in time," Leach said (1993, 4), and so is every human being, embracing an inevitably changing nature that opens itself to transformation. The ongoing process is often full of fragmentation and inconsistency, in contrast to a superficial belief in structural coherence. Borderlands, be they metaphorical or geographical, should therefore "be regarded not as analytically empty transitional zones but as sites of creative cultural production that require investigation" (Rosaldo 1993, 207–8), and the field of everyday practices should be the focus of inspection.

With regard to the southwestern China and Southeast Asia region, many recent works have discarded the unified state–oriented approach to shed light on issues of borderlands. For example, Thongchai Winichakul's *Siam Mapped* (1994) is a masterpiece on the nation-building of modern Thailand. He deconstructs the creation of the modern Thai "geo-body" and demonstrates the fixation of its national boundaries by appropriating mapmaking technologies. C. Patterson Giersch's *Asian Borderlands* (2006) looks into the political, economic, and social interactions between the indigenous people and Chinese official agents and immigrants in Yunnan during the Qing period and redefines the frontier as a "'middle ground' [a meeting place] in which social boundaries and cultural practices were in flux" (p. 7). Andrew Walker's *The Legend of the Golden Boat* (1999) examines cooperation in the Upper Mekong area. His ethnographic findings lead to the conclusions that the transnational movements of the Quadrangle region are the latest in a series of regimes of Upper Mekong regulation, and that "state (and non-state) regulation is intrinsically involved in the creation of the contexts in which markets flourish" (p. 14). From an ecological approach, Janet C. Sturgeon's *Border Landscapes* (2005) explores the landscape plasticity of two border Akha communities, located respectively in southwestern China and northern Thailand. She illustrates the appropriation processes by showing how these two communities turn their border landscapes from topography and land cover to "sites for maneuvering and struggle" by resorting to their sociopolitical tradition (p. 9).

---

14. Leach's *Political Systems of Highland Burma* is a milestone in ethnic studies; it looks into interacting social systems between groups and their consequent influences on identities. However, researchers working on the Kachin have since contested Leach's oversimplified construction of the two ideal political systems (*gumlao* and *gumsa*), as well as other flaws (see Robinne and Sadan 2007).

These works are geographically and theoretically related to my study of cross-border and transnational movement among migrant Yunnanese, between Yunnan, Burma, Thailand, and other places. The common thread uniting them is their consensus on the interlinking of forces that operate along constantly changing borders across time and space. They dismiss a simplified center-periphery model and look into borderlands in process. While recognizing the modern political trend in the formation of nation states, their analyses are not confined to the borders of a specific country. The other side of the border, in imagination or in practice, is also under investigation. Their works, in effect, articulate the subjectivities of borderlanders and offer new frames of analysis that go beyond the restriction of national boundaries.

Throughout history, Yunnanese mobility has resulted in the establishment of diasporic Yunnanese communities and transnational networks in a large stretch of land. Taking a transborder and transnational perspective, I look beyond governmental institutions and probe the migratory and mercantile agency of the diasporic Yunnanese. More specifically, I ask: Who are these Yunnanese migrants? Why and how have they undertaken ongoing movement and a range of underground and transborder trades? What have been their impacts upon local, regional, and transnational structures? And how has their persistent traveling affected Yunnanese diasporic communities? I use such concepts as friction, traveling culture, the transnational popular realm, gendered geography of power, and circulation to analyze this population's migration and economic engagements. Ultimately, I hope not only to make the voice of the migrant Yunnanese heard, but also to de-center Burmese national history and challenge the central state's political power in deciding inclusion and exclusion in social, economic, and political policy making.

The Shape of the Book

By choosing protagonists who belong to multiple generations, who have had different migration experiences, who practice a range of professions and are located in various places, I provide, in part one of the book, a grounding for an understanding of contemporary Yunnanese migration history. Chapters 1 to 3 cover the migratory experiences of four narrators through different life stages, providing insights into their inner selves as well as life in Shan State. Their narratives unveil the intertwinement of their subjectivities with historical contingent circumstances, infused with a range of sentiments (hope, loss, pain, desire, ambition, alienation, anxiety, ambivalence) and forceful tensions (love, hate, jealousy, anger, confusion). These intricate emotions are often tied to complexities involving their families, ethnic others, and states and societies. These protagonists speak about their ongoing attempts to realize their ambitions. Chapter 4 also deals with personal migration history, but among the Yunnanese Muslims. The narrators relate their marginality in Burma, owing to both their ethnicity and their religion, and talk about how they deal with this marginality through Islamic networking beyond Burma. Although these stories at first sight seem individual, on closer look they echo one another, demonstrating the narrators' motifs and strategies to overcome obstacles and adversities in order to reach their goals. Moreover, they thread together two common themes referred to by James Clifford—"roots" and "routes" (1994)—to portray how the narrators understand their life trajectories in relation to time, localities, peoples, and their multiple roles or positions. Concretely, I illustrate the craving (for certain places and people), crafting (of their narrated memories), and contrasting (of the inconsistencies and contradictions) in their narratives to reveal the divergent facets of their subjectivities as diasporans and the complexity of Burmese society in relation to its multiethnic structure and oppressive military rule.

After the delineation of these several peripatetic lives, part two of the book underpins the group's economic activities by exploring borderland livelihoods, gendered economies, and spatial flows. Chapter 5 examines the cross-border trade undertaken by male Yunnanese migrants between Burma and Thailand during the era of the Burmese socialist regime. It reconstructs the organization of the trade (mostly via mule caravans), its trading routes and traded commodities, and analyzes the sociocultural meanings underlying this venture. Although Yunnanese traders view borderlands as barbarous, their efforts to maintain reciprocity with autochthonous groups and respect their rules, in effect, negates the perception. Complementing this focus on the long-distance trade by Yunnanese men, chapter 6 examines the economic involvement of Yunnanese women. Their narratives illuminate the social construction of gender inequalities in relation to power distribution in both public and domestic spheres. Their engagement highlights an ongoing process of shaping and reshaping "gendered geographies of power" (Mahler and Pessar 2001) that reflects their mercantile keenness, frustration, and pain. While their practices contest existing gender categories, they also reproduce these categories. Chapter 7 explores the transnational jade trade dominated by migrant Yunnanese since the 1960s, owing to their well-connected transnational networks. My focus is on the traders' dynamism in the formation of their transnational networks and the flows of capital in response to the politico-economic policies adopted by different states. Their business extension to Guangzhou and Hong Kong since 2000 has resulted in the merging of traditional overland connections with newly established maritime links. Although coverage of the economic activities among the migrant Yunnanese in the second part is not comprehensive, the issues dealt with embrace an essential part of the group's economic life.

All the stories narrated here, flowing from individuality to a group concern, point to contemporary Yunnanese migrants' mobility and their relentless efforts in pursuit of a better life. Either the protagonists or their family members have experiences of flight. Repeated changes in environment result in status and class shifts and compel them to take up a wide range of jobs to make ends meet. In contrast to voluminous studies of overseas Chinese since the 1990s (e.g., Cohen 1997; Ma 2003; Ong 1999; Ong and Nonini 1997; Pan 1994), which have been critiqued as too "optimistic" and "class-based" (concentrating on the middle class) (Ty and Goellnicht 2004, 8), these stories of contemporary Yunnanese migrants attest to fluidity in social status and class. There was never an absolute division between traders and laborers, for the latter could also engage in small-scale trade, and the former could in turn suddenly lose all their profits and become muleteers or jade miners. In addition to status and class interchangeability, the protagonists cross a series of borders in relation to gender, body, and geography, highlighting their resilience. Borders for them hold different meanings in different situations, and their lives are marked by a series of border transcendences in their daily worlds (cf. Rosaldo 1993, 207–8).

Migrant Yunnanese mobility attests to the prevalence of travel by "many different kinds of people" (Clifford 1992, 107) rather than just the privileged. Their narratives of movement not only disclose individual life processes but also illustrate networks of connections, modes of transportation, gendered differentiation, and flows of diverse objects. Through traveling they have carried on the mobile livelihoods of their predecessors, who ranged over the historical borderlands between Yunnan and upland Southeast Asia, and they have even expanded overland travel to journeys by land, by sea, and by air.

By applying a personal narrative approach, drawing on different forms of narratives given by a range of Yunnanese migrants, I attempt to build a general historical background while digging into concrete lived experiences. My primary objective is to accomplish what the oral historian Alessandro Portelli has advocated, "to explore [the distance and bond between the personal experience and history], to search out the memories in the private, enclosed space of houses and kitchens and ... to connect them with 'history' and in turn force history to listen to them" (1997, viii). The stories that follow, I hope, open a window upon the migrant Yunnanese as well as the societies in which they are situated.

Part I

Migration History

1

The Days in Burma

Zhang Dage

> Last night, I dreamed about poppy farms; a whole field was full of blooming poppies.... They were red, white, and purple, dancing in the wind. I was like a wild horse running in the field. From exhaustion, I fell on the bed of flowers. I told myself repeatedly ... not to wake up if I still wanted to see the flowers.
>
> —Zhang Dage, 2002[1]

Zhang Dage, born in a mountain village in Shan State, Burma, in 1962, is one of my key informants. Like many Yunnanese migrants, his life has been marked by a series of migrations. Since 1980 he has settled in Taiwan, but every Chinese New Year he takes his family back to his parents' home in Reshuitang Xincun (often called Xincun), a primarily Yunnanese Han village in Chiang Mai Province in northern Thailand. We met there for the first time during the Chinese New Year in 1996 when I was conducting my doctoral fieldwork on the history of the KMT Yunnanese Chinese in northern Thailand (Chang 1999). At that time, many dependents of former high-ranking officers of the KMT Third Army still lived in this village.[2]

---

1. This is an extract from one of Zhang Dage's essays posted on his former weblog. *Dage* (senior brother) is an address for senior males of one's generation.
2. Xincun was founded in 1963 and named Ban Mai Nongbour in Thai. In 1995–1996 it was my major research site, with a population of nearly five thousand. The village has distinctive Yunnanese Chinese features reflected in its cultural organization and villagers' daily practices. I stayed there for approximately sixteen months, while making side trips to twenty-four other Yunnanese villages in Chiang Mai and Chiang Rai Provinces, gathering complementary data. Shu-min Huang published an ethnography on a KMT Yunnanese village focusing on its agriculture (2010).

When he heard about my Taiwanese origin and my research, Zhang Dage expressed great interest. He took me to his parents' orchard just outside the village and told me that in the future his parents would be buried there; he hoped to turn the orchard into a garden and open it to the public. I still remember Zhang Dage's words: "My parents' epitaphs would record Yunnanese history and culture and make the place a historical site. It is my wish to pass along our Yunnanese migration history to future generations."

Over the years he has shared a good number of his stories with me in person or by phone, and by letters, email, his weblog, and his Facebook page. These stories, with their references to mnemonic sites, persons, objects, and practices, reflect different stages of his life and provide valuable data regarding the migrant Yunnanese lifestyle, especially in the Shan State of Burma. Based on both his oral and written narratives, this chapter examines the localities, peoples, livelihoods, and times of Zhang Dage's early youth in Burma.

Letters from Zhang Dage

Dear Wen-Chin,

I'm very sorry for the delay in replying to you. It has been more than one month since I put your letter and the materials you requested in the briefcase that I carry from home to my clinic every day. You must have been waiting for my answer. I'm sorry to keep you waiting due to my busy schedule. How have you been?

I've asked my father for some documents for you. Regarding the flight from Yunnan after 1949, as I understand it, most people escaped in groups. The earlier arrivals helped those who came later. Before the Communist takeover, many Yunnanese had been involved in the border trade between Yunnan and Burma. Therefore, they were already familiar with the routes connecting the two countries. . . . While some Yunnanese who moved from the Shan State of Burma to the frontiers in northern Thailand found ways to migrate further to Chiang Mai, Bangkok, or even Taiwan, other Yunnanese kept moving inside Burma and Thailand. In a nutshell, the capable ones moved first and others followed. For human beings, the pursuit of a better life is anchored in persistent "hope."

[There were two general routes of flight from Yunnan to northern Shan State in Burma]. The first route connected Lashio via public roads [*gonglu*] with Taunggyi, Kengtung, Tachileik, then Mae Sai [in Thailand], and on to different Yunnanese villages in Chiang Rai Province [along the border] such as Mantang and Meisile. The second route connected Tangyan [or Tangyang] via mountain tracks with Nanpoliang, Bianliang, then Bingnong [in Thailand], and then other Yunnanese villages in Chiang Mai Province, such as Dagudi, Tangwo, Reshuitang Xincun, and Wanyang.[3]

. . . Yunnanese emphasize connections with others from their hometowns who often provide useful help in migration. Before leaving for a strange place, one is often told to look for fellow Yunnanese in that new place. I recalled hearing such references frequently. However, one does not always receive help when it is required. Sometimes these connections yield no assistance at all. Such cases often aggravate hardships for migrants that resemble tragic plots in novels. In other words, one may experience either a warm or cold reception when interacting with other countrymen.

. . . I am very busy, but I am still interested in the history of Yunnanese migration, although I am not able to study it myself. I anticipate that your field research will keep the record for us, and I greatly appreciate your work.

Late last June, my mother was hospitalized for four days in Fang [Chiang Mai Province] for bleeding in her stomach. She has returned home and is being looked after by my younger brother. On June 29, my father finally decided to build their *shengji* [grave] in our orchard, following Yunnanese custom. I was happy with the decision. My mother had been talking about this for a long time. Although my father knows a bit of *fengshui* [geomancy], and could have easily settled this matter earlier, he hesitated for several reasons. He was afraid that the construction of the graves in our orchard might inhibit the expansion of the village in the future and also conflict with Thai regulations on the usage of farmland. . . . Nevertheless, my mother's recent illness has made him change his mind. As I mentioned to you before, I hope to turn this place into a public garden. The idea has nothing to do with social status, but a wish to pass on our history to the next generation. We will never sell this piece of land. It will forever be the site of remembrance of my parents, the first generation of our family in Thailand.

---

3. From Bianliang to Bingnong one still has to pass through many places in southern Shan State. The Thai names of the Yunnanese villages in Thailand referred to here are Ban Tham Santisuk (or Ban Tham) for Mantang (Mae Sai District, Chiang Rai Province); Ban Mae Salong for Meisile (Mae Fa Luang District, Chiang Rai Province); Ban Piang Luang for Bingnong (Wiang Haeng District, Chiang Mai Province); Ban Anuro Thai for Dagudi (Chiang Dao District, Chiang Mai Province); Ban Tham Ngob for Tangwo (Chaiprakan District, Chiang Mai Province); Ban Mai Nongbour for Reshuitang Xincun (or Xincun) (Chaiprakan District, Chiang Mai Province); and Ban Yang for Wanyang (Fang District, Chiang Mai Province). Besides fleeing to Shan State, many Yunnanese refugees escaped from Yunnan to Kachin State.

Wen-Chin, I am writing this letter in bed as my child is sleeping sweetly next to me. In him, I see my past, my duty, and the continuity of the lives of the Yunnanese people. I wish you great success in your research. I will write to you further when I have more to share.

Best wishes,
Zhang Dage   *July 26, 1998, 3:00 a.m.*

Zhang Dage's parents are from Longling in Yunnan. His father escaped to Burma in 1951 with a few male relatives. Like many fellow refugees who maintained the hope of fighting their way back to Yunnan, he joined the KMT guerrillas in their headquarters in Mong Hsat (southern Shan State) that year and remained in the KMT Third Army until 1986. In 1958, Zhang Dage's father sent a few men to bring his wife out of Yunnan. After the Communist takeover, very few people were able to escape with their entire family at once. In most cases, males between fifteen and fifty years old left first, with the intention of exploring the new environment and returning to Yunnan if the situation in China improved. They believed the Communists would not harm women, old people, and small children. Many refugees more or less followed the direction of the caravan trade routes into Burma, bypassing main roads in some areas in order to avoid encountering Communists. These familiar trade routes were convenient for most Yunnanese refugees, and Zhang Dage's description of these escape routes gives a concise picture that accords with those of other informants (see chapter 2 in this volume; also Chang 1999, 21–49, 92–127; 2006a).

Zhang Dage's family moved several times within Burma. In 1978, an uncle took him to northern Thailand for schooling by following a Yunnanese caravan escorted by a troop of the KMT Third Army. In Thailand he was reunited with his father, a minor officer of the Third Army who had been dispatched to Thailand four years earlier. His other family members made the journey a few years later. Zhang Dage completed a Chinese education at the junior high school established by the KMT Third Army in Xincun, and in 1980 he went to Taiwan for further education.[4] He later

---

4. From 1971 to 1991, the Free China Relief Association, a semiofficial organization that worked closely with the Nationalist government in Taiwan, offered full scholarships to Yunnanese students of northern Thailand (from fifty to one hundred annually) to travel to Taiwan for further education.

graduated from a medical college, became a physician, and married a Taiwanese woman. They have three children.

Despite my Taiwanese background, I share the same family name with Zhang Dage[5] and have been affably treated as one with the same genealogy (*tong jiamen*). From 1997 to 1999, while I was writing my doctoral dissertation in Belgium, we corresponded through letters. His narration weaves nostalgia for the past with prospects for the future and a consciousness for maintaining a record of contemporary Yunnanese migration history. The letter quoted above especially expresses his earnest desire to learn about the flight experiences of his parents' generation and to establish a historical site that will carry their memory into the next generation.

Zhang Dage once set up a weblog and is now operating a Facebook page for information sharing and networking among migrant Yunnanese—a space for remembering common experiences. He also collects resources pertaining to the history of the KMT and Yunnanese migrants in Burma and Thailand that include reports, films, maps, novels, and biographies. All demonstrate his rootedness as a Yunnanese migrant, or what Basch et al. refer to as a "transmigrant" (1994, 7), predicated on maintaining a range of social connections between one's home society and the society of settlement. A central question arises: Where is home for Zhang Dage following his parents' and his continuous migrations? Is it Shan State where he was born and lived for sixteen years, Yunnan where his parents originated and his eldest sister still lives,[6] northern Thailand where his parents have settled for more than thirty years and will eventually be buried, or central Taiwan where his immediate family is presently located? Although these are separate locations, they are linked by a series of displacements and emplacements experienced by Zhang Dage's family members that embody multifarious strands of meanings in his memory. Shan State in Burma, which he talks and writes about most, seems to have particular significance.

---

5. "Zhang" is the pinyin Romanization in transliteration, whereas "Chang" is the Wade-Giles Romanization used in Taiwan.

6. When Zhang Dage's mother escaped Yunnan, his sister was eight years old. She was too old to be carried all the way and too young to walk by herself, so she was left behind with a grandmother.

We covered many topics through the years regarding this question of "home." The following extract from another letter is in response to my inquiry about Yunnanese women's lives as he witnessed them in Shan State during the 1960s and 1970s.

> Dear Wen-Chin,
>   . . . You must be anxious to receive a reply. I'm not too busy now and would like to answer the questions you have raised. . . .
>   Regarding the issue of Yunnanese women and their family life, it can be discussed from different perspectives. [In terms of family composition,] most husbands escaped Yunnan first and left their wives and young children behind. Some of the men were civilians; others were Nationalist stragglers or local defense guards. Many civilians joined the KMT guerrilla forces in Shan State after arriving in Burma. Many men went back to Yunnan a few years later and managed to take their dependents to Burma. A few who were better off settled their families in towns and cities. Most refugees settled around the military posts of the KMT troops [in rural Shan State] and engaged in farming. The lives of soldiers' wives were particularly hard. They had to sustain their families alone in the face of repeated battles. However, living within the power sphere of the KMT could at least guarantee protection against invasion by the Burmese army and other ethnic forces. Moreover, the KMT posts also functioned as nodes for trade caravans, and villagers could benefit from the trade. Life in Burma at that time was much better than it was in China, which was embattled by endless class struggles and a series of political movements. . . .
>   Most Yunnanese women in Burma spent a great deal of their time cooking, washing, taking care of their children, and raising a few pigs. In addition, they had to cultivate gardens [*zhong yuanzi*] and farms [*zhong di*]. The vegetables grown in gardens [next to their houses] were mostly for family use, but the produce planted on farms, including rice and opium, was largely for sale. Women were very busy throughout the whole year because they had to do everything themselves, including making clothes, pickled vegetables [*yancai*], soybean curd [*doufu*], sausage [*changzi*], ham [*huotui*], fermented soybeans [*douchi*], zongzi, and *baba*.[7] They observed every festival with specially prepared food. Festivals enrich life in Burma with beautiful memories

---

7. *Zongzi* are glutinous rice dumplings prepared especially for the Duanwu Festival during the fifth month of the lunar calendar. *Baba* are rice cakes, made especially for the Moon Festival in the eighth month of the lunar calendar and Chinese New Year.

of childhood [for the second generation]. Regarding the future, there was no particular plan. The essential concern [for women] was the maintenance of everyday life and the safety of their husbands and children....

... My biggest wish is that after Burma joins the ASEAN [Association of Southeast Asian Nations], its political situation will improve with the gradual growth of democracy and freedom, and that ethnic rebels will disarm. I dream of returning to my birthplace someday. It would be a great joy to walk again on those familiar paths that have sustained the footprints of many souls who preceded us in this foreign land.

Best wishes,
Zhang Dage   April 25, 1997, Tainan

In our correspondence and conversations, Zhang Dage often tells stories about the village life of his childhood in upper Burma. His narratives contrast with the memories of wars and fighting of the first generation, especially during the 1950s (see Chang 1999, 21–50). For him and many second-generation migrants who moved away later on, there is a sense of attachment to Burma, as over time memories of childhood and adolescence become nostalgic. Even today, Zhang Dage keeps transcripts of his scholastic records, stamps, notebooks, and postcards that he brought with him from Burma to Thailand and then to Taiwan, now invaluable treasures spanning time and place.

In line with Zhang Dage's narration, many informants also stressed how hard they tried to maintain a sense of normalcy in their everyday lives in spite of their mobility and difficult living conditions. Men were often absent because of military duties or trading activities, and women had to assume the responsibilities of everyday life. Their efforts to uphold a Yunnanese lifestyle illustrated their agency in counterbalancing external instability.[8] Scudder and Colson refer to "clinging to the familiar and changing no more than is necessary" in a strange environment as "conservative strategy" (1982, 272). Linkage with a former lifestyle entails the recovery of meaning and

---

8. In "Invisible Warriors" (Chang 2005), I have looked into the power relations embedded in gendered roles. By examining the life stories of three Yunnanese women migrants in northern Thailand, I discuss the manner in which these women coped with different predicaments in the past while adhering to traditional Chinese norms and values and simultaneously reinterpreting them with inner strength and creativity in their everyday life. Chapter 6 of this volume further explores the trading experiences of five Yunnanese women migrants in Burma in relation to gendered politics.

cultural continuity, which helps refugees reconstruct self-identity as well as form a basis of trust (Daniel and Knudsen 1995, 4). Daily maintenance of these efforts is typical for refugees (e.g., Daniel and Knudsen 1995; Fadiman 1998; Gold 1992; Hansen and Oliver-Smith 1982; Malkki 1995; Shami 1993) and calls for a range of strategies. Cooking native food is particularly essential. In the courageous and beautifully written autobiography *From the Land of Green Ghosts: A Burmese Odyssey*, Pascal Khoo Thwe, a student refugee from the Padaung minority in rural Shan State who had participated in the 1988 student movement for democracy, related his difficulty in adapting to the new diet and cuisine after arriving in England. Even "eating muesli with cold milk for breakfast for the first time was a shocking experience," he wrote (2002, 269). Regularly cooking native dishes became a necessary remedy to sustain his refugee life in a foreign land. Likewise, my informants commonly referred to cooking Yunnanese food as the most fundamental means for keeping up a Yunnanese lifestyle. As Zhang Dage's letter stressed, by observing traditional festivals with special food, Yunnanese refugees connected their past with the present, while transmitting Yunnanese beliefs, customs, and practices to the next generation.

Zhang Dage's Essays

Zhang Dage also wrote a series of short essays about his childhood in Burma, which he posted on a blog between 2000 and 2003. His narratives speak of the sociocultural meaning of Yunnanese family life, trade, education, and warfare in regard to ongoing movement. Here I quote from two essays that draw upon childhood memories, one dealing with a Chinese school and another about a battle.

Enlightenment of Education

After a diasporic Chinese community is founded, its first concern is transmission of Chinese culture to the next generation. This is not old-fashioned thinking, but perseverance in the face of external hardships.

When we moved to Bianliang (Figure 1–1), there was a primary school called "Bianliang Fuxing Xiaoxue" [Bianliang Revival Elementary School]. It was located on flat ground just outside the village center. The school was a straw long house divided into three rooms. The central one was

Figure 1–1. Zhang Dage's family photo taken in Bianliang between 1967 and 1968 (Courtesy of Zhang Dage)

the administrative office, and the other two were classrooms. The central office had protruding T-shaped eaves. Under the eaves, placed horizontally, appeared the name of the school. A couplet was posted vertically on its two sides. The line on the left stated: "Recover the motherland and wipe out national shame through the teaching and transmission of loyalty," and the line on the right said: "Regain and develop the nation with the cultivation of patriotic culture."⁹ Inside the office, above the doorway, there were four characters—"propriety, justice, honesty and sense of shame" [*li yi lian chi*]—and on each side a verse: "With feet planted on the ground and head supporting the sky" [*ding tian li di*] on the left, and "To carry on the heritage so as to pave the way for future generations" [*ji wang kai lai*] on the right. The national flag of the Republic of China and a photo of its founding father, Sun Yat-sen, hung centered on the front wall. Posted respectively on four poles on the left side of the classroom were four characters: "loyalty" [*zhong*], "filial piety" [*xiao*], "benevolence" [*ren*], and "love" [*ai*]. Those on the right side read "trust" [*xin*], "justice" [*yi*], "peace" [*he*], and "harmony" [*ping*]. These

---

9. Fuguo xuechi shouchuang zhongzhen jiaoyu / xingbang tuqiang peiyang aiguowenhua.

writings represented the great spirit of nature and the four ethical principles and eight cardinal virtues [*siwei bade*] in this rudimentary school....

I remember my first teacher's family name was Chang. Teacher Chang was not tall but had a stern face. An English teacher, surnamed Wu, joined the school later. Teacher Wu had an upright personality. The job in such a small school was too simple for his abilities, and he did not stay long. Before leaving, he gave me his English dictionary. I did not see him off on the day of his departure, but other students walked with him to the other side of the hill. They had prepared some dry food and boiled eggs for him. Even today, I do not understand why I did not join the other classmates to bid goodbye to Teacher Wu. Was I afraid of separation or was it simply due to my stupidity? I really do not know. Later on, the school hired Teacher Zi from a lowland town. He often told us stories about this town and inspired our curiosity about life there. Teacher Zi said that prior to his coming he had often heard about Bianliang. He traveled on a horse to our village. When approaching the village, he got off his horse and washed himself at a creek. However, after climbing over a hill, he was stunned to see our desolate village. Nevertheless, Teacher Zi stayed at the school longer than any other teacher. In the end, he moved to northern Thailand and resettled in a Yunnanese border village.

Zhang Dage was born in a village called Nanpoliang and lived there until 1967 when his father was dispatched to a KMT post, Bianliang.[10] After moving to this mountain village, Zhang Dage experienced many significant changes. One of them was attending a Chinese school. His essay quoted above reflects a strong cultural and political affiliation among the Yunnanese warrior-refugees with the KMT armies. When the guerrilla organization was disbanded in 1961, only the Third and Fifth Armies survived the disintegration. Subsequently, the Nationalist government in Taiwan ceased financial support of these two straggler armies and only sponsored intelligence work for Division 1920 headquartered in Chiang Mai Province (Thailand), which had supervised several posts in upper Burma since 1965.[11] While relocating their main forces to northern Thailand in the 1960s, General Li Wenhuan and General Duan Xiwen, the

---

10. The place is two to three hours' walk southeast from Mong Hsu (Maing Hsu), a place famous for its ruby mines (1990s).

11. The unit was commonly called the Intelligence Mainland Operation Bureau (*dalu gongzuochu*).

leaders of the two armies, left a small portion of their troops in Burma to facilitate the lucrative contraband trade across the border. Their major sources of income became drug trafficking, trade in jade stones, and escorting civilian caravans.

Although the interaction between the Third and Fifth Armies and Taiwan greatly diminished after the disbandment of the KMT guerrillas, and there were no more organized military actions against the Chinese Communists, anticommunism still served as the guiding ideology of the two armies, and the Republic of China on Taiwan remained the political fatherland vis-à-vis the native motherland of mainland China (Chang 2002, 2006a). These ideological beliefs were emphasized by the army leaders in the interest of community coherence, because they reminded the Yunnanese refugees in Burma of their common fate under the rule of a hostile host government and reinforced their morale in the face of harsh living conditions. By characterizing as devils the Chinese Communists who were responsible for their flight and the suffering of loved ones left behind, Yunnanese refugees perceived themselves as being on the side of justice. This political stance was further justified by their cultural affiliations and transmission of values to the next generation. In many Yunnanese villages in Shan State and the border areas of northern Thailand, Chinese education was organized by the KMT armies.

Zhang Dage's essay about the Bianliang Revival Elementary School indicates the KMT Yunnanese political identification during the Cold War period. Bianliang was a small mountain village with a population of about fifty households. Nevertheless, it was an important trading post of the KMT Third Army in Shan State, with around thirty troops stationed there. Armed caravans frequently passed through the village prior to 1973, either with transported goods such as opium from northern Shan State destined for Thailand or consumption merchandise from Thailand destined for the black market in Burma (see chapter 5). The name of the school, the national flag of the Republic of China, the photo of Sun Yat-sen, the verses and ethical values posted in a strong militaristic and nationalistic tone replicated those of schools in Taiwan. The four ethical principles (propriety, justice, honesty, and sense of shame) and the eight cardinal virtues (loyalty, filial piety, benevolence, love, trust, justice, peace, and harmony) were derived from Confucianism. Sun Yat-sen appropriated the eight cardinal virtues to enhance his philosophy of nationalism, and Chiang Kai-shek used the four ethical principles to promote the New Life Movement in 1934 that aimed to modernize Chinese society. These Confucian values thus served as a metonym of orthodox Chinese culture. In contrast with the Chinese Communist government, which aimed to destroy Chinese culture through the Cultural Revolution, the Yunnanese refugees took on the mission of cultural transmission.

Differing from the anticommunist propaganda found in nationalistic writings in textbooks published by the KMT government prior to the 1990s for use in Taiwan and abroad among ethnic Chinese communities, Zhang Dage's essay conveys a childlike tone regarding this particular political scenario. Together with his other essays, his reminiscences form a record of a precious social history for the Yunnanese refugees. His description of the things and people of his childhood suspends moral judgments inherent in discussions of contraband trade and political ideology. In spite of poverty and insecurity, it was a time of innocence for a little boy who appreciated life with his family in the mountainous Shan State. Apart from political affiliation, Chinese education was predicated on people's cultural attachment. Other informants have indicated that in areas where there were no Chinese schools, some parents hired private teachers to provide Chinese education for their children. This desire to transmit Chinese culture and identity to their offspring demonstrates this migrant community's determination to maintain their roots and counterbalance the external instability of living in a foreign land.

With reference to Tsing's analysis of the Meratus Dayaks' interconnections with a series of external forces (2005), Bianliang, with its confluence of multifarious elements generated from local, national, and transnational domains, involves political, cultural, and economic implications. Much like Tsing's interpretation, the frictions that arose from the interacting process, while it produced coercion and confinements, also yielded possibilities for alignment and cooperation that stimulated villagers' agency to respond. The above essay attests to their efforts to sustain their political and cultural identification via Chinese education, a prevailing strategy among Yunnanese refugees in Burma (and also Thailand). The following essay addresses a less routine aspect of life—a military conflict. Despite its intensity, in the eyes of Zhang Dage as a small boy, it brought unique excitement to the dullness of everyday life.

War

In the mountainous regions of northern Burma, military conflicts occurred incessantly.

In the third spring of our settlement in Bianliang [i.e., 1970], apprehensive rumors circulated. Adults appeared anxious. Father frequently went to Grandpa Luo's house to attend meetings.[12] An atmosphere of agitation seemed to permeate the whole valley.

A telegram arrived. It said that the Communist Party of Burma [CPB] was moving through the mountains north of Bianliang. They were bullying civilians with increasing threats. Negotiations were to no avail. A war was imminent. More troops were dispatched to Bianliang, and more supplies and weapons arrived. Military tactics were drawn up based on sand table exercises. Our troops had completed all preparations and were waiting for deployment.

The village was filled with the noise of troops and the neighing of war horses. In our house, soldiers filled the spare rooms and corridor. They polished their weapons with great enthusiasm. Mother, however, looked distressed.

In the early morning of the day of departure, Father wore a military uniform, looking dignified and unfamiliar. Uncle Zhang walked from his home, also fully armed and equipped. The whole military group set off north from the village. All the villagers were present to send off the troops and pray for their safe and victorious return. The atmosphere was intense. My attention was particularly drawn to a mule that was loaded with a pile of cotton cloth and a first-aid kit.

After the troops had set off from the village, Grandpa got a horse and rode with me to the top of a hill. He said we were going to watch the battle. I don't know whether Grandpa was concerned for Father's safety or simply curious, but I will never forget the view. In the far distance there was a large plain where I saw many farms, spires, houses raised on stilts, and smoke from kitchen fires. This place was Mong Zhang [northwest of Bianliang, about three hours' walk from there]; it was the main battlefield. The noise of the cannons resembled thunder, and gunshots were similar to the sound of firecrackers.

---

12. Grandpa Luo, the commander of the troop stationed in Bianliang, was only a few years older than Zhang Dage's father, but because of his higher official rank and according to Yunnanese custom, he was addressed as if he were a generation senior to his actual age.

Three days later, good news arrived. The enemy had surrendered, and our troops were returning victorious. All the villagers appeared to welcome their return. Soldiers told of their heroic deeds again and again. The troops returned to their respective battalions to receive awards.

A vast array of booty was displayed in the corridors of Grandpa Luo's house, including captured arms, leaflets for surrender, and printed pictures of Mao Zedong. The display was photographed. Some of the weapons were no longer of any use. Grandpa Luo gave this order: "You may use them as toys." We kids were exhilarated and fought to grab our favorite pieces. Everyone had a weapon. We launched our own fight over a local hill with incessant screams until evening when we lay down exhausted on the ground.

I remember there was a girl, the only one among the group. She was a tomboy and liked to play with the boys. She carried the only automatic rifle on her shoulder that day. Her distinctive appearance eclipsed the rest of the group. Years later she went to Taiwan for further education at a business junior college. It is funny to think back to the old days. The memories of childhood are sweet despite the vicissitudes of human affairs.

Contrasting the adult war with the children's mock battle makes an interesting juxtaposition. The story intertwines excitement with a sense of anxiety and highlights both instability and absurdity in the refugees' lives. It does not address the intricacies of the hostilities or the justification for going to war, as the author's intent is not to convince anyone or any political entity, but to share his nostalgia with his blog readers, mostly fellow Yunnanese migrants who came from Burma and Thailand to Taiwan. Given its focus on the villagers' reactions, Zhang Dage's narration brings the reader directly into the people's experience and simultaneously triggers their memories of similar experiences. The language tempo is succinct and fluid, resembling the script of a short film, and vividly portrays a process connected by five major scenes—the preparation for imminent war, the villagers sending off the troops, watching the war from the top of a hill, the return of the troops, and the children's mock battle.

Fighting was incessant at the time, and victory was only ever temporary. The expansion of the CPB as well as the increasing presence of the Burmese forces compelled the KMT soldiers and their dependents in Bianliang to withdraw to Mong Zhang in 1973. Very soon the troops retreated again from Mong Zhang to Piang Luang, a border post in northern Thailand, and their dependents gradually dispersed to different places. Zhang

Dage and his family then moved to Taunggyi, the capital of Shan State. During this period, many Yunnanese refugees in rural Shan and Kachin States also migrated to towns and cities in order to avoid the constant warfare. Slowly, they established their communities in many major towns and cities in upper Burma such as Muse, Namkham, Kutkai, Lashio, Hsipaw, Kyaukme, Tangyan, Taunggyi, Kengtung, Mandalay, Pyin U Lwin (Maymyo), Mogaung, and Myitkyina. Simultaneously, their economic influence became entrenched in its connection with the underground Burma–Thailand cross-border trade.

Zhang Dage's stories provide an insider's viewpoint that reveals refugees' dynamism as they reconstructed their lives in Burma. This dynamism not only inspired strategies for survival in different life domains, such as cuisine, education, economic engagement, and military action, but also created a new identity: anticommunist Chinese refugees in a foreign land who linked their past with the present and provided an outlook for the future through cultural continuity.

Zhang Dage's essays are primarily about his childhood in the rural areas, and his writing is distinctive and full of graphic images. He once explained this feature to me: "These images didn't appear suddenly but had been in my mind for a long time before I put pen to paper and wrote down the stories about them. It is like artists whose works are stimulated by inspiration. Prior to the flash of inspiration, these artists have actually been thinking for a long time." Zhang Dage's explanation indicates his artistic talent as a writer and also points to his conscious identification with his childhood in Shan State.

In addition, Zhang Dage's language communicates a strong sense of nostalgia that depicts a simple and joyful life. His other essays about this period are entitled "Life," "House Moving," "A Small Red Mule," "Mountain Spring," "Chicken Mushrooms," "Dream," "Mule Caravans," and "Li Dashu." By reconstructing memories of the beautiful old days, Zhang Dage acknowledged that his childhood in Nanpoliang and Bianliang often occurs to him, whether in thoughts or dreams, unlike memories of his later life in Taunggyi, Lashio, and northern Thailand. He said: "It was a kind of retroversion due to the pressures of studies and later on career development [in Taiwan]. For me, the time spent in Nanpoliang and Bianliang forms the roots of my life; times in Taunggyi and Lashio only form a part of the branches. The earliest stage was the hardest, but is also the most precious. People need roots. It is very sad if one doesn't have his or her own roots."

Through writing Zhang Dage crafts his longing for an enrooted childhood memory of rural Shan State. His essays reveal a strong desire to retain the past, which, however, is grounded on the awareness that the past will never return, and in any case, he cannot revisit these places, as the area is closed to foreigners. Life to him is a series of travels; after adapting to an environment, he often had to move to a new one. Consequently, he holds on to the memory of a happy childhood that gives him a feeling of rootedness in order to overcome the feeling of displacement.

In Taunggyi and Lashio (1974–1978)

Prior to the KMT troop's move from Mong Zhang to northern Thailand in 1974, Zhang Dage's father asked a cousin living in Taunggyi to take in Zhang Dage so he could study in that city. At the same time, a neighbor, Uncle Chen, contacted his brother in Taunggyi to take in his son, Xiaowei. Zhang Dage's uncle and Xiaowei's uncle both agreed. It was about a year later when Zhang Dage's mother, sister, and brother joined him there. On the afternoon of August 25, 2008, at his home in Taichung, Taiwan, Zhang Dage told me about some aspects of this transition.

"We rode horses from Mong Zhang and stayed one or two nights on the way. We crossed the bridge in Kunhing and arrived at a public road. We then transferred to a jeep. It was my first time sitting in a car. I was small and felt the car running very fast. I felt dizzy and didn't know which direction I should look. I turned to the left, to the right, and to the rear. But it was very scary looking to the rear and seeing the road moving so fast. If you are used to sitting in a car from a young age, you cannot imagine that feeling. You would say sitting in a car was just a simple matter, but it was not so in my case. My uncle noticed my discomfort and told me to look at the mirror at the front of the car. It helped. I felt more stable.

"The car reached Taunggyi. The house of Xiaowei's uncle was on the main road, *lanma*, and they alighted first. When the car took off again, my uncle said to me: 'Remember well where Uncle Chen's house is.' Attentively, I tried to remember every turn. But the roads were very different from those in our village, and the houses were different too. After two turns I had lost my orientation. When the car arrived at my uncle's house, I put down my luggage and began to miss Xiaowei. We came from the same village, and he was the only friend I had in Taunggyi. I immediately went to look for his uncle's house. But after two turns, I had lost my way. I cannot remember how I managed to find his uncle's house that day.

"My uncle registered me in the first grade at a Burmese school, and I started Burmese lessons. Before going to Taunggyi, I couldn't speak a word of Burmese. My uncle told the landlord's twin sons: 'You teach Jiayao Burmese; he will teach you Chinese.' My uncle taught me one Burmese sentence—'Daba khawlei? Zheshi sheme?' [What is this?] Whatever I saw, I pointed to that object and asked the twins: 'Daba khawlei? Daba khawlei?' I thus learned my Burmese from them. One of the twins was named Gugu and the other Bobo. By the time a month had passed, we had no difficulty communicating.

"Before going to Taunggyi, I had studied at the Bianliang primary school for nearly four years. The difference between these two schools was primarily the language used in teaching. Except for the class on the Burmese language, I had already studied the other subjects in Bianliang. I therefore scored the highest grades in the class. My class teacher seldom let me stay in class. She often assigned me errands such as going to the post office, buying things, or paying bills. She must have thought that I had studied those subjects before anyway, and that I was trustworthy and capable.

"I worked hard on the Burmese language because I refused to fall behind the other students. But maybe due to a Han chauvinist mentality which had been instilled in me by my grandpa and the teachers in Bianliang, I felt the Burmans were a less developed people and the Burmese language a less developed language. A year later, I asked my mother, who had just arrived in Taunggyi, to send me to a Chinese school in Lashio [the capital of northern Shan State]. She thought I was still too young and refused. I then asked my uncle repeatedly for the same thing. Finally he agreed to take me to Lashio. At that time I had yet to finish my second year at the Taunggyi primary school.

"We went by airplane, my first flight. My uncle gave me many first-time experiences. After arriving in Lashio, I was placed directly in Guowen Chinese School [*guowen zhongxue*] at the junior high level because of my age. My uncle took me to class on the first day. I was the shortest in the class and was thus assigned to sit in the first row. After I sat down, my uncle said to the class: 'This is Zhang Jiayao. He is from Taunggyi. You have to take care of him; he is still small.' After the introduction, he returned to Taunggyi and left me alone in Lashio.

"I stayed at the school dormitory with students of different ages. The older ones took care of the younger ones. Some kids still wet their beds. The beds were made of bamboo and were placed at two levels, one higher and one lower. The sides of these beds did not have railings, and students frequently fell onto the ground while asleep. Those who slept on the lower-level beds often found their heads covered with white powder in the morning. It was from the upper-level beds, where worms were eating the wood.

"At Guowen, the happiest hour was after school. The older students took the younger ones to the river. We wrapped our dirty clothes in a bundle with a piece of *longyi*.[13] We washed the clothes and dried them on the grass by the riverbank. We swam for one or two hours and then picked up the dried clothes and went back to the dormitory. Occasionally, we went out for a movie or wandered around the town. I spoke Burmese when we were out, but basically, my life in Lashio was a return to the familiarity of Han community life. The Han population in Lashio was much larger than in Taunggyi."

Leaving the mountains for Taunggyi and later Lashio was transformative for Zhang Dage. It was a leap from rural to urban and from contact with other ethnic minorities to encounters with the ethnic majority, the Burmans, and their culture. In Tsing's words, it was a process of "encounters across differences" (2005). While adapting to a much more advanced lifestyle in a material sense, he was also aware of different ethnic politics. In the mountain villages, in association with the KMT troops, the Yunnanese Chinese were politically predominant and economically more resourceful. Although fighting with ethnic-based armies or the CPB sometimes occurred, basically they governed their own areas and led their own way of life. But in the lowlands, all the official agencies were controlled by the Burmans. When Zhang Dage had to attend the Burmese school and learn the Burmese language, he was aware of the shift from being in a ruling group to a ruled group. As told in the story, before long his ethnic pride propelled him to go to Lashio for a Chinese education. He was there for

---

13. *Longyi* is a sarong-like skirt commonly worn by both men and women in Burma.

only one and a half years before making another leap to Thailand and later on to Taiwan to pursue grander opportunities.

While Zhang Dage was in Lashio, one individual influenced his decision to go to Thailand and then Taiwan. This was an outstanding student who had graduated from Guowen Chinese School several years before Zhang Dage's arrival. That student received a scholarship from Taiwan and went there for further education. While he was studying at a medical college, he published a magazine critical of the Burmese government. This angered the government and made the student a hero to the Chinese community, especially the teachers and students at Guowen. "Our teacher told us that that graduate was our model. I thus decided to go to Taiwan. At that time my father was in northern Thailand. It was easier to go to Taiwan via Thailand. So I decided to go to Thailand first."

Going to Thailand (1978)

Zhang Dage returned to Taunggyi and waited for two months until there were vehicles going to Kengtung. They were government trucks that transported supplies to the border areas for the Burmese troops and, at the same time, also secretly served as a means of transportation for civilians. The fees collected from the passengers provided extra income for the drivers. These trucks were blue and rounded in the front, and were called *lantouche* by the Yunnanese. Several informants said that they were bullnosed Hino trucks that Japan donated as a part of postwar compensation for its atrocities in Burma during the Second World War.

Zhang Dage left Taunggyi with Uncle Chu,[14] a fictive relative who was going to Thailand for business. They were among several hundred passengers in a caravan of more than forty trucks. They gathered at Hopong, a village outside Taunggyi, before setting off on the journey.

"The sight of the cars going around the mountains was spectacular. While our truck was on this side of a mountain, I could see other cars on the opposite side of another mountain. Unfortunately, the trucks were stopped

---

14. Uncle Chu was married to a woman from a Zhang family. Though his wife is not genealogically related to Zhang Dage's family, because they shared the same family name Uncle Chu was considered kin by affiliation.

at a checkpoint before reaching Loilin [ninety-two kilometers from Taunggyi]. All the passengers were chased out of the trucks and forbidden to go any farther. I understood Burmese and remember a military officer shouting to the crowd: 'What do you Chinese intend to do? Why are you all going to the border? Are you going to subvert the government?' The passengers had to look for their own transport. Some people decided to return to Taunggyi by hiring tractors, but most of them decided to go to Loilin and see what could be done the next day. It was already dark as we walked toward Loilin dragging our luggage. We were like a swarm of fleeing refugees, distressed and dirty. When we arrived in Loilin, we went to a school. We put aside the desks and chairs in a classroom and made our beds on the floor. Uncle Chu said to me: 'We sleep here tonight. Do not be afraid.'

"After lying down, I put my hand into the pocket of my shorts to check on the money I had carried. I couldn't find my money. I panicked. I had carried eleven hundred kyat. That was several years' savings from my family. I must have dropped it on the way while walking to Loilin. I ran outside to look for the money, but was stopped by a soldier. '*Dikaung* [kid], where are you going?' Many Burmese soldiers were on guard outside the school. I replied: 'I've lost my money. I'm going to look for it.' He said: 'Where on earth are you going to find it? You can't find it. Wait till tomorrow morning.' But I didn't listen to him and kept running. I searched the ground with my flashlight. I came upon a small package wrapped in cotton paper. I grabbed it and felt the weight. I didn't know what it was, but thrust it into my pocket. I ran forward and found another similar package. I thrust it into my pocket too. Do you know what I had found? Sixteen pieces of old silver Chinese coins [*laoyinyuan*]. It was a lot of money. I didn't know what to do with them. If I was found in possession of these illegal coins, I would be put in jail. I walked back to the school and threw the two packages under a green hedge; I was afraid the Burmese soldiers would search us during the night. I prayed that I would be able to find the coins the next morning.

"I couldn't sleep the whole night. I was troubled by many thoughts. I had lost my own money but found those illegal coins. And I didn't know if I would be able to make my trip to Thailand. Around six o'clock in the morning, I got up and went to look for the money. It was foggy. I pretended that I was going to urinate. I walked to that hedge and put my hand underneath to search. The two packages were still there. I put them in my pocket and went back to the classroom. I then told Uncle Chu about the loss of my money and about finding the coins. Uncle Chu said to me: 'I know someone in Loilin. His name is Cao Dapeng. We will go to the station to ask his whereabouts.'

"We went to the station and told a *saikka* [trishaw] driver to take us to Cao Dapeng's house. Uncle Cao was startled to see us. His house was very shabby and had nothing in it. He went to the chicken coop in the backyard and got two eggs. I spotted his nervous looks to his wife, expressing his embarrassment over their poverty. After the meal, we hired a tractor and went to Pinlong.[15] We stayed in Pinlong for two days and then went to Xunding [a Shan village that was three to four hours on foot from Pinlong].[16] We waited for a period of *sangai* [three rotating markets] before setting off from Xunding to Thailand with a caravan.[17]

"I met Uncle Zhang Han in Xunding. His house had been next to ours in Bianliang. He and his troops were stationed in Xunding. He was very happy to see me and asked a soldier-messenger to take me every day to his office. He would chat with me while lying in bed, smoking opium. In addition, the family of that soldier-messenger lived in Reshuitang Xincun, the village that I was traveling to in northern Thailand. After learning of my destination, he was very nice to me. Generally speaking, I was very happy in Xunding, except in my dealings with our landlady, who was a snob. It was a Yunnanese custom to accept requests for accommodation from fellow travelers. However, the terms of payment were not discussed at the beginning. Sometimes when I stayed in the kitchen to help the landlady prepare meals, she would complain acrimoniously that too many people stayed at her house. I dared not tell Uncle Chu about this, but he must have observed the landlady's coldhearted manner. When we were leaving, Uncle Chu purchased a big sack of rice and a whole preserved pig's leg. He asked a few soldiers to carry the rice and ham to the landlady's house as

---

15. Pinlong is the town where an agreement initiated by Bogyoke Aung San that guaranteed a union form of government and the right of secession to ethnic minorities was signed in 1947.

16. Xunding was a primary starting point of the caravans traveling to Thailand (for further information see chapters 3 and 5).

17. *Gai* was the Yunnanese pronunciation for *jie* in Mandarin, which means a marketplace. It was a tradition in Yunnan and upper mainland Southeast Asia that a market was held every five days in rural areas. *Gai* thus became a unit of time. *Sangai* referred to three units of *gai* at one place, meaning fifteen days.

gifts of our appreciation for the board and lodging. The gifts amounted to more than half a year's accommodation. This incident taught me how to treat people generously.

"We set off on our journey to Thailand with a small caravan of thirty to forty mules. I remember there were eleven escort soldiers and a commanding officer. We walked for ten days. The experience was very significant for me. Even after all these years I remember several scenes vividly. During the journey, we had to pass several rivers that flowed through valleys. The riverbanks were precipitous [*xia jiangbianpo*]. One time I saw a man carrying a big load of flip-flops with a bamboo stick, walking downward to a river. From a distance, I couldn't see the man, only a load of moving slippers. Another time I saw a man carrying a big roll of corrugated zinc plates on his back. They were for use in roof construction. I also saw another man carrying a bicycle, walking down a slope. After reaching flat ground, he rode the bicycle. That bicycle was loaded with commodities. These scenes startled me. If I had still been living in mountain villages, I may not have felt shocked. But I had been to Taunggyi and Lashio, and had the experience of traveling by airplane, train, and car. I had watched movies, and our house in Taunggyi had electricity. I had experienced civilized life and was used to buying smuggled goods transported to the cities by Hino trucks for the *hmaungkho* market [black market]. When I saw how hard these porters worked to make a living, I felt pity for them. I knew I could not do what they did. Their profits from these demanding trips were small.

"During the journey, I also saw oxen that were being herded to Thailand for sale. But some oxen die on the way because of illness or old age. When this happened, they were abandoned. It was pitiful to see oxen dying on the way. They knelt down unable to move. I walked farther and saw oxen that had just died. Swarms of flies circled around the carcasses. When approaching the Thai border, I saw whole skeletons of oxen, and farther down, scattered skeletons.

"Once we had to pass a track. We knew enemies were entrenched on the other side of the mountain, but we had to pass there, as it was the only way. The atmosphere was intense. Nobody made a sound, not even the animals. Another time, while passing a place at night, a troop emerged suddenly from behind. They had hidden themselves in dense grass. Luckily they were not enemies. After recognizing our troop, they emerged to greet us. Each time, before setting off on the next stage of the journey, our escorts had to send two soldiers ahead to check if it was safe. Every day, the distance we walked varied. If the track condition was good, we walked a longer distance. If conditions were bad, we walked a shorter distance. When there were no villages on the way for a few days, we had to prepare extra food in advance. The knowledge of long-distance trade was obtained through the accumulated experiences of many generations. It was precious wisdom."

Zhang Dage's group arrived in Thailand safely. Despite the challenges that arose from political suppression, material scarcity, social unrest, and topographical dangers, Zhang Dage mapped out his future through mobility. While his father and uncle initiated going to Taunggyi, his later journeys to Lashio, Thailand, and then Taiwan were his own decisions. They reveal his internal drive in response to external challenges and his pursuit of a better life. Travels, in effect, bring him into contact with diverse people and environments and also cultivate his outlook as he compares different ways of living. In his narratives the reflections on the contrast between rural and urban lifestyles on the way to Thailand are particularly heartfelt and reveal his conscious forward-moving or upward path and his choice not to return to his former way of life. This longing for a better future through movement is common among migrant Yunnanese youth.

By narrating his lived experiences, Zhang Dage relates his involvement with a series of environments and events in meaningful sequence. Looking back on his life in Burma, he is conscious of complex forces that have impacted how he understands the world and himself: those originating from places, people, and things around him, and from ideologies of anticommunism and Sinocentrism. While the last two factors urged him to migrate and finally go to Taiwan, where he could discard his refugee status and be fully Chinese, the former ones have always reminded him of his identification with the Shan State of Burma and motivated him to seek connections and to write and talk about them. Through these practices he has been trying to unify the various impacts arising from his migratory life in order to assuage his state of ambivalence as a diasporan. While he values his roots and native places that live only in his constructed memory, he exerts himself to find the best in his current habitat. In Taiwan, he is a physician, a prestigious profession that has transformed his original status—from refugee to returned overseas Chinese (*guiqiao*), and from a child of an ethnic military family to an upper-middle-class elite. By crossing several national borders, he has also transcended the borders of his former social status and class. Yet, can we answer the question raised at the beginning of the chapter: Where is home for Zhang Dage?

On his former blog, Zhang Dage posted his favorite poem, entitled "Miscellaneous Poem," written by a famous Chinese poet, Tao Yuanming (365–427 CE).

> Life has no roots / Like dust floating on a footpath / Scattered by the wind without a destination / The physical body is not eternal / Having been born to this world / We are all brothers / There is no need for bloodshed / Enjoy life whenever possible / Drink with neighbors / This life will not come again / Just like a day passes by / Act now / Time never awaits you.[18]

This poem, characterized by an understanding of life's uncertainty and a carefree attitude, seemingly contrasts with Zhang Dage's craving for roots. His fondness for the poem, however, reflects his diasporic subjectivity that straddles the divide between attendant prospects and a lost feeling when traveling. It is an interstitial state of mind that commonly exists among immigrants and refugees whose lives are stranded in dislocation and exile (e.g., Anzaldúa 1987; Khoo Thwe 2002; Krulfeld et al. 1999; Lorente et al. 2005; Malkki 1995; Said 1999). They continuously struggle to reconcile the friction generated by the gap between their past and present.

Again, take Khoo Thwe's flight to England as an example: although the new environment granted him physical safety after his dreadful experiences fighting the Burmese army in the jungle, he was not able to regain peace of mind. While he worked strenuously as a Cambridge University undergraduate during the day, at night he was preoccupied by his native "ghost culture." In his autobiography he wrote:

> The space between being awake and asleep, the gap between the physical and metaphysical or subliminal worlds, between East and West, were eerily interlocked in my mind. All I needed was to go to sleep and I was in another world—whether of nightmares or visions of my friends and my home in Shan State. When I woke up I was thrown back to the lonely reality of exile. I was worried about my friends and family in the wrong way, because my feelings for them were mixed up with guilt and frustration. (2002, 279)

---

18. Rensheng wugendi / Piaoru moshangchen / Fensan zhufengzhuan / Ciyi feichangshen / Luodi weixiongdi / Hebi qingurou / Dehuan dangzuole / Doujiu jubilin / Shengnian buzailai / Yiri nanzaichen / Jishi dangmianli / Suiyue budairen.

Although Zhang Dage has never referred to such opposing forces, he acknowledges an enduring in-between feeling that is intensified by his multiple concerns: worry for his aged parents in Thailand, missing his eldest sister in Yunnan, nostalgia for his native places in Shan State, and caring for his own family in Taiwan. These feelings have driven him to go to Thailand annually despite his busy career. In 1993 he went back to Burma to visit his uncle's family who had moved from Taunggyi to Mandalay, and in 1997 he went to Yunnan to see his ninety-four-year-old grandmother[19] and his eldest sister, and to worship at the ancestors' graves. Still, he hopes to go back to Nanpoliang and Bianliang in Shan State for a visit someday, although he knows that all Yunnanese migrants have moved away from these places. While physically he may not be able to return to his native places, like Khoo Thwe he travels there in his dreams.

---

19. The grandmother passed away the year after Zhang Dage's visit.

2

Entangled Love

Ae Maew

> I just wanted to move on from my life in Burma. I believed if I studied hard, I would get a chance to go abroad. Education was the only way to change my life.
>
> —Ae Maew, January 30, 2005

Cat Girl

Ae Maew, meaning cat girl, is the Shan nickname of a Yunnanese graduate student I met in Taiwan in 2004 when I was invited to lecture at her university on the diasporic Yunnanese consciousness of time and space. After the lecture, Ae Maew came to see me and shared briefly her own migration experience, which sparked my interest in her Yunnanese origins and her effort to come to Taiwan for higher education. She was a second-generation migrant in Burma who had grown up in Laikha in Shan State. I hired her during two winter breaks (2005 and 2006) to assist me in fieldwork. Through her connections, I extended my ethnography to a few places that I had not visited before in Shan State.

In January 2005, after completing part of my fieldwork in northern Thailand, I flew from Chiang Mai to Yangon to meet with Ae Maew, who flew in from Taiwan. We did a few interviews in Yangon and then flew to Mandalay, the last royal capital, to which the Yunnanese immigration, mostly from Tengchong, has a history of several centuries.[1] Because of my limited research budget, we had to stay in a cheap hotel in the downtown, not far from the Yunnanese Association. We took a room with twin beds. Its old green carpet emitted a slight damp smell, and the showerhead in the bathroom continually dripped. I apologized to Ae Maew for the rough living conditions. We borrowed two bicycles to navigate the city during the day. It is organized in a grid, with numbered streets that makes it easy to locate addresses, but getting around is a challenge, with trishaws, coaches, motorcycles, cars, and bicycles moving through intersections with very few traffic lights. Even in early January the city was very hot and dusty.

Ae Maew had some friends whose relatives were in the jade business in Mandalay. With her help, I visited a few jade companies and interviewed several jade traders to trace their transnational networks as well as learn about their diverse lives outside of work. The Yunnanese husband of Ae Maew's best high school friend, a Shan lady, took us to explore the jade marketplace frequented every day by numerous small traders. When we were not conducting interviews, Ae Maew often told me about the joys and sorrows of her life. Despite her young age, she has experienced much adversity, complex tensions and conflicts involving family, ethnicity, society, and state. She expressed contrasting and contradictory feelings and seemed unreconciled to the divergent facets of her subjectivity in relation to her multiple positions—a daughter, a sister, a second-generation Yunnanese migrant in Burma, and a Chinese trans-migrant from Burma to Taiwan. Lila Abu-Lughod stresses exploration of this question of positionality in ethnographies of the particular by looking into how individuals live their "'cultural' complex" in order to "subvert the most problematic connotations of 'culture': homogeneity, coherence, and timelessness" (1993, 13-4).[2] Her viewpoint is in accord with the philosophical school of

---

1. Some surviving stone tablets of a Yunnanese Han temple, Jinduoyan tudici, located near a port on the Irrawaddy River in Mandalay, record its founding more than three hundred years ago. Another temple in Amarapura, Dongmiu guanyinsi, eight miles south of Mandalay, was completed in 1773 (Wu and Cun 2007b). About a hundred years later (in 1881), the Yunnanese Association was established there on a piece of royally granted land (Wu and Cun 2007a). Most of the early Yunnanese immigrants in the city were merchants and clerks.

2. This orientation is in line with that of a number of anthropologists since the 1980s who have discussed the significance of polyphony and of individuality and challenged traditional interests in using collective structures for the presentation of a coherent society (Clifford and Marcus 1986).

phenomenology that endeavors to recover the meaning of subjective consciousness and explore how the subjective consciousness opens toward the world from different angles (Natanson 1973; Watson and Watson-Franke 1985, 13). Corresponding with Abu-Lughod's phenomenological insight, my focus on Ae Maew's life and her changing relationships did draw me to see and also experience the whirl of "frictions" that drive her to transgress a range of structural forces relating to gender, class, community, and nation, simultaneously causing her intense pain and frustration. Moreover, it challenged my academic positioning's thin veneer of "neutrality." The story that follows not only illuminates Ae Maew's life but also my personal limitations during an ethnographical process.

On our last night in Mandalay before we set off for Taunggyi, we were, as usual, battling the heat and mosquitoes before falling asleep. The wall fans did little to help. Ae Maew assured me that after we reached Taunggyi, which is located on a plateau, it would be much cooler and there would be no more buzzing mosquitoes. Maybe it was the anticipation of going home that triggered Ae Maew's childhood memories that night. She spoke of Laikha, the place where she grew up before moving to Taunggyi:

"I love animals and have raised cats since I was a little girl. I often carried a cat in a cloth bag while taking our buffalo to graze. Sometimes I carried a cat wrapped in a *longyi* on my back. That is why our Baiyi [Shan] neighbors called me Ae Maew, meaning cat girl. . . .

"From childhood I saw mules silently carrying heavy loads. My family began breeding mules when I was in junior high school, seventy to eighty in the beginning. The number grew to over a hundred later on. They were born from the mating between horses and donkeys. Mules can't give birth themselves.[3] You have to keep on mating horses and donkeys in order to get mules. When I heard that purchasers had arrived in the village, I knew which of our mules would be sold. My heart saddened. Despite the fact that the mothers were horses and their young were mules, they were very attached to each other.

"The selling took place every year during the advent of Chinese New Year. Young mules were taken away one by one as the merchants set off on

---

3. I found a source that mentions that male mule foals are castrated after birth so that they can be tamed and take on the work of transportation (Li 2008, 111). In any case, the offspring of cross reproduction cannot reproduce.

their trade journeys. My heart was with these mules that wailed for their mothers while being taken away. I recognized their individual cries even after they had gone some distance, and each one was branded in my mind. But this was how we made a living. I wanted to break free of such a life. I was aware that the only way this could happen was to study hard in order to leave the village for further education in the city.

"During the summer, the livestock were taken to the mountain to graze. At that time, all farms grew rice; animals had to be kept away. Every household knew approximately where their animals were grazing, and about every two weeks, they had to check on them. Sometimes the animals couldn't find water and could die of thirst. Therefore, it was important to monitor them and drive them to a place with water. Villagers helped each other in this task. If I chase my animals today, you come to help me. Tomorrow, I help you in return. Every household's livestock was kept at a different site, so there was no risk of mixing with the neighbors' stock. Each herd had a lead female horse.

"After the rice harvest, it was time to lead the animals back to the village from the mountain. Villagers called this *kaibazi* [opening the valley]. They tore down the wooden rails around the farms and let their animals stay there for the winter.

"I was attached to the animals I looked after. I touched them and talked to them. After the mares gave birth to baby mules, the mothers and babies were cared for in the stable. I could tell the mothers were feeling uncomfortable with swelling breasts. Sometimes, I milked the mother horses and saved the milk in bottles. Out of curiosity, I would stare at the bottles for a long time, and then bottle-feed the baby mules. They were lovely, but when they grew older they were sold off. I cried for them. I cried. My father and mother didn't know about this. Oh, I didn't want to have this kind of life. It was very sad. Although these animals didn't speak, you could read their emotions by looking at them.

"I named every horse and mule. We had one horse that was wild and often had stomachaches, so I named her Chenshui.[4] Early one morning when Mother had gone to the market and my brothers were away I saw her in the distance walking home. Her steps were unstable, and with each one she stumbled, raising clouds of dust. She was bringing her two baby

---

4. *Chenshui* in the Tengchong dialect means stomachache.

mules with her. I knew it was her. I opened the gate of our pen to let her and her children in, and then I ran to my auntie's house to borrow medicine. My cousin came with me to give Chenshui a shot.

"The livestock had their own instincts. When they were sick, they found their way home and we gave them some salt or medicine. After eating, they would wander around for a few hours or an afternoon and then go back to their own place again. Sometimes they cried too, and when they did, I would wonder if they also felt sad."

Ae Maew's captivating account of the horses and mules reminded me of a faraway world that is intimately connected to my research on the long-distance caravan trade that relied on mules (chapter 5). Yet it was an aspect of that world and way of life that I had much neglected before. For years, I had listened to numerous accounts narrated by retired caravan traders and muleteers. To me, this traveling trade was an adventurous male undertaking, but Ae Maew's narrative reveals an intimate female role behind the trade. Her sentiments toward the animals contrasted sharply with the ventures of the male traders and complemented their "history" of the trade. I anticipated exploring a new world, the rich lives of Yunnanese women, during our upcoming trip to Taunggyi. I would stay at Ae Maew's home, which would guarantee an anthropological methodology of participant observation.

Multiple Star Residence

The next morning, Ae Maew and I joined two other passengers in a small shared van bound for Taunggyi. We left at eight-thirty in the morning. The road was bumpy from time to time, and when another car approached from the opposite direction, we had to roll up the windows to keep out the dust. After one and a half hours we entered a highland region on a winding mountain road. The landscape was barren, composed of limestone mountains. There were no villages on the way. I tried to picture trains of mule caravans in the past passing through this desolate track. Around noon, the car stopped in front of a small restaurant for lunch. The driver poured buckets of water on the engine to cool it down, producing clouds of hissing white vapors. After lunch, the car continued its journey, eventually leaving the barren mountains for colorful slopes and valleys. We passed through several villages, their entrances marked with large bamboo groves. The road became wider and smoother, flanked on either side by an endless succession of rolling farms that cultivated barley, rape, beans, wheat, and other crops I could not name. Ae Maew pointed out the cinchona (*jinjina*) that grew along the road and said she liked their slim, tall shape very much. Intermixed with cinchona were many *Bombax ceiba* trees with crimson blossoms. Ae Maew said that during the rainy season, the scenery was even more beautiful.

Around five in the afternoon, we finally arrived at Ae Maew's home in Taunggyi. It was an old two-story teak house that Ae Maew had purchased for 2.46 million kyat in 1994, one year before she went to Taiwan, using her savings of twenty years, plus some loans from friends. She said she bought the house for her father, who had been teaching at a Taunggyi Chinese school since 1989 and had been staying in the school dormitory. Her aunt and her eldest brother from Pinlong soon moved to the house, and then her sister. Her two other brothers came often as well. However, Ae Maew's mother was left behind in Laikha to take care of their farms and livestock. In 1998, her father was diagnosed with late-stage throat cancer. After the end of a school term in January 1999, Ae Maew hurried home from Taiwan. She first went to Bangkok, where she met up with her sister who had gone to Thailand a few years earlier. Together they went back to Burma via northern Thailand by secretly crossing the border. It was only upon arriving home that Ae Maew learned that her mother had not been informed of her father's illness. At her insistence, her mother finally moved to Taunggyi from Laikha. Ae Maew then returned to Taiwan to continue her studies. About a month later, Ae Maew's father passed away.

Ae Maew had told me something of her family's conflicts when we were in Yangon and Mandalay. Once she said: "My mother was always treated as an outsider by my aunt, a domineering figure who meddled in my family's affairs. She took my brothers, one by one, from Laikha to Pinlong when they were school age. My father had also lived with my aunt. He had been teaching at the Chinese school in Pinlong before going to Taunggyi. He went home only two or three times a year for short visits. All my brothers were alienated from my mother. My aunt tore apart my family."

Ae Maew's aunt and father were from a family of the landlord class back in Yunnan. Her grandfather had been a high-ranking official in Kunming, the capital of Yunnan. The aunt had been engaged once, but the flight after the Communist takeover had resulted in separation between her and her fiancé, and she has remained unmarried. Ae Maew's father respected this unmarried elder sister very much and asked his children to address her as "Beibei"—the Chinese address for a senior brother of one's father—instead of "Gugu" (a sister of one's father). The preference for a male form of address points to the tradition of gender inequality but also to the aunt's high power and status in the extended family. She raised Ae Maew's brothers and several of Ae Maew's male cousins. Consequently, a deep hatred exists between Ae Maew's mother and aunt. Nevertheless, they have been living together in the house in Taunggyi since 1999. When Ae Maew took me home, there was only her mother, her aunt, and a cat living in the house. Ae Maew's eldest brother has been in a Mandalay jail since 2003 for the crime of gambling. Her second elder brother died of AIDS in connection with drug addiction two years after their father's death. The third brother is married and living with his wife's family in Taunggyi. Ae Maew's sister was working in Bangkok at a Chinese newspaper publisher.

When we entered the house, Ae Maew was upset with its dusty condition. We only saw her aunt, who was nearly eighty years old. She was very thin and small and greeted us warmly. I called her Gugu (auntie) instead of Beibei (uncle). Ae Maew briefly introduced me to her and started to complain about the house. She said that she had transferred one hundred thousand kyat to her third elder brother a few months earlier (through a friend's connection) to hire a domestic worker for one year to look after the house and her mother and aunt. But there was no sign of the worker. Ae Maew apologized to me for the disorder. I tried to calm Ae Maew and said it was not bad at all; it only needed some cleaning.

Ae Maew took up a gray tiger cat that was squatting on the cooking stove in the kitchen. She held it lovingly and said she had brought the cat home from a friend's house about a year earlier. Ae Maew showed me around the house. Actually, it was a lovely wooden house. Downstairs were the living room, the kitchen, and two bedrooms. Upstairs were another living room with the family altar, two other bedrooms, and a small balcony facing the road. There were only a few pieces of wooden furniture in the two living rooms—a cupboard, some chairs, and two tables—emphasizing the empty spaces. In my eyes, they resembled two small ballrooms. I loved the simplicity. In the backyard there was a toilet and a bathroom, but the latter was only used for water storage. Ae Maew's mother also kept a small garden in the backyard where she planted some vegetables and herbs. At a corner of the backyard was a hut made of pieces of wood from torn-down rails. Ae Maew said that this was her aunt's kitchen. A chain lock was placed on the door. On seeing this extra kitchen, I wondered if Ae Maew's mother had gained a superior position in the household (having the main kitchen for her own use). I thought of a Chinese saying—a kitchen does not accommodate two women (yige chufang rongbuxia liangge nyuren)—describing the tension between a mother-in-law and a daughter-in-law. I saw that it applied to Ae Maew's mother and auntie as well.

Having placed our luggage in the room next to her mother's on the second floor, we started to clean the house. A few minutes later, Ae Maew's mother came back. I greeted her and called her "Dama" (senior aunt).[5] She was in her mid-seventies, and, in contrast to Ae Maew's aunt, was tall and stout. Ae Maew looked very much like her. They had beautiful eyes. Yet, Dama had a sorrowful face; the lines revealed the adversity she had undergone. On seeing her mother, Ae Maew complained again about the condition of the house. Dama was quiet and went about her own work. I could not tell whether she was happy to see Ae Maew home or not. "This is my mother. She doesn't know how to please people," Ae Maew sighed.

By the time we finished cleaning, it was nearly seven o'clock in the evening. After a day's traveling and the cleaning, we both needed a good shower. There was no hot water in the house, so Ae Maew took me to a neighborhood bathhouse. She explained that most people went to a bathhouse when they needed a shower. After the shower, I put on a Burmese *longyi* I had purchased in Mandalay. We walked home slowly. The night had become very dark; there was no electricity. The air was cool and the sky full of stars. I had not seen such a beautiful sky for some time. Taunggyi was a charming mountain town (Figure 2–1), very different from dusty and bustling Mandalay. I told Ae Maew her wooden house was lovely; I wanted to name it the "House of Many Stars." She laughed.

We lit candles in the living room downstairs and discussed our work for the next day. The government provided electricity for different quarters by turn. Even when there was electricity, the power was weak and unstable. Dama had gone to her room to rest. Gugu sat with us in the living room.

---

5. *Dama* (senior aunt) is an address for female adults whose husbands are older than one's father.

Figure 2–1. A part of Taunggyi

She called me Teacher (*laoshi*) and praised my beauty. "Teacher's face is plump and her cheeks are red, very good looking," she said. A plump face symbolizes fortune in Chinese society. However, my face has never been plump. I tried to remain polite. Ae Maew told her I had come to learn about the history of the Yunnanese people, how they had come to Burma and what they did for a living. "Oh, Teacher is a Bodhisattva, Teacher is a Bodhisattva," Gugu said. I felt the praise absurd, and joked, "Oh, yes, I make magic." Gugu laughed heartily. I then urged her to tell me about her family background. She said:

"Our father had been an official [*dangguande*] in Kunming. He came home once every three years. He was a member of the Yunnan Provincial Assembly for three terms. My eldest brother had been the General Chief of five townships."

Ae Maew added: "My aunt was the second girl in the family and was addressed as *erxiaojie* [the second young lady]. She had one elder sister, two elder brothers, and two younger brothers. My father was the youngest son in the family. My aunt had been powerful in the old home in Tengchong. She was in charge of stamping official papers. She had all the keys to the house."

"How did you and your family come to Burma?" I asked.

"My brother [Ae Maew's father] carried our mother on his back from our hometown. He carried her for many days until he was not able to walk anymore. He cried and cried. Our mother said: 'Go, go, leave Mother alone; you go.' But he still carried our mother. We passed a village of barbarous people [*yiren zhaizi*]. They grabbed our mother's clothes and left her nearly naked. My brothers' clothes were grabbed too. My third niece's clothes were tattered and hence not grabbed. She took off her coat and gave it to a brother. I took off my coat and gave it to my mother."

Ae Maew said: "My father and his two elder brothers had fled Tengchong earlier than other family members. After arriving in Burma, my father joined a KMT guerrilla unit in Shan State and later on led a troop back home to take the rest of the family members out. He carried his mother for eighteen days. The grandmother's feet had been bound since childhood and she could not run. My father was twenty-seven years old. He took more than one hundred people out."

Ae Maew and I went to bed late. I could see numerous stars through the window while lying in bed. While I was pondering the day's experience, Ae Maew said: "My father used to say in his late life that he had killed many people when he took the troop back to Tengchong. He felt guilty. My brothers were disobedient. He said this may have been due to his sins; those dead people came to demand the debt. But my father was a very kind person; he treated people warmly. He was a learned man. He taught his children ancient Chinese literature, such as *Xishi xianwen*, *Sanzijing*, the works by Ouyang Xiu and Su Dongpo."

"You mean he taught your brothers?"

"Yes, my brothers. They all lived in Pinlong. There was no Chinese school in Laikha. My father only stayed in Laikha for two or three years as a traveling trader. Using two mules he transported goods for sale to the rotating market of different villages in the mountains. Afterward he was invited to be a Chinese teacher in Pinlong. He often said he didn't know trade. Teacher, you should meet one of my elder cousins. He lives in Pinlong. He knows my father's history."

Songs of Morning

At five in the morning I was awakened by Dama's sutra chanting. She had begun her devotions for the day with worship at the family altar, and the wooden structure of the house transmitted the sound of each movement. Ae Maew was awakened too. She pulled her comforter over her head and tried to sleep as the bed was warm and it was a cold morning. Later, the striking of a gong from the road announced the begging of alms, and I struggled to get up and put on my coat so I could take some pictures. The balcony on the second floor was a good spot for a clear view of the street. A few minutes later a group of monks passed by chanting sutra, and I saw neighbors, none of them Yunnanese, giving them cooked rice.[6] Afterward, there came the sounds of hawkers selling various morning foods, including sticky rice, fresh milk, fried noodles, and fritters. Female sellers walked elegantly by with pots of food on their heads. Their hawking was a kind of singing that accentuated and prolonged one syllable of the name of the food they sold. More groups of monks passed by. The tea shop across the road was now playing popular Shan songs aired over a loudspeaker. Many guests were having their tea and breakfast in the shop. The morning had become lively.

At nearly seven o'clock, Ae Maew took me to the market, and on the way I asked her why Yunnanese neighbors did not give alms as their neighbors did. "No, Yunnanese don't. They go to Chinese temples; there are several in Taunggyi. The Guanyin temple is the biggest one. My mother goes there the first and fifteenth days of each month following the lunar calendar."

My studies among Yunnanese migrants in northern Thailand indicate similarities in this respect. While ethnic Chinese originating from Guangdong (Canton) and Fujian in southeastern China have largely assimilated to local Theravada Buddhism, the Yunnanese still practice their traditional religion, a conflation of different elements derived from Confucianism, Taoism, Mahayana Buddhism, and folk beliefs (see Chang 1999, 226–93) of a "highly eclectic nature" (Yang 1994, 25). Like their fellow Yunnanese in Thailand who tease ethnic Chinese coming by boat as having become Thai, the Yunnanese in Burma like to say the Cantonese and Fujianese have become Burmese and cannot speak Chinese. Differentiated by migration routes, most "overseas" Chinese were originally concentrated in lower Burma and the "overland" Yunnanese in upper Burma. However, after

---

6. Ethnicity can be identified by style of clothing; the Yunnanese normally do not wear *longyi*.

completion of the railway extension to Myitkyina and Lashio (respectively in 1898 and 1903), many maritime Chinese moved to northern cities and towns to make a living.[7] Most Cantonese worked in the fields of carpentry and construction or the restaurant business. Most Fujianese were involved in trading produce and sundry goods. As for the Yunnanese, most of them came to Burma after 1949 and have been concentrated in upper Burma. According to information provided by both Yunnanese and maritime Chinese in Taunggyi, there are more than ten thousand Yunnanese in the city, while the number of Cantonese and Fujianese is around three thousand. The Yunnanese perceive themselves as being more traditional than the Cantonese and Fujianese in terms of maintaining "Chinese" culture. While this point has been largely acknowledged by their maritime counterparts, they are also perceived as risk-takers in illegal business. In contrast, the Cantonese and Fujianese see themselves, and are also perceived by the Yunnanese, as being more conservative in business dealings.

That morning, on the way to the market in Taunggyi, we passed a few ethnic Pa-O (also known as Taungthu/Dongsu) compounds and saw workers in many houses busy packing dry tobacco leaves into bamboo baskets. Ae Maew said most Pa-O in Taunggyi cultivate tobacco and sell it to different parts of the country. They are known as hardworking people, and many of them have become big bosses in the tobacco business. The Shan, too, are considered diligent workers, mostly in farming and petty trade. The Yunnanese have lived peacefully with these two groups, but intermarriage has been uncommon, except in the early days when the number of Yunnanese women was limited. In the early 1970s, when instability in rural areas caused Yunnanese to begin moving to Taunggyi, they received much help from local Shans. Informants pointed out that Shan headmen were kind to them and covered up their illegal status. Many Yunnanese rented houses from Shans and later applied for citizenship with Shan identities.

Every morning, Ae Maew and I started our day by going to the market. Sometimes we had breakfast there and then went on to interviews in different locations; other times, we brought fresh vegetables and meat home and made our own breakfast. One morning, while frying rice in the kitchen, Ae Maew was happily singing a Burmese song.

---

7. See Wikipedia http://en.wikipedia.org/wiki/History_of_rail_transport_in_Burma and http://en.wikipedia.org/wiki/Lashio.

I asked her what song she was singing, and she said it was a song with rhymes about rain that is taught to children. It says: "When rain comes, we take a shower in the rain. When mama comes, we drink milk from her. When daddy comes, we eat the coconut he cuts for us" (Mo-ywa-yin mo-ye-cho-meh / Me-Me la-yin no-so-meh / Pe-Pe la-yin oun-thi kweh-sa-meh). Ae Maew smiled and said, "Everyone learns this nursery rhyme at school when they are small." After finishing the song, Ae Maew said, "While studying at university, the only subject that I didn't need an extra class for was Burmese. My Burmese was even better than my Burman classmates', and I earned a very high grade."[8] I was intrigued by Ae Maew's attachment to some aspects of things Burmese and her dislike for others, revealing her different sentiments connected to Burma and intertwined in her subjectivity in an interstitial state that embraces tensions, ambivalence, love, and hatred toward the same or related phenomena in different situations.

A good example of her contempt for Burmese society was our encounter with a collector of tolls in Mandalay, after we rode our bicycles on an overpass. The collector, a young boy around fourteen or fifteen, accused us of transgressing the law by riding bicycles on the overpass and demanded angrily that we pay a fine of a thousand kyat each. (The toll for a car was only twenty kyat.) He pointed to an obscure sign that had been painted long ago that forbade riding bicycles on the overpass, although walking with a bicycle was allowed. People from other places would have no way of knowing about this regulation. We tried to explain this to the boy, who threatened to send for the police. In the end, Ae Maew became quite provoked and shouted at him: "How old are you? How many years of education have you received? Why have you become so wicked at such a young age?" I did not know whether he was shocked or hurt by Ae Maew's words, but they seemed to curb his anger, and he shouted back: "Go! Go! *Tayoke soe* [damned Chinese]!" Upset by this incident, Ae Maew cursed "*silaomian*" (damn old Burman) as we were compelled to walk our bikes back to the other end of the overpass where we had started. Ae Maew lamented: "Teacher, how can I stay in such a society? It's so corrupt. He is just a boy. I hate this government and society."

---

8. It is common that students have to take extra classes at their teachers' homes, a way for the teachers to earn extra income. This happens from primary school to university. Several informants remarked that what appears in exams is only taught during extra classes.

Moving Upward

After finishing high school, Ae Maew stayed in Laikha for another two years in order to save money to go to university. Apart from working on the family farm growing garlic, rice, beans, corn, and sesame, she worked on other people's farms. On several occasions while we were cooking, taking a walk, or chatting before falling to sleep she recounted her work experience since childhood:[9]

"From a very young age, I have been looking for different opportunities to earn money. I started selling fruits from our yard in the second grade. I often climbed trees to pick fruits, put them in a bucket, and took them to school to sell. I could climb trees like a monkey. Sometimes I sold fried sunflower seeds. I purchased twenty-five packages at a time and put them in my cloth bag. After class, I took them out to sell to my classmates and earned a profit equivalent to five packages. Other times, I cooked corn from our farm and carried it to school. No matter what kind of goods I found, I tried to turn them into money. I didn't like poverty. I wanted to get out of it...."

"I was a child laborer, working on other people's farms during vacations since age eleven or twelve. In the summer, the weather was scorching hot, and I worked from seven in the morning until five in the afternoon. The first year I earned six kyat a day; the second year eight kyat, and then ten kyat. I often picked on higher-paying farms which were so wet my feet were covered in water. I was just a child, but I worked with adults to harvest rice and pick garlic...."

"Our family purchased our own farm when I was in junior high school, around fourteen or fifteen years old. It was my sister and I who repeatedly asked my father to buy livestock and to farm. From the time I was small, I observed other people's ways of living and tried to learn how they earned money. I saw that some families raised horses. The mares gave birth to foals which were sold for money, so I asked my father to raise horses. I saw other families with farms and thought of having one of our own. I then pestered my father to buy one.

"Look at my thick calves. They are because I have done heavy tasks from a very young age. Our house was located at the edge of a village, and every

---

9. A space separates the occasions on which we talked in the excerpts that follow.

morning my sister and I had to walk a long way, each carrying ten *dan* of water.[10] We then cut plants for our pigs; we raised nearly twenty of them. We had to walk one hour each way to cut wild plants, and each full basket weighed ten kilos. I miss the experience of talking with my sister on the way. When we were tired, we would take a break or get water from a well. The taste of water was sweet. After arriving home, we boiled the plants, rice bran, and residue of soybeans into a big pot. This was the food for the pigs."

"I sold lottery tickets when I was fifteen or sixteen years old. At the beginning I sold lottery tickets for other ticket sellers. But later on, I became an independent seller myself. I rode a bicycle to tea shops in different villages to look for customers. I earned tens of thousands of kyat in one lottery cycle. The year before coming to Taunggyi, I went to the ruby mines in Mong Hsu and panned for rough rubies in the river. I stayed there for three to four weeks. . . .

"I hid the money I earned in shoes, old clothes, and in the cracks on the back of our cooking stoves. This was how I saved money. But in 1987, there was demonetization. I lost two-thirds of my savings. Teacher, I didn't want to do all these jobs. I wish I could have simply been a student."

Ae Maew moved to Taunggyi in 1990 (at age seventeen) to prepare for the entrance exam to go to university. Her father had come to this city a year earlier. She entered the Department of Animal Science at Taunggyi University in 1991. Meanwhile, in the evening, she attended the Chinese school, where her father worked, at the junior high level. As there had been no Chinese school in Laikha, it was her first time attending a Chinese school. Her father had taught her some Chinese each time he went home. More often she had learned Chinese from one of her cousins and her own dictionary. She said:

"The first Chinese novel I read was written by Jin Yong when I was fifteen or sixteen. It was *Yitian tulong ji* [Heaven sword and dragon sabre]. A lot of words I didn't know, but I combined them with the words I knew and tried to guess their meaning. After Jin Yong, I read Qiong Yao's *Xin you qianqianjie* [The heart with a million knots].[11] I got these novels from

---

10. The act of carrying water by placing a carrying pole on the shoulders with one bucket hung on each end is called *danshui*, and one *dan* of water refers to two bucketfuls.

11. Both Jin Yong and Qiong Yao are popular novelists based in Hong Kong and Taiwan respectively.

my two cousins and learned new words by reading them. While taking Chinese class at the junior high level, I also taught at the primary level. I started with the fourth grade. Whenever there were words I didn't know, I asked other teachers."

Visit to Taunggyi University

On the fourth day of my stay in Taunggyi, Ae Maew proposed to take me to Taunggyi University, where she had studied for about three years. The university was on the outskirts of the city, and it took two buses to get there. On campus, Ae Maew pointed out many cinchonas, trees we had also seen on the way to Taunggyi from Mandalay. She said every university in Burma grows this kind of tree, which she likes very much. I asked her if she missed being on the university campus. To my surprise, she shook her head and said no. As we passed the first building, the administration building with offices for all departments, we heard music. Looking through the windows, we saw students rehearsing a performance. This jogged Ae Maew's memory of the opening performance for the freshmen of her year. She said: "The welcoming performance was grand, different from those in Taiwan. It took place two months after the arrival of the first-year students. It was a very happy occasion, and all the professors and students participated. The concert was big. I remembered everyone was given a package of *danpauk*[12] and a Pepsi in a glass bottle. The final and most anticipated event was selection of the most beautiful girl and the most handsome boy from the first-year students of each department. They represented their departments and needed to have good grades." We stood outside that room for some minutes. Ae Maew was engrossed in her observations.

We came to a tree with blossoming yellow flowers. Ae Maew said: "This is British jasmine. I picked many flowers from this tree and put them inside several books that I took to Taiwan." I picked one flower and put it in my notebook. Ae Maew continued: "After my first term at the university, the school was closed by the government until 1993. When it

---

12. *Danpauk* is Indian *biriyani*. It was a dish Ae Maew and I enjoyed very much while we were in Mandalay.

reopened, we had three terms in 1993, one to make up for the second semester of the first year and the other two for the second year. When I was in the third year in 1994, I took an exam to go to Taiwan. I was selected and offered a scholarship."[13]

In Taiwan, Ae Maew first studied at Qiao Da, a college that offers preparatory courses to Chinese overseas students before they are assigned to universities. Two years later, based on her results, Ae Maew was sent to the department of history at a national university. She worked part time during the semester and full time during winter and summer vacations. Two years after her arrival in Taiwan, she cleared all the loans she had taken out for the purchase of the house in Taunggyi. From time to time, she sent money home. "I have worked as a librarian, shop girl, domestic nurse, and restaurant employee. One summer I washed dishes thirteen hours a day for one month in a noodle shop. I am amazed at my own past," she said.

Ae Maew received Taiwanese citizenship when she was a junior. Her application was granted because of her father's military service in the KMT guerrilla force in the 1950s. After graduation from university with a degree in history, Ae Maew worked for three years and then went back for graduate studies in business management.

"My brothers didn't go to university. They were not interested in Burmese," she said.

"Why were you interested in Burmese?" I asked.

"I was not really interested in the language. I just wanted to move on from my life in Burma. I believed if I studied hard, I would get a chance to go abroad. Education was the only way to change my life. It was strange how I, a girl from a rural village, had such a thought. My mother didn't even know what grade I was in at school," she replied.

We walked around the campus. Ae Maew introduced each place to me: "This is one of my classrooms. All the buildings here are named after different places in Taunggyi District. This one is named Inle; that one Loilin; the other one Linke. They are all beautiful names. After finishing one class, we had to rush to another one."

"How was the teaching here?" I inquired.

---

13. The Taiwanese government organized the exams in upper Burma and northern Thailand each year.

"Not bad. The professors here are not bad. This is the Department of English; further on is the Department of History, and then the Department of Myanmar. It was originally called the Department of Burmese," she said.

"Look," Ae Maew pointed to a construction site. "They are building the ceremonial hall for graduation. The university had no ceremonial hall before, and the commencement had to take place at Mandalay University. The ceremony here is grand, even grander than the ones in Taiwan. The female students go to the beauty parlor in the early morning to get their hair and makeup done. Each one looks like a bride." Ae Maew joyfully described the occasion.

When we reached the campus border, there were very few trees, and the grass was dry. Ae Maew said: "One thing I have regretted is that I did not have a romance here. At that time, I didn't like boys of other ethnic groups, and there were not so many Chinese students." Ae Maew became deep in thought.

The temperature had risen at noon. As we walked toward the campus entrance under a serene blue sky, Ae Maew seemed to be trying to retain as many memories of the campus as possible. She stopped walking and said: "Look at the mountains."

I directed my gaze to the nearby mountains that partly surrounded the campus and said: "Your university in Taiwan is also surrounded by mountains." I was happy to find a similarity.

"No, it is not the same. This was my first university, and it has a different feeling. It's winter now, very dry. In the summer, the campus will become greener, and so will the mountains."

Ae Maew's Father, Mother, and Aunt

One morning Ae Maew and I were looking through two wooden boxes of books left by her father. Among them, I found a pile of letters and poems written by Ae Maew's father, whom I should address as "Dadie" (senior uncle).[14] I asked permission from Ae Maew to read them. Dadie had kept all the letters he had received as well as many letter drafts he had written. Ae

---

14. *Dadie* (senior uncle) is an address for male adults who are older than one's father.

Maew loved her father dearly and wanted me to know more about him. She then contacted one of her cousins who lived in Pinlong to come to Taunggyi in order to tell me his father's history. This cousin, whom Ae Maew calls "Tangge" (cousin from the paternal side), was born in 1934. In 1958, he followed Ae Maew's father and other family members to Burma. He said:

"My uncle [Ae Maew's father] finished *gaoxiao* in Tengchong, an equivalent to today's middle school education. After that he went to Xiaodong High School [*xiaodong zhongxue*] in Longling for three years. When the local Communists [*tugong*] came in 1949, he joined them for the liberation of China. However, he soon discovered that they were abusing their power by bullying civilians. In 1950, he escaped to Burma and joined the KMT guerrilla forces. While serving in the Fourteenth Division of the Third Army, he received training at the headquarters in Mong Hsat for half a year. In 1958, he and a troop of more than three hundred fought their way back to Yunnan and brought out a few hundred people, around thirty of them his family members. He carried his mother, who had bound feet, on his back for eighteen days. The group fled from Tengchong, passed Longjiang, and then hid in a Kachin village. The Communists caught up with them and took part of the group back. It was during the rainy season. We arrived in the Jiangdong area and hid in a forest for more than one month while the Communists blocked our way out, living on corn that was ground into powder. When the blockade was relaxed, we found a guide to take us out. We walked during the night, passed Chefan, and then crossed the border and arrived in Hemonglong in Burma. Later on we moved to Muse. I was fourteen years old. My uncle took me to work with him in a textile factory in Kutkai, and a year later he returned to the KMT guerrilla forces and stayed there until 1961."

I pictured Dadie as a patriotic young man ready to dedicate his life to his country. He joined the KMT after having escaped to Burma with a hope of recovering the homeland someday. Ae Maew's mother (Dama) did not join the flight in 1958; she had arrived in Burma a year earlier. She was not from the same village as Dadie. One night while she, Ae Maew, and I were sitting in the living room, she related the story of her flight at my request:

"Ae Maew's father and I got engaged before the Chinese Communist takeover. After he fled Tengchong [in 1950], I waited for him until my family urged me to get engaged to another man [in 1957]. Seven days prior to my marriage with that man, I secretly received a letter from Ae Maew's father.[15] He asked me to flee to Burma and told me to stay with certain people in different places during the journey. With a niece and a nephew, I made my way to Burma and arrived at a place called Panghu, which was near Jiegao, adjacent to Ruili [in Yunnan]. A year later, his family also escaped to Burma, and I went to stay with them. They gave me food, but I also worked on a tea farm. Ae Maew's father was in the army. In 1961, he sent a letter to me and told me to go to Laos to meet him. I was twenty-nine years old that year."

Dama thus made her journey through Muse, Lashio, Mandalay, Taunggyi, Kengtung, Tachileik, and Mae Sai to Laos. Dadie's troop had been pushed to Laos by the Burmese army and temporarily encamped there. She said: "We got married in Laos and stayed there for two months. The troop had negotiated with the Thai authority and paid two hundred thousand baht as a bribe to enter Thailand by [crossing the Mekong River]. We took a big ship. A group of dependents went to Laoxiangtang village [Ban Huae Pai], a group went to Mantang village [Ban Tham Santhisuk], and another went to Mae Sai." These are border villages and a town located in Chiang Rai Province. Dama and Dadie stayed in Mae Sai for one year and then went back to Burma where most of Dadie's relatives remained. "We crossed the border from Mae Sai to Tachileik and then went to Kengtung. We took an airplane from there to Nansan and then went by vehicle to Pinlong. We stayed in Pinlong for a few days, and then moved to Xunding, where we stayed for five years. I gave birth to three boys there. Afterward, we moved to Laikha, where I gave birth to Ae Maew's sister, Ae Maew, and another daughter, who only lived for a few days."

Although the narration was simple and straightforward, it revealed Dama's inner strength that enabled her to undertake these risky journeys to reunite with her fiancé. Was it out of love, obligation, social convention, or mere circumstance? Dama and Dadie seemed to be very different types of people, and their marriage had been arranged by their parents. Dadie was an educated man who loved literature and composed poems. After his military engagement, he took up trade for a couple of years and then

---

15. Informants said that villagers on both sides of the border were sometimes allowed to cross over to trade in local markets (leaving in the morning and returning in the late afternoon). Letters or other objects could be smuggled back and forth through this channel.

dedicated himself to Chinese education for the rest of his life. In contrast, Dama is illiterate, although her family's modest holdings place her in the landlord class. After fleeing to Burma, she labored at heavy tasks in the countryside until she moved to Taunggyi in 1999. How did they interact with each other? I tried to persuade Dama to tell me about her relationship with Dadie, but to no avail.

One day I was looking at a photo of Dadie taken with his students that hung on the wall in the living room downstairs. When Dama came over and stood beside me, I took a chance and asked her if she missed Dadie. "He's already dead [*rensiluo*]," Dama replied. She paused and then added: "Taiwan sent eight hundred US dollars to him as a prize for his dedication to Chinese education for thirty years—a prize from Taiwan [*taiwan laijiang*]."

"Do you miss him?" I persisted.

"He's already dead." That was all Dama would say. My question was too contemporary, too modern, and perhaps too naive for her.

Between Dama and Dadie, there was Gugu—Dadie's sister. Ae Maew said her aunt was too smart and cunning and her mother too simpleminded. They did not talk to or interact with each other while I was staying with them, and I learned that this was due to years of accumulated hatred between them. Gugu converted to Christianity in 1995, following the conversion of Tangge, who lives in Pinlong. Tangge has five sons and one daughter. His third son was once addicted to drugs and squandered most of his savings, but then his addiction was cured in a church in Mae Sai. Afterward, he not only converted to Christianity but dedicated himself to theological studies. His parents and grandaunt eventually became Christians too, and now every Sunday Gugu dressed herself neatly to go to church.

Ae Maew and Her Brothers

Among the pile of written materials Dadie left were many letters from his former students that had been sent from Taiwan, Thailand, and Burma. All the students expressed their gratitude for his earnest teaching, praised him as an excellent teacher, and stressed how much they missed him. I asked Ae Maew why her father, such a respected teacher, had disobedient sons. Ae Maew sighed and said: "My father was busy educating other people's children and didn't have much time for his own. He said that he had spent the least time with my sister and me, but we had not become bad or caused our family to worry about us."

If Ae Maew's father had spent the least time with Ae Maew and her sister and they had not become problematic, then responsibility for the failure of Ae Maew's brothers cannot be placed entirely on their father. Among the letters, I found the first one that Ae Maew had written to her parents from Taiwan.

> Respected Laoye[16] and Mother,
> Since I arrived in Taiwan I have not written to you yet. How have you been? I miss you very much. Ye and Mom, please do not worry about me. I have been very well here. Everything goes fine. I have returned the money that I borrowed earlier from Mr. Yang by working during last winter vacation. In addition, I have saved another 30,000 NT. I can send the money to you if you need it now; otherwise I will send it together with the money I will earn during the summer vacation. . . . I passed all the subjects last semester, but the grades were not very high. I will work harder this semester. At the end of the school year, if I can be sent to an ideal department at a national university, I will go. Otherwise, I will stay one more year at Qiao Da. Going to a private university is too expensive. Please do not worry about me; I will try my best. . . .
> Laoye, you must have confidence in me. I will work hard. You and Mom, please take care of your health. . . . Wait for my success. Tell elder sister that the outside world is complicated. I will try to look for a chance to bring her here. . . .
> Peace to the whole family.
> Your daughter,
> Ae Maew   *April 3rd*

I also found the draft reply from Ae Maew's father.

> My Dear Daughter Ae Maew,
> I have received your letter. I am very pleased with your life and work in Taiwan. I still teach at [the same] Chinese school. My health is all right. I am already over sixty years old. You are my hope. You must work hard. . . . Your sister left for Thailand with your [eldest] brother [earlier this month]. After your departure, she lost interest in taking dressmaking classes. She

---

16. *Loaye* (or *ye*) is an old-fashioned way of addressing one's father.

stopped teaching at the Chinese school, as well, and remained idle at home. I had to let her be; she is already twenty-nine years old.

Your [eldest] brother's business has gone bankrupt. He asked for money from me. I dared not give him much as I have no confidence in him. This has resulted in tension between us. I cannot care so much anymore as I am already old. . . .

As you know, being a Chinese teacher in a foreign land is not easy. Having been born in this age, we have to persevere in our belief in the Three Principles of the People.[17] We should not impute faults and wrongs to others, but work hard for our own duty. However, I am more than sixty years old. My mental and physical strength is declining. I feel sad about this condition. Earlier, your mother came to Taunggyi to get a set of artificial teeth. She has returned [to Laikha]. She is fine. Do not worry.

Looking back on my former military experience of more than ten years when I fought against the Communists with my life, I lament my present situation. You have the chance to go abroad for further education. You must persist with high moral principles and strive to excel. Persevere with your will and win glory for your old father. We will talk more next time. Take good care of yourself.

Your father   April 26th

The letter shows that Ae Maew's father was upset with the family's situation as well as his own condition. He had great expectations for Ae Maew—his only hope in his old age. Once he was a passionate and patriotic young man, but as he aged, he saw his family falling apart. Concern from his former students and Ae Maew might have been his only consolation. He served Chinese education for about thirty-five years in total. Actually, Chinese education was banned in Burma in 1965, although Chinese lessons were secretly organized and given in private homes in upper Burma. In 1978 the restriction was relaxed but not removed, and many Chinese schools were reestablished using religious names. The major Chinese school in Mandalay has been registered as Confucius School (*kongjiao xuexiao*) and the one in Taunggyi as Buddha School (*dacheng baodian xuexiao*).

---

17. The Three Principles of the People (*sanmin zhuyi*), created by Sun Yat-sen, contain the ideas of nationalism, democracy, and livelihood. This political philosophy used to be the official ideology of the Chinese Nationalist Party. However, it is considered outdated, and even the party has stopped referring to it since the 1990s. The citing of the ideology by Ae Maew's father reflects the influence of political propaganda during his times.

Statues of Confucius and Buddha are placed in these schools. Informants explained that this method of registration was strategic in order to get approval. Because Burma is a Buddhist country, the government allows the establishment of schools of Buddhism or a similar religion. Many Chinese schools in major cities provide lessons up to the high school level. After graduation, many students continue their studies in Taiwan or China.

In contrast to Ae Maew's status as a filial daughter and her efforts to live up to her father's expectations, her three brothers were failures. I only found letters from her third elder brother to his father. In these letters, the brother, Lin San, persistently requested money from his father. The following is an example.

> Dear Father,[18]
> After departing from home, I have safely arrived in the [jade] mines. The situation is more or less the same as before. However, the money I took with me was not sufficient. I was very happy that my buddy, Dawen, is going to visit you. I have borrowed 50,000 kyat from him. I hope, Father, you can return the debt to him. Your son's business will straighten out. I will face reality. Please do not worry.
> Your son,
> Lin San   *June 1st*

Lin San finished his junior high education at a Chinese school in Pinlong, and he then helped on the family farm in Laikha. He also took charge of selling their produce in Taunggyi. However, very often, Dama did not know his whereabouts when the farm required help. Under such circumstances, Dama had to ask a neighbor to write a letter on her behalf to her husband or Lin San. In these letters, Dama complained of Lin San's disobedience and her helpless situation. The following two extracts are examples.

> Dear Husband,[19]
> It is time to sow seeds on the farm, but Lin San is nowhere to be seen. Please find him as soon as possible; otherwise I will have to rent the farm to other people. I have no capacity to take care of it myself. . . .
> Your wife   *April 10th*

---

18. Lin San used a formal address here—*fuqin daren*.
19. The address to her husband in Chinese is *fujun rumian* after his name.

Dear Son,
   You have left home for a long time without sending back any word. I wrote to you some time earlier, but why have you not replied?
   I'm writing to you again. I hope you come home immediately on receiving this letter. It is time to harvest the rice and also to cultivate the garlic. You must come back with your sister [Ae Maew's elder sister]. I'm too old to do all the work by myself.
   Your mother   *October 28th, 1996*

These letters show that Dama had no authority over Lin San. Ae Maew said: "Before I finished high school, my brothers were seldom at home. Sometimes, my third elder brother came back to sell produce or mules, and wanted to keep the money from the sale. He often had conflicts with my mother."

Lin San got married in 1996 and then lived with his wife's family in Taunggyi. This is unusual among the Yunnanese, who follow a patrilocal practice. He helped his parents-in-law look after a chicken farm. After marriage, he seldom visited home except when he wanted something. Around 2000, he went to Hpakant in Kachin State to work in the jade mines. (According to the letter, he had been there once earlier.) This is a popular undertaking among Yunnanese men (chapter 7). Everyone who goes there dreams of becoming rich in this venture, although very few people have such luck. Many fortune seekers not only use up all their money there but become drug addicts. Lin San was one of them. Ae Maew and her parents had spent much time and money in different places to help him with his drug problem, but so far to no avail.

As for Ae Maew's eldest brother, Lin Yi, he finished his high school education at a Chinese school in Lashio. He then started cross-border trade between Yunnan and Burma, purchasing clothes in Yunnan and taking them back for sale in Burma. He did this for only two years and then around 1983 shifted to northern Thailand. The major commodities he purchased were packages of monosodium glutamate, an illegal trade. Though risky, the profit was high, and he became quite rich in a couple of years. However, demonetization in 1985 suddenly brought him to bankruptcy. He then went to Thailand again and stayed for nearly ten years working in tourism and construction. In 1994, he moved to Taunggyi and stayed at the house Ae Maew had purchased. He did not have a job but sometimes went to Mong Hsu to buy rubies. While living at home, he often went gambling, and his father was not able to control him.

Whenever Ae Maew came home from Taiwan in the 1990s, her eldest brother quarreled with her fiercely. He kept asking her for money, and this hurt Ae Maew greatly. She said: "From a very young age, he went to Pinlong for studies, and later on to Lashio. I rarely saw him, but whenever he came back to Laikha, he would talk to me a lot. His visits always made me very emotional. I was happy that my eldest brother came home, but I felt sad that he would soon leave again. During his stay, he used to tell me many stories about his life, including his romances. He even showed me his love letters. He liked to tease me because my way of speaking and dressing were very unrefined, and he would tell me how I should dress myself. While he was away, I often carved words on the trunk of the banana tree near our pig pen—'I miss my eldest brother.' However, the eldest brother in my mind was different from the real one. He was originally the best child in our family, but when he grew up, he became the most disobedient."

In 1998, Lin Yi went to Laogai, a border town in the region of Kokang in northeastern Shan State, to start a business. He opened a shop and sold clothes that were imported from Mae Sai in northern Thailand. Apart from running the shop, he worked at a gambling house owned by a Fujianese boss. Many gamblers were from China. In 2003, a Burmese officer gambled there and lost a lot of money but refused to pay. Lin Yi was called to negotiate with the officer, who became very angry and fired a shot just above his head. That officer then called the police to raid the gambling house, and Lin Yi has been in prison ever since.

Ae Maew's second elder brother, Lin Er, also took up the cross-border trade between Burma and Thailand in the 1990s. He too became addicted to drugs. In 1999 Ae Maew arranged for him to stay in the church where her cousin's son worked in Mae Sai in order to help him get over his drug addiction. Before that, she had sent him twice to a private hospital in Taunggyi for abstention.

Through religion, Lin Er finally stopped using drugs, and he was baptized as a Christian. He continued to stay and work in that church. However, one and a half years later, he was diagnosed with AIDS. He then went home to stay with his mother and aunt in Taunggyi. Ae Maew said: "It was a difficult period for my mother. During his stay, he was often very emotional. Though he was repentant, he couldn't accept the fact that he had contracted the illness. In the last few months of his life, he was sent to a private hospital. I called him from Taiwan every day to console him and spent a lot of money. I sometimes wonder if our family has been cursed."

I felt Ae Maew's helplessness. The more I learned about the drug problem in her family, the deeper my frustration grew. Many Yunnanese families are haunted by the problem.[20] Once a family member is addicted to drugs, the whole family lives in an abyss of pain. Job opportunities are rare, and drugs are available everywhere in the country. Well-off families try to send their children abroad in order to isolate them from this dangerous temptation.

The certificate of Lin Er's baptism still hung on the wall in the living room in a glass frame. It quotes two passages from the Bible:

> So if any man is in Christ, he is in a new world: the old things have come to an end; they have truly become new. (2 Corinthians 5:17)

> I am the vine, you are the branches: he who is in me at all times as I am in him, gives much fruit, because without me you are able to do nothing. (John 15:5)[21]

Unhappy Chinese New Year

Chinese New Year's Eve of 2005 arrived on the fourteenth day after my arrival in Taunggyi. I was scheduled to visit a Yunnanese Muslim woman that morning, and as we were leaving the house, Dama, displeased, said to Ae Maew: "Why are you still going out today? Go and paste the New Year's couplets [*chunlian*]." Ae Maew shouted back: "I told you I would do that after coming back. Why didn't you understand?" She walked out of the house. I hurried to catch up with Ae Maew, surprised by this unexpected scene. We had to go to a nearby market to take local transportation, a kind of pickup truck, which was always jammed with passengers. We sat

---

20. Mandy Sadan tells about the drug and drinking problems of her husband's family in Kachin State (2014).

21. The English translations of the two passages are from *Bible in Basic English*, http://www.o-bible.com/bbe.html.

tightly next to each other in the car, but with lingering tension in the air, we did not talk to each other.

Since my arrival in Taunggyi, I had been working every day. Most of the time Ae Maew accompanied me to interviews. While I rewrote my field notes in the house, Ae Maew was always doing housework, especially cleaning and reorganizing. I noticed Ae Maew had become more and more impatient, often blaming her mother for not keeping the house tidy. One day Ae Maew had an argument with her mother while I was out conducting an interview, and that night Ae Maew asked me to take a walk with her. She said, "Teacher, I feel my life is too heavy, both mentally and physically. That's why sometimes you see me lose my temper. I have to vent the pressure. My relationship with my mother used to be good. I am the youngest child; wherever she went, I followed her. However, after I received more education, the gap between us became larger. In the home of Laikha, I worked on our dining table next to the cooking stove. Every night I lit small bundles of pine wood to do my homework, as we could not afford to use an oil lamp. I was afraid to be alone and always asked my mother to keep me company. After studying awhile, I would raise my head to look at her." We walked in the neighborhood, which was in deep darkness. Thousands of stars were shining in the sky. A few Pa-O boys were playing guitar and singing love songs.

After my interview with the Yunnanese Muslim woman, I decided to go to the nearby mosque to meet a Yunnanese Muslim man whom several people had recommended to me. I told Ae Maew to go home first and assured her that I knew the area quite well. When I got back to Ae Maew's house, it was nearly three o'clock in the afternoon. A table with several dishes had been placed in the front yard as Dama, Gugu, and Ae Maew were preparing to worship Heaven and Earth (*baitiandi*).

Although Gugu had converted to Christianity, she participated in the worship by repeating prayers of good wishes for the offspring. After the worship of Heaven and Earth, Ae Maew and I moved the table to the second floor for the worship of ancestors. During the preparation, Ae Maew had disputes with her mother because of different opinions about worship arrangements. The custom here is to finish the worship of Heaven and Earth and ancestors before noon and have the New Year's Eve meal at lunchtime. However, when we completed the worship and warmed up the dishes, it had passed four o'clock in the afternoon. We placed the food on the folding table in the living room downstairs. The table was set against a wall, and Dama insisted on pulling it out and opening it to its full size. Maybe she considered this the most important family meal of the year, although her family had fallen apart many years ago. Ae Maew tried to stop her, saying that the table was not stable. Gugu kept reciting prayers and scattered uncooked rice on the floor for prosperity and good luck. The whole situation was disturbing and the atmosphere tense. Dama managed to pull out the table, but suddenly one extended side collapsed; a bowl of rice fell to the floor. Dama shouted: "Stop reciting [*bie nian le*]." The intensity seemed to reach its climax and then dissipate.

Gugu went to sit in the backyard next to her kitchen. Ae Maew went to her room to cry. I stayed in the living room to accompany Dama. She was eating the New Year's Eve meal alone. I sympathized with Dama and disliked Gugu. From the very beginning, I had chosen my allegiances. There is no complete neutrality in ethnography. I felt Dama's anger and Ae Maew's frustration. My thoughts were in disarray as I tried to understand what had just happened. "Why does Gugu participate in the worship? She is a Christian. Is she trying to demonstrate her position in the house? Does she not know her participation generates tension?" I pondered these questions. Suddenly, Dama shouted again: "Do not create disturbances here [*bielai zheli nao*]." The words were aimed at Gugu, whether she heard them or not.

After dark, New Year's Eve was as quiet as usual, with no sign of celebration in the neighborhood. Lighting firecrackers had been banned by the government. That night Ae Maew said, "I pity my mother, but I cannot agree with her stubbornness. She doesn't understand I need my own space. I know she's a straightforward and honest countrywoman. But she simply doesn't know how to manage the house. My father always paid much attention to appearances. He was always neat. However, my mother doesn't know how to dress up at all. Maybe that was why my father stayed away from home most of the time. When I choose a boyfriend, his appearance and social position must enhance my status. If not, I will not give him any consideration."

"If you meet an ideal Yunnanese man here, would you consider marrying him?" I asked.

"No, absolutely not. I cannot stand this place or this country. I prefer to stay in my small apartment in Taiwan. I hate this environment. I hate poverty. I want to give my family a hand, but I have never succeeded in pulling them up. I have never been satisfied with my family."

Ae Maew's third elder brother, Lin San, came to the house on the second day of the New Year. Since we came to Taunggyi, he had been around the house often. On the third day after our arrival, he asked Ae Maew for money. Ae Maew told him she had no money. "Not even a thousand or two thousand kyat?" he questioned her. Ae Maew felt his demand distasteful, but gave him one thousand kyat. On the seventh day, Lin San took away a comforter that Ae Maew had brought back from Taiwan. On the eleventh day, he took away a basket. He may have exchanged these things for money to buy drugs. He did not talk to his mother or Ae Maew, only Gugu. Every time he came, he stayed in Gugu's little kitchen and did not come inside the house. On the second day of the New Year, he came to the house several times, creating an uneasy atmosphere.

A few days later, Ae Maew and I went to the market to buy many things for the house. We were leaving soon. On our way back, we passed a neighbor's small shop; that family had also moved from Laikha. The mother of that family hurried to us and said Lin San had been demanding money from Dama and destroying some things in the house. We rushed home. After entering the house, we saw Lin San and Gugu sitting together in the living room. Lin San stared at Ae Maew and me angrily with a frightful gaze. A teakwood chair had been smashed, and a window was broken. There were some pieces of stone on the floor. Though we had not witnessed Lin San's violent act, the scene was intimidating. I was a foreigner, staying illegally in the house, as the Burmese government prohibits foreigners from staying in civilian houses. I had already been worried that Lin San might report me to the authorities, and this new situation intensified my fear. Quietly, Ae Maew went to the backyard to take a broom and a basket to clean up the mess in the living room. Lin San then went to the backyard followed by Gugu. After cleaning, Ae Maew sat in the living room and started to cry. That was the second time I had seen her crying.

That day, Lin San did not go back to his wife's house but moved into Ae Maew's house and slept in Gugu's room. He demanded Ae Maew and Dama give him the deed for the family's farm in Laikha. Later, Ae Maew told me that what her third elder brother had done that day had already been done before by her first and second elder brothers. It was all for money. I did not know Lin San's potential for violence and felt very insecure.

The next day I went to say good-bye to several friends. I was leaving alone the next day for Inle Lake, a beautiful tourist area in the plains, about half an hour from the plateau of Taunggyi. I needed to give myself a break before going back to Thailand for further fieldwork. I tried to persuade Ae Maew to come with me. She said she still had to arrange several things, but she promised to return to Taiwan in time for her studies. I told her to start packing both her and her mother's things, in case Lin San tried to do something dangerous to them and they had to leave the house immediately. Yet Ae Maew stubbornly said she had purchased this house with her savings of twenty years and would not give it up.

The next morning, before getting up, Ae Maew and I were chatting. A few days earlier, her sister had called and said she was coming back in a month's time. There was no telephone in the house, but her sister had called a neighbor, and the neighbor had come over to call Ae Maew. Ae Maew said her sister was always jealous of her progress in Taiwan and blamed Ae Maew for not taking her there. "I told her the easiest way is to go as a student, which means she has to take an exam. I passed all the information to her, but she did nothing. What could I do? She called me to help her arrange a few things, and I said I would try. Teacher, I felt exhausted mentally and physically. I'm the only one supporting this family. My siblings think that I can find money easily in Taiwan, and my brothers keep asking me for it."

Undercurrent

The beautiful Inle Lake is famous for its floating vegetation and stilt houses that sit high above the water. The fishermen propel their boats by rowing with one leg while standing on the other leg. The picturesque serenity alleviated my anxiety. I reflected on how the entangled "frictions across differences"—different statuses, different ethnicities, different societies—had impacted Ae Maew's life. Tsing perceives the power of differences: "Difference can disrupt, causing everyday malfunctions as well as unexpected cataclysms" (2005, 6). Though causing much pain and frustration, the frictions Ae Maew experienced have stimulated her to seek new possibilities and directions abroad rather than keeping her in Burma suffocated with rage. Her strong will contrasts with her brother's indulgence in vices and failures. Her sister too leads an independent life abroad. Both her mother and aunt were also brave women, fighting against numerous vicissitudes (and also against each other) in order to survive (and protect their power). In this family, the women seem to be much stronger than the men.

Ae Mae's anger and devotion to her family reminded me of Ruth Behar's *Translated Woman* (1993), an ethnography of an uneducated, socially marginal Mexican woman, pseudonymed Esperanza, whose life is also replete with rage, suffering, and persistent efforts to improve her and her children's lives. By "choosing" Behar, an American academic, to "hear her story and to take it back across the border to the mysterious and powerful otro lado" (p. 6), Esperanza remakes herself and figuratively traverses the borders of class, language, and nation to the American academic world. She relates her replication of her mother's role and life, enduring endless hardships originating from male gender dominance. Conscious of gender inequality, she states: "There's nothing like a daughter. God gave me daughters, thank God. Between a daughter and a son, a daughter is thousands of times better than a son" (p. 160). Comparatively, Ae Maew seems also thousands of times better than her brothers. She and her mother have also been suppressed by patriarchal demands (although different from Esperanza's)—to be a filial daughter, supporting sister, good wife, and caring mother. These roles have compelled them to endure ongoing toils and distress in addition to repeated traveling. Their bravery in facing unknown environments and the future is beyond my imagination. While recognizing this similarity in Ae Maew's, her mother's, and Esperanza's unrelenting perseverance in coping with structural forces, however, I did not see Ae Maew's and her mother's experience in what Behar writes about Esperanza's redemption via her devotion to a spiritual cult and narrating her life stories to an ethnographer (paralleling Catholic confession). Perhaps Ae Maew chose me to tell her stories, but I doubted if her telling or my listening produced any concrete benefits. Although her move to Taiwan has provided her with higher education and better life prospects, she is still trapped by her family's relationships and problems. I wondered if there would ever be redemption for Ae Maew.

I planned to stay in Inle for three days and then catch my flight from Heho Airport to Yangon and from Yangon to Chiang Mai. I took a long walk in nearby villages the first afternoon. The silhouette of mountains reflected in the lake and the paddy farms. A group of villagers, mostly women and children, were working on a road carrying pieces of rock on small bronze plates placed on their heads. They placed these rocks onto the road and went back to carry more. The manual work was incredibly slow. I wondered how long it would take to finish the construction and felt sorry for these possibly unpaid workers. In the evening I made a phone call to one of Ae Maew's friends, Ajuan, and asked her to pass on the address and phone number of my guesthouse to Ae Maew.

The next day, I took a boat trip with two tourists from the guesthouse. We visited craft shops, temples, and a rotating market. In my worry about Ae Maew and Dama, the trip seemed surreal. On the third day, the two tourists and I hired a guide to do a one-day trek through the mountains. We passed tobacco farms, a few Pa-O, Shan, and Intha villages and several temples. Part of the climbing was hard, but I was grateful for the physical workout.

When I returned to the guesthouse, it was already half past six in the afternoon. A boy working there handed me a note. He said a friend had come to visit me that afternoon, waited for an hour, and then left. My anxiety rose as I opened the note; it said:

Dear Teacher,
    This is Ae Maew. I've come to see you. You must have been at the lake. I'm sorry that I didn't inform you in advance. I just wanted to see you.
    Since you left the house, a series of things happened as you had predicted. Well, they are all over. However, I felt hurt in my heart. My brother cut one of my palms with a knife. I have to stay a few more days with my mother. She needs company. I'm going back. I'll call you tonight.
    I wish you a peaceful journey.
    Ae Maew   *February 19th, 15:50*

I was enraged. What a beast! I felt like I wanted to do something violent as well. I needed to vent, too. I questioned myself: "Have I become involved too much or simply not enough in Ae Maew's family's affairs? What is the boundary for an anthropologist?" I felt terrible that I had left Ae Maew alone at this critical time. I could not wait until she called, and I hurried to a nearby shop to make a phone call to her friend Ajuan. Ajuan told me Lin San had destroyed more windows and doors of the house. Ae Maew asked Ajuan's brother-in-law to mediate, and the result was to let Lin San sell the family farm. He promised to give a share to his elder brother who was in jail, although this promise had no guarantee at all. I asked Ajuan why no one had called a policeman. "Everyone said they should, but no one really did it," she replied.

My thoughts were in disarray; I could not think of a solution. Slowly, I walked with heavy steps back to the guesthouse. The heat was unbearable, stifling. At the guesthouse, I wanted to wash my face in a shared bathroom, but some wet tissues left in the hand-basin by the previous guest were disgusting. I felt like running away from this place and this country as soon as possible. Ae Maew's words echoed in my mind: "I hate this environment. I hate poverty." I took off my glasses with their thick lenses, intending to place them on a corner of the basin. Accidentally, I dropped them, and they broke. A sense of deep unease swallowed me as my world suddenly blurred; things around me seemed to fade away.

3

Pursuit of Ambition

Father and Son

> I was young and ambitious.... My troops and I received training at the headquarters [the KMT Third Army in northern Thailand] for one month and then returned to northern Burma to recruit more soldiers.
>
> —Mr. Li—Father, June 5, 2007

> It is hard to imagine that I, born in a mountain village in Burma, could have become a manager in a Taiwanese company.
>
> —Guoguang—Son, June 6, 2007

I met Mr. Li and his eldest son, Guoguang, during my third field trip to Taunggyi in June 2007. Zhang Dage had mentioned the father to me two years earlier. He told me that Mr. Li had been in the Ka Kwe Ye (KKY)[1] force and could tell me much of its history. Zhang Dage originally tried to arrange a meeting for me with Mr. Li in 2006 while I was conducting fieldwork in Taunggyi, but electronic communication was not convenient in Burma at that time, and when he finally got in touch with Mr. Li via one of Mr. Li's brothers who also lived in Taiwan, I had already left Taunggyi for another city. The following year, as I was planning another trip to Burma, Zhang Dage gave me Mr. Li's phone number. The day after my arrival in Taunggyi, I called Mr. Li from a shop. Luckily, he was home. I told him

---

1. The Ka Kwe Ye, or People's Volunteer Force, were auxiliary local defense troops officially recognized by the Burmese government between 1963 and 1973 (Smith 1993, 95). However, a former KKY officer told me that his unit was established in 1962 in northern Shan State.

briefly about myself and my wish to visit him. Strangely, he said he had not heard about me, but he invited me to visit him that morning. Not knowing Mr. Li's neighborhood well, I asked the shopkeeper (also a Yunnanese) for directions. He told me it was not easy to locate Mr. Li's house, which was some distance away, but Mr. Li's eldest son lived nearby. He suggested I go to the son first and let him take me to see his father. He then kindly sent a shop girl to take me to the son's house.

Mr. Li's eldest son and his wife ran a bookstore that also provided copy services. After I introduced myself and told him about my phone call with his father, the son immediately agreed to take me by motorcycle to see him. The father's house, located in an alley, was a medium-size two-story building with a front yard. When I arrived, Mr. Li was sitting in the yard smoking a Yunnanese water pipe (*shuiyantong*) and chatting with a friend. I greeted him, gave him a tin of cookies[2] that I had purchased in the shop earlier and my name card. He looked at the card and told his son to take me to the living room. A housemaid brought me a glass of hot tea. Many photos and certificates hanging on the walls immediately captured my attention. These certificates attested to Mr. Li's important positions in various organizations, including several local Chinese temples, Chinese schools, and two Kokang associations. Mr. Li entered the room and saw me looking at them. He smiled and invited me to sit on the sofa. I repeated again my wish to learn of his personal history. He sat down in good spirits, lit a cigarette, placed it in a water pipe, and started to smoke. Punctuated by the distinctive sound of the water pipe, he began: "Whatever you want to know, you may ask. My history is very long; not even three days and three nights could exhaust my whole story [wode gushi santian sanye ye shuo buwan]. You can write slowly. You can ask me the history of the [KMT] Third and Fifth Armies, the history of the caravan trade, the history of Shan armies. Do you know Bo Kanzurt?[3] I entered the troop at the age of fourteen or fifteen."

Mr. Li's opening was a declaration of his importance and personal involvement in the making of history in Shan State in Burma and the border areas of northern Thailand. This is an intricate history that involves various ethnic forces and state authorities beyond national borders. I was

---

2. Among the Yunnanese in both Burma and Thailand, it is customary on a formal visit to bring a tin of cookies for the host.

3. Bo Kanzurt was the secondary leader of the Shan United Revolutionary Army. He was in charge of the army's affairs in Xunding, while the founder of the army, Bo Moherng, camped with another section of the troops in Piang Luang, a border village in northern Thailand.

impressed by his openness and pondered how to begin my inquiries. I was familiar with the common description of one's history as "very long," with a narration that would extend "beyond three days and three nights." While pointing to the richness of one's life history, simultaneously the informant can also mean "my story is too long to tell." Experience had taught me that unless I built a base of trust and familiarity with my interviewees, it would be difficult to gain insight into their lives. A link with a person's close relatives is always good preparation, but I was not sure what had gone wrong with the earlier connection via Mr. Li's brother.

What I was more interested in getting Mr. Li to tell me was the concrete social history of the past, rather than a general description of leadership in different ethnic insurgent groups. To avoid sensitive questions right away, I started to ask Mr. Li about his family history.

"When did you come to Burma?"

"It wasn't me. It was a very long time ago. At the end of the Ming dynasty, a son-in-law of the emperor, from a family named Chen, took troops to Kokang. There have been seventeen generations in my clan since the immigration. The troops first arrived in a place in Kokang named Shangliuhu [area of upper six households]. My great-grandfather moved the family to another place, named Alapi [also in Kokang]. My grandfather and grandmother moved again to Changqingshan [mountain of evergreen, which is next to Kokang across the Salween River]. My father was born there; I was born there too, in 1943. Changqingshan is a big mountain. There were many villages, forty to fifty of them. Ours was called Dashuitang [big water pond].[4] My father was a division chief [*quzhang*]. Our ancestor originated from Nanjing Yingtianfu. My wife's ancestor was also from Nanjing. He was dispatched to a military station in Zhenkang. The clan of my wife had been there for many generations. Her family fled Zhenkang to Kokang in 1958."

"Do you have a clan genealogy book?"

"No."

"Are Kokangs and Yunnanese the same?"

"The speech is the same. We speak the same dialect as the people of Zhenkang and Gengma [in Yunnan]. But we are Kokangs. There are in total eight hundred thousand to nine hundred thousand Kokangs [spread

---

4. Another place also named Dashuitang is located inside Kokang.

in different places] in Burma.⁵ There is an Ethnic Kokang Cultural Association [*guogan minzu wenhuahui*]. The current association president, Luo Xinghan, is seventy-three and the richest person among the Kokang. I'm the first vice president of the association, in charge of the affairs of Kengtung and Taunggyi Districts."

Mr. Li's narration is drawn from different sources, mingled with popular social history. Kokang, a primarily ethnic-Chinese-inhabited area, is located in the far northeastern corner of Shan State, bordering China's Yunnan Province. Across the border on its east are Zhenkang and Gengma. Its western border reaches the Salween River and its southern border the Namtim River. It is a mountainous region, famous for the production of high-quality opium. The total geographical area is about fifty-one hundred square kilometers (Cai 1989, 1; Luo 2006, 19). Local people tend to attribute the origin of their ancestral migration to the flight of the last Southern Ming emperor, Yongli (also commonly known as Gui Wang),⁶ to Burma in 1659. The emperor was captured in Mandalay in 1662, then delivered to Kunming and executed there by strangulation (Shore 1976; Thant Myint-U 2006, 84–87; Yu 2000, 89–112). Some of the loyalists and troops accompanying him were said to have escaped to Kokang, where they settled.⁷ Despite the historical fact of Yongli's flight to Burma, there is no record that verifies its Kokang origin.⁸ Throughout history, the region has been under the sphere of influence of different political entities—China, Great Britain, and Burma.⁹ However, its remoteness and rugged terrain have

---

5. The number seems to be exaggerated. According to Kokang Cultural Association in Lashio, there are about three hundred thousand Kokangs in Burma—four thousand to five thousand in Mandalay, fifty thousand in Lashio, more than one hundred thousand in Kokang, and the rest dispersed to other places in upper Burma and Yangon. Many Yunnanese migrants who hold a Kokang identification card are actually arrivals to Burma after 1949; they are from a range of places in Yunnan.

6. Yongli was the emperor's era name. His original name was Zhu Youlang, and he was commonly referred to as Gui Wang (Prince Gui), although historically he was never entitled to this position (Shore 1976, 249). I am indebted to Sun Laichen for the reference.

7. Research on Kokang is meager. A few major works are by Cai (1989), Kratoska (2002), Sai Kham Mong (2005), and Yang (1997). Historians have disputed the resettlement of the surviving loyalists and troops of Zhu Youlang in Burma; see Nin (1987).

8. I am indebted again to Sun Laichen's confirmation of the lack of historical records regarding this question.

9. Kokang (or Guogan), called Maliba in earlier times, was incorporated into Chinese territory in the early Ming period, under the administrative supervision of the native official (*tusi*) of Meng Gen. Later on, control switched to the native official of Mu Bang. In 1897, the British extended their colonial rule to Kokang. Following the independence of the Union of Burma in 1948,

guaranteed its de facto autonomy and the people's self-identity as Kokangs (*guoganren*), or people of Maliba in earlier times (*malibaren*). Nevertheless, the region is not completely isolated. Because of its geographical location, for centuries many artisans and laborers from nearby areas of Yunnan arrived every year to take miscellaneous jobs during the dry season and returned home before the advent of the rainy season (Cai 1989, 37). Following the Communist takeover in China in 1949, many Yunnanese refugees fled to this essentially Chinese-inhabited region.

Apart from connecting his ancestor's arrival in Kokang with the last Ming emperor, Mr. Li's placing his and his wife's ancestry in Nanjing prior to migration to Yunnan and Kokang is also derived from a popular social memory that stresses Han Chinese origins. Yunnan (and also Kokang) was originally inhabited by non-Han ethnic groups. As mentioned in the introduction, beginning with the Ming dynasty, massive Chinese resettlement in Yunnan was carried out to consolidate the central government's rule in this frontier area. The Han influx was accompanied by Chinese colonial rule. The rhetoric of imperial historiography highlighting Sinocentrism underlines the official records (Wade 2000), and in practice the Chinese expansion in Yunnan through "successive stages of conquest, occupation and assimilation" (FitzGerald 1972, 77) has essentially been remembered by the Han population as civilizing (*jiaohua*) native barbarians (Chang 2006a, 67). Accordingly, only by attributing one's ancestral emigration as being from China proper can one justify his or her Han identity. As the founding capital of the Ming dynasty, Nanjing has historical significance. Large numbers of Ming troops gathered here before they set off to Yunnan for military occupation.[10] Moreover, since Emperor Yongli fled from Nanjing to Burma, Nanjing is often appropriated as one's original ancestral locality, especially among those clans that did not pass on a genealogical book.

Mr. Li went on to tell me the function of the Ethnic Kokang Cultural Association, which was founded in 1976 in Lashio. He referred to it as a legal institute that helps mediate all kinds of disputes among fellow Kokangs. It even has the authority to grant divorce and to mete out punishments to

---

Kokang became a constituent part of Shan State. The Kokang were recognized as an ethnic group later and granted citizenship (Cai 1989, 10–19; Chen 1996, 180; Kratoska 2002). Until 1965, the place was under the rule of the Yang family, which had established its control around 1880 (Cai 1989, 25).

10. However, most of the troops were recruited from neighboring provinces in the Yangtze delta area (Chang 2006a).

drug addicts and criminals. In a nutshell, it is a very powerful organization among the Kokang, with branch offices located in various places.

"Whatever you want to ask, you may ask," Mr. Li repeated again. I was encouraged and suggested he tell me about his youth. I wanted to learn more of his personal story. He said: "We [he and his group of friends] went to a local school in [Changqingshan] for two years, and then transferred to another Chinese school in Lashio. We were older than the other students of the same grade, so we jumped to the fourth grade. I was eleven years old at that time. I studied in Lashio until I finished junior high in 1961. In Lashio, I went to Zhong Hua School. We had to practice Chinese calligraphy and keep a diary every day. Our teachers and textbooks were all from Taiwan.[11] Ideologically, we affiliated with the right wing [the Chinese Nationalist government]. Another school—Zhong Shan School—belonged to the left wing [that identified with the Chinese Communists]."

"How were the textbooks transported from Taiwan?"

"Possibly they were transported to Yangon and then distributed to different places inside the country.[12] The left-wing Zhong Shan School used Nanyang textbooks from Malaysia. They had three hundred to four hundred students; we had more than six hundred students. The students of the two schools often got into fights. Sometimes I took out my gun and fired a shot in the air. That scared those Zhong Shan students and they ran away. My father was a division chief in Changqingshan, so he had guns. After graduation in 1961, I went to join the [KMT] Third Army, which had just retreated to Thailand from Shan State in Burma. At that time, Chiang Kai-shek was the president [in Taiwan]; Chiang Ching-kuo was the minister of national defense;[13] Chen Cheng was the vice president. The

---

11. The school may have had connections with Taiwan, but it was quite impossible that the teachers were sent from there. During the Cold War period, there were intelligence agents working in upper Burma for the Taiwanese government, but most of these agents were local Yunnanese.

12. Another informant said that Chinese books from Taiwan were banned, as Burma did not recognize the KMT government in Taiwan. However, prior to 1965 many textbooks from there were transported to Yangon via Hong Kong by sea. In Hong Kong, a new cover was added to these books that changed the place of publication to Hong Kong. Other sources were Chinese textbooks published in Singapore and shipped from there to Yangon. After the ban on Chinese education in Burma in 1965, the government forbade the entry of Chinese textbooks. The mule caravans from northern Thailand then smuggled a small number of Chinese textbooks to Shan State. Most Chinese schools, now underground, also printed their own textbooks using steel plates.

13. Chiang Ching-kuo was the eldest son of Chiang Kai-shek. He became the minister of national defense in 1965.

Third Army had its registration number in Taiwan. I was appointed the commanding officer of the Second Independent Regiment [*duli diertuan tuanzhang*]. I left the Third Army and returned to Burma in 1968 to lead a Ka Kwe Ye troop in Changqingshan of more than three hundred soldiers. I led the troop until 1973."

By connecting his personal experience with group and national history, Mr. Li seemingly tried to emphasize his significance. As I grew more interested in the details of his military career, his recounting, however, became sketchy. He quickly changed the subject and referred briefly to his movement from one place to another as a civilian businessman after 1973. Though a civilian, he stressed his leadership among the Kokang and his contribution to the community, without giving much explanation. Maybe he was tired; maybe he was cautious about revealing too many details. I sensed it was time to end my visit. Before leaving, I asked him if I could come the next day to learn more of his story. He said I was welcome. I was pleased with the answer and told him I would go to his eldest son's house next morning by nine o'clock and let his son take me to his house again. With this arrangement in place, the eldest son, Guoguang, sent me back to my place.

The next morning I arrived at Guoguang's small two-story wooden house. The front part of the first floor was a bookstore, and Guoguang was sitting there smoking a cigarette. He invited me to come in and gestured to me to sit on a wooden chair. A maid brought me a glass of hot tea. While waiting for him to finish smoking, I started to chat with him. Guoguang was born in 1966 in Dashuitang village in Changqingshan. He has two younger sisters and three younger brothers, all married except the youngest brother. Guoguang's family moved to the present house only a year ago. Guoguang and his wife, a teacher at a Chinese school, have two children. They first stayed with his parents, but two years ago they moved out to open a Chinese restaurant. The business was poor, however, and he closed the restaurant and moved to the present house to start a bookshop. The shop sold and rented out novels, magazines, and cartoon books, many of them from Taiwan. Most of the time, the shop was looked after by a Shan girl. Guoguang said he also brokered jade stones from time to time for buyers from China and Taiwan who are mostly acquaintances through business connections. When they came, he would take them to see jade stones and help in price negotiations. To my surprise, he suddenly told me that a year ago, his uncle in Taiwan had contacted the family about my coming. "So," I thought, "the family has known about me for a year." I pondered this in my mind.

"I have been to Taiwan. I was there for many years," he said slowly. He lit another cigarette and continued smoking. I sensed he had something to tell me, but I was also a bit anxious about the appointment with his father. I kept quiet and waited to hear what he was going to say. I ended up sitting in Guoguang's shop for the next three hours completely absorbed by his story and struck by his eloquence. I raised very few questions and tried to write down everything I heard in my notebook. Guoguang narrated his story structurally, mapping out his account progressively through time and space. His voice was low and his tone quiet. It seemed the story had been growing inside him for a long time, and finally he gave birth to it by telling it to a stranger, a stranger he had heard about a year before, a stranger who was researching the history of Yunnanese migrants in Burma and Thailand and possibly would publish it.

As Guoguang neared the end of his tale, his father appeared. He had come to check on why I had not shown up and found me sitting in the shop taking notes of his son's story. I felt a bit awkward. He did not say anything but gave a few nods. I was not sure what his nodding meant. I apologized to him and said I would visit him the next morning. He agreed and then left. Guoguang seemed undisturbed by his father's arrival, and after his father left, he carried on relating his story. Around half past twelve, his wife, Chunmei, came home from school. She is from Taiwan, where they had met and gotten married. It is unusual for a Taiwanese lady to follow her husband back to Burma. I had lunch with them that noon.

The following week, I visited Guoguang and his wife several times. I checked with Guoguang on some parts of his story and learned from Chunmei about the family's interaction with her father-in-law. "He still lives in the past," Chunmei said to me. "The whole family disagrees with his way of doing things. Most of his children live in separate places, but he has not divided the family property yet. He still thinks of buying a big piece of land in Taunggyi and having all his sons build their houses next to each other on the land."

That week, I also visited Mr. Li three more times on my own. Apart from relating his life story to me, he and one of his friends took me to visit three local Chinese temples, the Taunggyi branch of the Ethnic Kokang Cultural Association, and two Chinese schools. Ostensibly he was giving me a tour of Taunggyi; in reality, he was demonstrating his wide social connections. "I have cared for my people my whole life. I have suffered a great deal. I do not aim for money but for name,"[14] he stressed while we were visiting the Ethnic Kokang Cultural Association. He told me details about his military life that reflect a precious part of the social history of Shan State since the 1960s. The "incident" when he saw me interviewing his son seemed to have generated a positive push. I sensed that there was a slight tension between father and son and that perhaps Mr. Li was competing with his son in narrating his story to me. During our interviews, he hinted a few times that he was more experienced than his son.

From my perspective, both the father and son told wonderful stories, illustrating their movement and evolution over time and space and how they as actors make their own history by repeatedly battling external constraints and adversities. The significance of their accounts rests not on authenticity, but on their viewpoints on the world they have lived in and their commentaries on their life processes, bearing facets of determination, ambivalence, and even regret. They wanted me to listen to their stories and to write them down. Both their narration and my writing metaphorically give new life to their past and bring meaning to their present. Through narration, they reconstruct the past as well as themselves.

In the following sections, I juxtapose accounts narrated by the father with those of the son. Belonging to different generations, father and son have related their stories from different perspectives. Nevertheless, as they have shared a part of life together, their narratives overlap to some extent. Their stories are far from complete; there are many fragments, discrepancies, and even mistakes or contradictions. Nonetheless, these defects also reveal their personalities and motives in transmitting their stories to me.

The Father: Arrival in Thailand in 1961

On my second visit, Mr. Li began his story with the military engagement of the 1960s:

"My father was a division chief in Changqingshan, an area which had been under the administrative supervision of Mu Bang *tusi*. Before 1965, Kokang was ruled by the Yang family. In 1959, the Burmese government

---

14. His words in Chinese are: "wodeyisheng dou aihu renmin chile henduoku women shi buaiqian ai mingyi."

demanded the handover of political power from the native officials of Shan State. Yet, the Yang family refused to comply. In 1962, General Ne Win seized the reins of power through a coup. The next year, the government captured several members of the Yang family, including Yang Zhencai, the incumbent native official. Yang Zhensheng [*alias* Jimmy Yang], a brother of Yang Zhencai, led a local defense guard to fight against the state army. In 1965, he brought a remnant of the guard numbering about one thousand to northern Thailand and collaborated with the ousted former Burmese prime minister U Nu. His troops were camped near the headquarters of the KMT Third Army in Tham Ngob.

"In 1961, several years prior to Yang Zhensheng's military action, I had already led about forty soldiers from my home village to join the Third Army in Tham Ngob. I was young and ambitious [*nianqing zhiqigao*]. General Li Wenhuan was a good leader, despite his being authoritarian.[15] He gave me three machine guns—one from Taiwan, one from Canada, and one from Czechoslovakia—and forty rifles. Later on, he gave me another American A64 machine gun. My troops and I received training at the headquarters for one month and then returned to northern Burma to recruit more soldiers. My troops were code-named the Second Independent Regiment. In 1963, forty to fifty of my troops went to Tham Ngob again for training. They stayed for nearly a year and then returned to Changqingshan."

Mr. Li did not mention his unit's mission. It is quite possible that it assisted General Li in drug trafficking from northern Shan State to Thailand. Although they had retreated to Thailand, Generals Li and Duan respectively deployed a part of their forces in Shan State to facilitate drug trafficking. According to Chao Tzang Yawnghwe, their military bases were scattered across an area of some 20,000 square miles (32,187 square kilometers), covering nearly one-third of Shan State (1990, 124–49). Li and Duan led two major opium-trading groups in the region during the 1960s and 1970s.[16] Mr. Li further described the financial aid General Li provided his forces in Burma:

"The Third Army had several supply bases in Shan State. With money brought from Thailand, these bases purchased rice in Burma for the troops

---

15. For the organization of the KMT Third and Fifth Armies and their leadership see my paper "Identification of Leadership among the KMT Yunnanese Chinese in Northern Thailand" (Chang 2002).

16. For more information on the drug issue see Chao Tzang Yawnghwe (1993), Lintner (1994, 239–71), and McCoy (1991).

stationed in the state. Apart from rationed rice, each soldier was provided thirty kyat per month for non-staple food [*fushifei*]. The money was given to the adjutant in charge of buying food in each troop. The adjutant could use the money for trade; for example, he could invest it in buying opium. After the commodity had been sold, the profit belonged to the troop. In addition, every soldier received twenty kyat as pocket money per month. At that time one Burmese kyat could be exchanged for two Thai baht. One chicken was valued at about one kyat. The commanding officer of a regiment received two hundred kyat per month and another fifty kyat for food.

"The Third Army had its best time from 1967 to 1970. Its total number of soldiers in Burma and Thailand reached four thousand to five thousand. The Fifth Army was weaker. It had one thousand to two thousand soldiers. The two armies levied taxes on businessmen in the drug trade, and they helped escort traders' caravans back and forth between Thailand and Burma. Whenever a drug caravan was leaving for Thailand, their troops in Burma would send a telegram to their headquarters in Thailand. The headquarters would decide on the number of soldiers required to escort the caravan. The size of a caravan varied each time. Usually it was between one hundred to two hundred mules. Sometimes it may have amounted to several hundred. One mule was loaded with forty *zuai* of goods.[17]

"The armies recruited soldiers from different parts of Shan State. Their military bases were not fixed. They moved from place to place depending on the situation. When a troop was on the move, every soldier carried a bag of rice, a suit of clothes, a water pitcher, two pieces of tarpaulin (one to put on the ground, and the other above) and three blankets (one to put on the ground tarpaulin, the other two to cover the body). The size of a tarpaulin sheet was two meters by two meters. Each regiment had a few mules that carried kitchenware and food.

"In 1965, I went to Tham Ngob again for training and stayed there until 1968. That year I told General Li of my decision to leave the army to return to Burma and join the KKY forces. Northern Shan State had become a battlefield. The Communist Party of Burma [CPB] was gaining control in Kokang and Changqingshan. The KKY unit I led had about 300 soldiers. About 150 were in charge of growing opium; the other 150

---

17. One *zuai* (in Shan) or one *peittha* (in Burmese) is traditionally known as a *viss* in English, equivalent to around 1.6 kilograms.

were on guard. Fifty of them followed me around. But when the situation required it, all troops participated in fighting.

"Changqingshan produced the best opium. Half of the harvested opium grown by my troops became the common property [of our unit]; the profit from the other half was divided equally among all the soldiers, including those who planted the crop as well as those on military duty. Between 1969 and 1972, there were a lot of battles. Our troop fought alongside another Burmese troop, also numbering about three hundred soldiers. They did not grow opium, but were financially supported by the government. However, the Burmese troops were bad; they often troubled civilians. Yet, within my sphere of influence, they dared not misbehave. My ruling philosophy was to 'suppress the bully and assist the weak' [*yaqiang tiruo*]. Once I joined the KKY, I could buy supplies from the Burmese government cheaply, and then resell part of the goods to civilians. In 1973, the government disbanded the KKY,[18] and I moved to Mong Nai [or Mone]. There were eight hundred Kokang households in Mong Nai."

In the course of the interviews, while delineating a sociopolitical picture of Shan State and northern Thailand in the 1960s and early 1970s, Mr. Li portrayed himself as a hero who bravely pursued his military career for the good of his people. Since the mid-1960s, the situation in Kokang had become more and more unstable. The area was torn between three major military forces—the CPB, the KKY, and Yang Zhensheng's troops (Cai 1989, 21; Sai Kam Mong 2007, 267).[19] The KKY were supposed to fight against the CPB alongside the Burmese army, but many of them were more interested in the drug trade. A great advantage to joining the KKY was obtaining permission from the government for this trade. Despite the wartime situation, the trafficking persisted. Several KKY troops were in alliance with the KMT armies for this highly lucrative business. In 1969, the CPB took control of Kokang. Thousands of Kokangs fled to other places, such as Lashio, Kutkai, Pinlong, Nansan, Mong Nai, and Taunggyi.

---

18. The change of policy was because of the KKY's inability to fight the Communist Party of Burma and also because of pressure from the US government, which accused these ethnic militias of engaging in drug trafficking (Chen 1996, 193–94).

19. Sai Kham Mong wrote: "In the Northeast Military Region of Kokang, Wa and Kachin sub-state, there were altogether twenty-three groups of Ka Kwe Ye formed with 4,211 men" (2007, 267). Among them, the unit led by Luo Xinghan was most powerful. The CPB in Kokang was led by Peng Jiasheng (or Pheung Kya Shin) (Chen 1996, 186–203; Lintner 1994, 201–37).

A portion of them escaped to northern Thailand and resettled in a range of Yunnanese villages founded by the KMT Third Army. Fighting went on in northern Shan State until the late 1980s.

The Son: Life in Changqingshan and Mong Nai

Complementary to his father's account that referred to the complex geopolitics in Shan State during the 1960s and the early 1970s, Guoguang talked about its impacts on civilians' lives. He said:

"While living in Changqingshan, whenever we saw airplanes coming, we rushed to *tudong* to hide. Every household had its own *tudong*. It was a cave dug in the ground; the mouth was covered with a wooden board, and some earth was put on the board. The size of a *tudong* correlated with the size of a household. Everyone had to hide in his or her own household's *tudong*. If you had tried to enter someone else's, they would not have allowed you in.

"Because of ongoing fighting in Changqingshan, many families gradually moved away. My grandfather had two wives. He took the first grandmother, the fourth, fifth, and seventh uncles, and the second, third, fourth, and fifth aunts, totaling more than twenty people, to Reshuitang Xincun [Xincun] in Thailand. Later on they all moved to Taiwan. My father moved us to a village named Nakhan [in 1972], sixteen kilometers from Mong Nai. I was about seven years old, the age to go to school. We lived there for a few years.

"When we first arrived, there were only twenty to thirty Chinese households in the village. Gradually the number increased to four to five hundred. At that time, the Burmese government did not allow Chinese education. My grandfather on my mother's side taught us some Chinese at home every morning before we went to the Burmese school. Our village bordered a river. On the other side of the river was a Shan village. The Burmese primary school was located in that village. Chinese students and Shan students did not mingle, and sometimes we got into group fights. We felt we were from one side, and they were from the other. We were very young, but the distinction existed. Whenever we were in a fight, the Shan students would say: 'We are going to call the Shan army to beat you.' We would shout back, 'We are going to call the Kokang troops to beat you.'

Since childhood we felt like refugees lacking state protection. The Burmese government did not allow self-rule in Kokang. Even if you carried a *hmatpontin* [identification card], the policeman still made trouble for you and insisted the card was a fake.

"One night, when I was around [nine] years old [in 1974],[20] Khun Sa's troops fought their way to our village. Possibly a Kokang troop had attacked one of their Shan villages earlier. They regarded our village as being connected with that Kokang troop and came for revenge. Our village was not armed at all, and villagers had to run when the troop came. It was around seven o'clock in the evening. Some villagers shouted: 'Shan soldiers have come to fight us.' Behind our house was a field of tall corn. Our whole family hid in the cornfield. My youngest sister who was still small was scared and crying. Adults had to cover her mouth. We had no time to take anything with us from the house. We had to let the Shan soldiers rob us of whatever they wanted. Hiding in the cornfield, we heard a lot of shooting around us. That night forty to fifty people were injured. The next morning, all the villagers fled to Mong Nai to ask the local government for help. However, the Mong Nai government was afraid of provoking an attack from the Shan troop if they helped us. They didn't want us to stay, but after a long negotiation, they allowed us to settle temporarily in the market, which had many stalls used for selling goods in the daytime. After the market ended, we could use those stalls. All the villagers, two hundred to three hundred people, slept in them that night. Those who were better off left the market the next day. Slowly, the rest moved to other places too. Some went to Pinlong, some to Laikha, and some to Lashio. My father took us and a few other households to Loilin."

Guoguang's memory of his childhood was replete with fighting and fleeing. Shan State (as well as many other parts of Burma) was torn apart by different military groups; the people were compelled to side with one group or another. Sai Kham Mong wrote, "While some locals like Kachins, Shans, and Kokang were enlisted in the [Ka Kwe Ye] groups and fought alongside [government troops], some locals joined the [CPB]" (2007, 267). Fighting occurred among the KKY forces and ethnic insurgent groups, often not because of political differences but because of conflicts over the

---

20. Guoguang originally said twelve years old. However, I double-checked with his father, who said the incident occurred in 1974. Guoguang would have been nine years old then.

94   Beyond Borders

opium trade. The most prominent example was the opium battle of 1967 between the KMT forces and Khun Sa's troops.[21] Prolonged warfare caused people great hardship. A large number of civilians became refugees in their own country, running away from one military group to the protection of another and from one place to another, as Guoguang told in his story.

The Father: From 1969 to 1975

Notwithstanding the ongoing warfare, underground trade continued. Many ethnic insurgent groups and the KKY forces undertook this lucrative business to empower themselves. Mr. Li related his involvement in the trade:

"The state provided a limited number of old weapons to the KKY forces, so they basically had to arm themselves. Most weapons were purchased in Thailand and Laos. The war in Indochina was going on, and many American arms were stolen and smuggled out for sale. General Li of the KMT Third Army controlled a good number of smuggled arms. He traded them with allied KKY forces and some other ethnic rebels connected with him. Sometimes he gave weapons to these groups as a token of collaboration.

"Our lives were very harsh then. It was pure luck that we survived those days. The government sold us goods cheaply, and we then sold them again. Goods purchased with one hundred thousand kyat could be resold for two hundred thousand kyat. Sometimes the profit was more than double. As we were a KKY troop, we could apply to the government to buy various kinds of goods, including textiles, rice, gasoline, cement, tires, salt, sugar, tobacco, clothes, flour, peanuts, corn, bicycles, jeeps, and so on. The jeeps were left over from the Second World War. One jeep cost only about one

---

21. Khun Sa was regarded as the biggest drug warlord in Southeast Asia in the 1980s. He founded the Shan United Army and claimed to fight for the independence of the Shan people in Burma. Yet his claim was regarded as a pretext for his engagement in drug trafficking. Many of his officers had been KMT guerrillas. It was said that in the early stages of his career, he received some weapons from General Li. With an increased grip on power, he wanted to control the opium trade, and he refused to pay Li and Duan taxes when passing through their territories. Li and Duan collaborated to punish Khun Sa for challenging their authority. For details of the battle, see Lintner (1994, 245) and McCoy (1991, 333–34).

thousand kyat. At that time, a big truck was only a few thousand kyat. We also levied an opium tax on the local people, at the rate of 20 percent of their production. In addition, the troop grew its own opium. The state army enlisted people by force, but the KKY didn't do so. My troop protected people within my domain."

"How did the KKY recruit their soldiers?" I questioned.

"If a household had two sons, then one was recruited. If a household had four or five, then two of them were recruited. In 1971 or 1972, we fought a big battle. A part of my troop was stationed in a post named Shuangkengshan, located in Changqingshan. There were about fifty soldiers. A Burmese troop with around the same number of soldiers was stationed nearby. One day the CPB attacked us. They had more than twenty-four hundred people and surrounded our post. Our troop had prepared well, and all the soldiers hid themselves in the trenches. We fought for seven days and nights. We didn't even have time to cook. The CPB had a large number; they took turns firing arms day and night. Our number was too small, and the soldiers were not able to rest. Some were too tired and fell asleep even while fighting. Our machine guns kept smoking because of nonstop firing. One of my soldiers was especially brave. He alone killed more than fifty CPB soldiers. The CPB troop leader ordered him caught alive. On the seventh day, my soldiers became exhausted. The CPB troop then stormed us. They stood up and ran at us directly, not even trying to cover themselves. In the end, we were not able to sustain the defense. The whole barrack was destroyed. Only a few soldiers managed to escape, including that very brave one. We had killed more than 150 CPB soldiers. Our side had about 30 soldiers dead and another 15 captured."

"How about you?" I asked.

Mr. Li smiled and said: "I was not in this battle. I was lucky. I had been away in another place. We had radio communication at that time, but the CPB force was too strong. It took time to recruit support. The Burmese army finally sent three brigades and other KKY troops, including Luo Xinghan's troop, to the battlefield. The number totaled about three thousand. They fought for forty-two days to chase away the CPB."

I was surprised to learn of Mr. Li's absence after having listened to his narration of the battle and the bravery of his troop. If I had not questioned his whereabouts, would he have revealed his absence? Perhaps not. His speaking about the war was very much done to demonstrate his troops' bravery and the importance of his leadership. As he did not participate in the battle, he must have crafted the story based on what he had heard from his surviving troops as well as his understanding and imagination. The sharp contrast between the number of his troops and that of the CPB seems to be unbelievable. Yet the important point is how he has remembered the event. Through remembering (and perhaps distorting some of the facts) and recounting the experience, Mr. Li gives new meaning to the former hardship and suffering that he and his troops had gone through during a chaotic time. But why did he not tell me of a fighting experience he personally encountered? Was he involved more in the underground trade than military action? Before I got a chance to express my doubt, Mr. Li went on to tell me about the intricate relationships between armed ethnic groups. He said:

"We had contact with different groups—the Third and Fifth Armies, Khun Sa's army, and Luo Xinghan's army. We were all together."

"But didn't you fight against one another?"

"Sometimes we did, sometimes not. When we were not at war, we were friends." Mr. Li laughed.

Obviously there was no continuity of alliance or enmity between armed ethnic groups. It was the groups' interests that determined conflict or collaboration. Subsequently, I asked him about the 1974 attack of Khun Sa's troops on Nakhan village, which Guoguang had related. He said:

"They were not Khun Sa's troops. It was another Shan unit. We had stayed there less than a year when the incident occurred. They killed eight villagers and captured twenty-five that night."

"Where were you?"

"I was in Pinlong. I went there for business. I was lucky again."

"Why did you move your family to Nakhan?" I asked.

"The KKY forces were disbanded in 1973. I then left Changqingshan. Actually before Nakhan, I had moved my family to Lashio a year earlier. It cost a lot of money to live there. There were always people who came to ask for help."

"How was life in Nakhan?"

"We grew crops—rice, corn, peanuts, and sesame."

"No opium?"

"No, not after 1973. The land in Nakhan was fertile. You sowed one bucket of seed; you would harvest one hundred buckets later. I took care of the other Kokang households who followed me there. Young people came to help on my farm voluntarily. After the attack by the Shan troop in Nakhan, I moved my family to Loilin.[22] About ten households followed me. Prior to my arrival, the Kala [of South Asian origin] in Loilin didn't allow Chinese to live in the village. They were Muslim. They forbade the Chinese to eat pork. I was not afraid of the Kala. I told my people to retain the habit of eating pork. Because of my persistence, the Kala dared not trouble us. In Loilin, I started my business of selling clothes and textiles in the market. I went to Taunggyi to purchase the commodities and brought them back to Loilin for sale. My house in Loilin is still there. My second son's family lives there now."

Mr. Li's narration provides more information on trade than military action. This seems to suggest that his priority at the time was business. Moreover, his mention of the Kala at the end made me think of Guoguang's narrative of the conflict between the Chinese and Shan students. Although many informants described reciprocal interaction with other ethnic groups in their everyday lives and economic undertakings, an ethnic boundary existed and resulted in tension under different circumstances (as also shown in Zhang Dage's and Ae Maew's stories).[23]

With reference to Tsing's interpretation (2005) of "friction across difference" grounded in the case of the Dayaks' overlapping relations with the Indonesian government, transnational enterprises, international nongovernmental organizations, and local environmentalists and nature lovers, Mr. Li and his troop's connections and clashes with multiple military groups and their participation in the opium trade point to a comparable history involving different layers of power structure. It was an intriguing history of politico-economy against a backdrop of Burmese isolationism, ethnic division, and the Cold War, which were activated by continuous "illicit" flows of people, resources, commodities, capital, and information (McCoy 1991; Lintner 1994). The question of legality was overshadowed by competition for power. While being shaped by this gigantic historical process, Mr. Li and his group, despite their borderland origin and relatively small-scale

---

22. According to Mr. Li's narration, he moved his family from Changqingshan to Lashio in 1972, from Lashio to Nakhan in 1973. The attack on Nakhan took place in 1974; the family fled at that time to Mong Nai. Mr. Li moved the family from Mong Nai to Loilin in 1975.

23. I will probe this subject further in the following chapters.

military force, also reacted to it with their adaptive strategies in various domains of everyday life—farming, trading, and fighting wars. Mr. Li's narration together with Guoguang's account above gives a nuanced picture of how various military entities' entrenchment affected local people's lives, resulting in continuous migration and shifting affiliations with these forces. Both the civilians' and armed groups' activities in effect intersected state and nonstate powers beyond Burmese national borders.

Later I made a visit to Loilin with Guoguang. The trip was four hours from Taunggyi by motorcycle through a mountain road with endless turns. This road had been used in the past for transporting black market goods between Taunggyi and Loilin. The landscape of mountains, valleys, pine forests, paddy fields, and rivers was impressive, but the road was very bumpy. During the 1970s and 1980s, Taunggyi was the center of the black market trade in upper Burma. Traders came here to buy wholesale goods that were mostly smuggled from Thailand by mule caravans.

Guoguang took me to the market at Loilin. He pointed out the location where his family had once owned two shops. His mother, sisters, and a few workers looked after the shops, and his father was in charge of replenishing goods from Taunggyi. While in Loilin, I stayed at their house. It has partly been rebuilt. Guoguang showed me the original site of the kitchen and a section for workers and soldiers. Despite the KKY's disbandment, Mr. Li had maintained around twenty soldiers. The kitchen had been torn down, but two big cooking stoves still remained, evoking images of life in the past.

The Son: Leaving for Thailand in 1985

Guoguang lived in Loilin from 1975 to 1985. Not long after his graduation from high school, he left home for Thailand. He said:

"One day two young men from Changqingshan arrived at our house. One was eighteen years old, named Changshou [long life]. The other was twenty, named Qiwu [seven five]. Qiwu was born the year his grandfather was seventy-five years old. The family thus named him Qiwu. They were on their way to Thailand. My father was in charge of the Ethnic Kokang Cultural Association of the area, so they came to stay at our house for a couple of days. I was nineteen years old and had just finished high school.

They asked me to join them on the journey to Thailand. Changshou had seven thousand kyat with him; Qiwu had about ten thousand kyat. They said to me, 'Guoguang, you come with us. We will take care of your spending on the way. We young people should go out into the world to explore our future [*dao waimian quchuang*].' I was very keen on the idea. In fact, I had been thinking of going somewhere before meeting them. I thus left a letter for my family telling them I had gone and asking them not to look for me. I was afraid I would attract attention, so I didn't take any clothes or luggage with me. We took a government truck that transported supplies to the border area. The fare for one person was two hundred kyat.

"The road was bumpy, and public security was bad. The truck went slowly, sometimes only seven or eight kilometers a day. The driver stopped frequently for security checks, sending a person ahead to make sure there was no ambush by Shan rebels. Then the truck went for a short distance and stopped again to check. We proceeded very slowly in this way. On the fourth day after my departure from home, our truck was attacked. Two Burmese soldiers were shot dead. On the seventh day, the truck finally reached its last stop—Mongton—which was one day's walk from the Burmese-Thai border. I had an aunt living in Mongton. I went to look for her. On seeing me, she chided me for leaving home without telling my family. My aunt's living conditions were not good. She had been 'stolen' [*tou*] by my uncle when he was serving in a rebel troop.[24] She had been to Thailand before. She gave all her husband's money to me, two hundred kyat. She also stole a pair of sneakers from him. They were the shoes he wore to weddings. She then gave me a traveling bag with some of her husband's shirts inside. I was still young and didn't think much about this. When her husband discovered later what she had done, he must have beaten her.

"We hired an oxcart to take us to Dagudi.[25] There was a checkpoint near the border. On seeing Burmese soldiers, we were scared and started to run. The Burmese soldiers fired shots at us. Luckily, the bullets didn't hit us. We abandoned our luggage while running. When we reached Dagudi, we did not have a change of clothes.

---

24. It occurred often in Shan State that women were "stolen" for marriage. In some cases, the action was prearranged between the man and woman; in other cases, it was carried out by force (see chapter 6).

25. Dagudi (Arunotai in Thai) is a Yunnanese border village, which has been the first stop in Thailand for many Yunnanese from Burma.

"When we were in Mongton, my aunt told me to look for one of my father's former subordinates—a company commander [*lianzhang*]—once I arrived in Dagudi. I found the house of that company commander. He let us stay and suggested we plant potatoes in the village. That day he killed a chicken for us. Changshou decided to stay in Dagudi. However, Qiwu's and my ambition [*zhiqi*] was not to plant potatoes in Dagudi. Our ambition was to go to Chiang Mai or Bangkok to explore the world [*datianxia*]. We were naive at that time. We couldn't speak a word of Thai, and we had no Thai identities either. Three days later, Qiwu and I went to Xinchun by taking a pickup truck.[26] The fare was fifty baht for one person. Before leaving the village, the company commander told us to look for Teacher Li when we arrived in Xinchun.

"When we went to Teacher Li's house, he told us that we could both work in his lychee orchard. He would provide board and lodging, but no salary. Qiwu had an uncle who lived in Chiang Mai. He called him, and few days later his uncle came to take him to Chiang Mai. The three of us thus stayed in separate places—one in Dagudi, one in Xincun, and one in Chiang Mai. We wrote to one another about our lives. Qiwu often described the bustling life of Chiang Mai, while I related my days in the orchard. As for Changshou, he often complained about the harsh work in Dagudi, and about how many days he had not been able to take a shower. We told our tales in letters that we handed to drivers for delivery.

"In Teacher Li's orchard, there was another worker who had arrived before me. He was also from Burma. His name was Caobin. The boss paid him eight hundred baht a month. He was very kind and caring to me. Each time he received his salary, he gave me some money. Sometimes he took me to a noodle shop for a treat. The food provided by our boss was very simple: cold rice with some fermented soybean curd and vegetable pickles. Our job was to guard the orchard. When lychees became ripe, Thai people would come to steal. They were organized and came in trucks. Each Thai worker was given a basket and would quickly pick lychees and then leave

---

26. Guoguang's grandfather and many family members had migrated to Xincun earlier. There used to be private pickup trucks that offered transportation between Xincun and Dagudi every morning. As more and more villagers own cars, this transportation service has gradually declined since 2000.

in the truck that brought them. Our boss gave us a rifle. He said that when we saw lychee branches shaking, we should fire the rifle in the air. I was very thin at that time and dared not fire the rifle. I let Caobin do the job.

"At that time, Xinchun was quite disorderly. Many people were drug addicts. While walking in the village, you were sometimes approached by drug dealers. They put heroin in cigarettes and sold them for ten to twenty baht each. However, Qiwu, Changshou, and I were resistant. None of us became drug addicts.

"Later on I met an important person [*guiren*] in Xincun. It was a turning point in my life. His name was Ahao, from Fujian in China. He had flown to Thailand with a Chinese passport. He had a rich uncle who owned a business in Bangkok dealing in water pipes. He had a quarrel with his uncle and came to the north to relax. Maybe someone had told him about Xincun. I was having a drink in a shop. My table still had a spare seat, and he sat next to me. We started to chat. Later on I took him to my orchard. Ahao then asked me, 'Guoguang, would you like to go to Bangkok with me?' I said OK. We were together in Xincun for a few days and got to know each other better. I saw him as a trustworthy friend.

"So I told my boss that I was leaving for Bangkok. By then, I had worked there for three months. The boss said OK but didn't give me any money. Caobin accompanied me to the provincial road to wait for the bus. He was sad about my leaving. He cried and gave me an envelope to open after I was on the bus. In it was a letter and fifteen hundred baht. He was paid only eight hundred baht a month, and every month he had given me one hundred to two hundred baht. He must have saved this fifteen hundred baht over several months. I was very touched and cried. Ahao was sitting next to me. He didn't know what had happened and patted my shoulder.

"When we arrived in Chiang Mai, we bought tickets for the night bus that went directly to Bangkok. Ahao told me that if the policeman got on the bus to check, I should just pretend to be sleeping. He had a legal identity. He sat on the aisle seat and let me sit next to the window. A policeman came by once, but luckily, he didn't check on me. I fell asleep, and seven or eight hours later Ahao woke me up. I opened my eyes and suddenly saw a prosperous world full of high-rise buildings and overpasses. There was a lot of noise and smoke from cars, different kinds of cars, unlike those in

Burma, which were mostly left behind from the Second World War. I was dazzled. My fear of encountering police subsided.

"After getting off the bus, Ahao hired a *tuk-tuk*[27] that took us to his factory site. His one-room lodging was crude. It was a bit slanted, and behind it were a detached kitchen and a toilet. It was the rainy season, and water had accumulated around the lodge's stilts. His uncle owned the factory. He didn't want to live with his uncle and had asked to stay alone on the factory site.

"The next morning, Ahao took me to eat *kuaytiaw* [noodles] at a nearby corner stall. Afterward, he told me to stay at the lodge and went to work. That noon he brought back a lunch box for me. I was not related to him at all, but he took care of me. I was very grateful. A few days later, I asked Ahao to give me some money to go to the market. I told him I could cook for him. Anyway, I couldn't stand eating out of a lunch box every day. He gave me fifty baht and told me to tell him when I had used up the money. Every morning I went to the market. Before going, I would ask the Thai names for the items I wanted to buy. But very often by the time I got to the market, I had forgotten the correct names. Sellers couldn't understand me and were amused by my way of speaking. On figuring out what I wanted to buy, they would teach me the correct terms. I gradually learned some Thai.

"Every day I cooked and waited for Ahao to come back to eat. I calculated the time and had the meal cooked before he returned. After eating, he often fought with me over the dishwashing. I told him: 'You have worked all day and are tired. Let me do the dishes.'

"One Sunday, Ahao took me to Yaowarat [the Chinatown in Bangkok]. Before going there, he said: 'Guoguang, you must be missing your hometown a lot. I am going to take you to a place where there are *xidoufen, yancai,* and *babasi.*'[28] Having stayed on the factory site for a few weeks, I was excited about seeing this Chinatown. It was packed with people on Sunday. I was interested in different kinds of Chinese food. Ahao bought a shirt for me. While eating *xidoufen* in a shop, I met Acao, a friend from Loilin. He had come to Thailand a year earlier. I was very happy to see him. We talked a long time. Acao told me he would ask his boss if he would hire me. He asked me to meet him a week later at the same place.

---

27. *Tuk-tuk* is a motorized tricycle used as a type of local taxi in Thailand.
28. These are common Yunnanese dishes. *Xidoufen* is gruel cooked from ground garden peas; *yancai* is pickled vegetable; *babasi* is Yunnanese cooked noodles.

"At that time, the bus fare was two baht each time, notwithstanding the distance. I took the bus to Yaowarat alone the following Sunday and met Acao. He said I could work at his factory. He then accompanied me back to Ahao's place to pick up my luggage. Ahao was hence left alone in his lodge. I had stayed with him for two months.

"Acao's boss was in the scrap metal business. There were sixteen workers at the factory who were all Yunnanese from Burma around age twenty or twenty-one. Our boss was from Taiwan. He hired us because we were cheaper and we spoke Chinese. I got eight hundred baht a month. The salary was paid once every week, two hundred baht each time. The boss provided lodging but no food. After each paycheck, every worker put twenty to fifty baht away as the common fund for food. We took turns going to market. We cooked Yunnanese dishes and spoke with each other in our own language.[29] The factory was a small Yunnanese society. I was happy there. Every weekend, Acao, Ahao, and I went to Yaowarat for fun. Ahao worked for his uncle, but he didn't go to the factory every day. Sometimes he came to our factory and hung out with us. However, he had good pay—seven to eight thousand baht a month.

"I was in that factory for six months. One day our boss was caught by the police for drug trafficking. He was found possessing fifty kilos of heroin in his car. After he was caught, the Thai police surrounded our factory and carried out a search, but nothing was found. We were not aware of his involvement in drugs at all. Later on we heard that he had several cars that he used for transporting narcotics from Chiang Mai to Bangkok. All the workers were illegal immigrants. When the police came and surrounded the factory, everyone tried to run away, but eleven were caught; only five escaped. I was taking a shower at that time, so I hid myself in the bathroom and was not found. Acao also got away. Those who were caught were delivered to Mae Sai to await expulsion. The five of us didn't know what to do next. Acao called Ahao. Ahao came and proposed we sell all the scrap metal in the factory. He said if we didn't sell it, the Thai police would take it anyway. The boss had no relatives or friends in Bangkok. His wife was in Taiwan and dared not come to Thailand for fear of being caught as well. Ahao spoke Thai well and was experienced. He contacted buyers and hired trucks to transport the scrap. We got more than three hundred

---

29. Yunnanese is similar to Mandarin Chinese and belongs to the same language family.

thousand baht from the sale. We gave fifty thousand baht to Ahao. He had helped us so much. At first he didn't want to take the money, but we insisted. We divided the rest of the money equally among sixteen people, with nearly twenty thousand baht for each one. We took a bus to Mae Sai to look for our friends. Ahao helped to find out their whereabouts just before they were expelled, and he gave them the money. They were very grateful for the unexpected money.

"Acao and I used our share of the money to start a small business selling *youtiao*.[30] We first learned how to make it with a Yunnanese friend from Xincun, who spent two weeks teaching us. Then we started to sell *youtiao* from a small cart. While selling it, we had to keep an eye out for the police. Whenever they came, we had to run. In the third month, a policeman came. We quickly took our money and ran. But when we returned to look for our cart, it was already gone.

"Two weeks later, I met a lady typist who worked at Xianluo [Huaqiao] Ribao [a Chinese newspaper company in Bangkok]. Thanks to my earlier Chinese education, she found me work there as a data caretaker. I got eighteen hundred baht a month, pretty good pay. I then rented a small studio of my own. The rent was six hundred baht a month. Every day I spent two baht to get to work by bus and another two baht to get home. The work started at nine o'clock in the morning and ended at three in the afternoon. I also bought myself a few shirts and two pairs of trousers. Before going to work I put some pomade on my hair. I had become a white-collar employee. Every weekend, I still met Ahao and Acao. I had better pay now, although not as good as Ahao's. So, I fought to pay for food and drinks each time. In the past, they had always paid for me.

"One day, when we were drinking beer together, Ahao suddenly said he was going back to Fujian because he missed his family a lot. I thought Ahao might have been feeling low or drunk and didn't take much notice of what he said. But two days later, he went to the police station to report himself as an illegal alien. His visa had already expired. We dared not visit him because of our illegal status. Later on he was expelled. Since then I have lost contact with him.

---

30. *Youtiao*, a fritter of twisted dough, is a Chinese specialty for breakfast. It is also common in Thai cities because of the influences of ethnic Chinese.

"I worked at the newspaper company for more than a year and saved a few dozen thousand baht. I didn't want to keep on working at the company. I wanted to go to Taiwan. Through a friend's connections, I spent twenty-five thousand baht on buying a Thai passport. It was a real passport. I used someone's name and birth information, but the photo on the passport was mine. When going through customs, I was scared. I spoke Thai with an accent. Whatever questions the officer asked me, I kept on answering 'khap, khap, khap.'"[31]

I was very much taken by Guoguang's story, especially by the camaraderie he shared with his friends. It displays the human kindness, joy, and courage generated and supported by difficult living conditions. The story underlines the youthful propensity for pursuit of ambition in the outside world that drove Guoguang, Changshou, Qiwu, Ahao, and Acao to meet and care for each other. The part about Guoguang and Ahao is particularly poignant, indicating an intimate connection. In contrast to bustling Bangkok, the crude lodge they stayed in provided warmth and protection.

Since I started my research in 1994 among Yunnanese migrants in northern Thailand, I have met many young Yunnanese people from Burma. They had risked their lives on perilous journeys and entered the country illegally. After arriving in Thailand, most of them stayed a short period in Yunnanese villages along the border that functioned as their transfer stops for later journeys to Chiang Mai or Bangkok. While in these villages, most men worked as farmworkers and women as domestic servants. Their goals and experiences were similar to Guoguang's. Thailand was a dream and a future for them. However, some were not so lucky and failed to reach their destinations or even died on the way.[32] For those who had entered the country, more challenges awaited them.

The movement of migrant Yunnanese was greatly facilitated by their intragroup nexuses, as Guoguang's (and also Zhang Dage's) story has shown. Many informants often stress that Yunnanese are close-knit and commonly trust only people who are known to them. These are usually *laoxiang*—countrymen, preferably from their home village. I was told this

---

31. *Khap* is an affirmation used by men in Thai.
32. The death of fifty-four Burmese illegal migrants on April 9, 2008, due to suffocation in the back of a freezer truck during transportation to Ranong, a border town in southern Thailand, highlights the tragedy of and risks undertaken by illegal migrants from Burma.

tendency is geographic in origin, as the mountainous topography naturally isolates places in Yunnan from each other. The KMT Third Army was traditionally known for its regional solidarity and was referred to as "younger dependent troops" (*zidibing*), placing emphasis on their kinship and territorial loyalties, since most of them came from Zhenkang, Gengma, and Kokang. External instability and involvement in transnational trade, paradoxically, have made migrant Yunnanese a mobile people, leading them far from home. I have often observed that when two Yunnanese meet for the first time and find they have roots in the same region, they form an immediate bond and compare notes as to whom they know in common. They quickly form networks of *guanxi* (connections). For the Yunnanese in a strange land, these regional connections make up an invaluable web that draws them together in mutual support.[33]

Guoguang's account highlights this feature of kinship and territorial bonds. He was helped in every place by people related to his father or the family in one way or another. These connections are based on references rather than face-to-face familiarity. In other words, one need only refer to a mutual link when seeking help from someone one has never met before. However, one should keep in mind the indebtedness to others and find suitable occasions to pay it back. Guoguang's insistence on paying for food and drinks for Ahao and Acao when they went out illustrates his desire to express his gratitude and return the favor he owed. (The story of Zhang Dage's uncle bringing rice and ham to the landlady also illustrates this reciprocal relationship.)

Although Yunnanese tend to emphasize intragroup bonds, establishing connections with strangers is not impossible. I have observed many cases when they develop networks of connection with non-Yunnanese in trade and even for personal friendship, though to a lesser extent than with Yunnanese fellows. In terms of business transactions, one needs to be flexible, and one is often dependent on institutional organizations that facilitate connections with outsiders. (This type of interaction is especially seen in the jade trade, which I will explore in chapter 7.) With regard to personal friendship, Zhang Dage made friends with Burman neighbors in his

---

33. The role of kinship and regional networks in migration is not exclusive among Yunnanese or Chinese communities. Scholars of migration studies have explored this subject in a wide range of migrant societies (e.g., Akanle 2013; Jarnigan 2008; Kyle 2003; Wilson 2009).

childhood. Ae Maew's best friend during her high school years was a Shan girl. In this chapter, Guoguang treasured his companionship with Ahao. Such friendship also attests to individual openness that is not entirely constrained by intragroup bonding.

After Guoguang left Thailand, he never again saw these friends mentioned in the story. He said:

"They had no fixed residence. I heard Acao died because of some kind of lung disease. It was from his work that he had inhaled too much poisonous stuff. I heard Changshou returned to Burma later and Qiwu was in Chiang Mai. But I don't know exactly where they are now. I miss Ahao most. I do not have a photo of him. I don't even know his full name. At that time I just called him 'Ahao, Ahao.'"

I could hear the regret in Guoguang's voice. The friendship was of short duration yet deep. Perhaps he blamed himself for not having tried to locate Ahao's contact information in Fujian. He could have gone back to the uncle's factory and asked for the information. What prevented him from doing so? Perhaps it was his continuous pursuit of his goal of going to Taiwan, and perhaps this makes him feel sad now whenever he thinks of the past. Although Guoguang had a wealth of new experiences in Taiwan later, the memory of those youthful days in Thailand has never faded from his mind.

The Father: 1992 Onward

In 1992, Mr. Li led the whole family (except Guoguang) to Mong Hsu to participate in ruby mining. It was a booming enterprise that had started only two years earlier when rubies were discovered there. He said:

"At that time, Mong Hsu was very insecure. There were many different militia groups, including the Wa, the Shan, the Taungthu [Dongsu/Pa-O], and the Karen. More than one hundred thousand people flocked to the place to seek their fortune. The government was not able to control the region. These militias often oppressed the civilians. I couldn't bear the situation and organized a Kokang troop in 1993 to maintain order. In less than a year, more than thirteen hundred soldiers joined. I took charge of excavation in Mong Hsu. My wife took my eldest daughter to Tachileik to sell excavated rubies from our mines. On each occasion, they stayed in a hotel, and Thai dealers would come to buy the gems. I left Mong Hsu with my family in 1996. During the years of excavation, we made a fortune of over two hundred million kyat. But my youngest son had a gun accident later, and his medication cost the better part of the fortune."

"How did the accident happen?" I asked.

"My son was a bodyguard for a militia leader. He carried his gun while sleeping. The gun accidentally dropped to the ground and went off. The bullet hit his belly and went through his lungs. I sent him to the best hospital in Thailand. I told the doctor to cure him, no matter how much it cost. He has more or less recovered now. My life has been like the rains. Sometimes the drops are big, and sometimes small. But I have never wasted my name."

Just as he skipped over details of his life in Loilin, Mr. Li offered a narration about ruby excavation in Mong Hsu that is sketchy. In contrast to Guoguang's narration, which stressed horizontal friendship, Mr. Li's emphasis on his leadership and accomplishments portrays a world of hierarchy, influenced by relations of power and domination. This contrast illuminates their different positions, personalities, and perspectives on the world. Mr. Li consistently portrayed himself as a leader, not only a leader of his troops but also a leader of his family and his people. I understand that this is what he wanted me to write and how he wanted to be remembered. He may have considered accounts of friends, family, or everyday life to be too soft and trivial. Nevertheless, the extent of his leadership may have been exaggerated. While in Changqingshan, his KKY troop was only a small unit among many other KKY forces. After disbandment in 1973, he handed over most arms to the government, while larger KKY groups, such as the one led by Luo Xinghan, resisted the order and went underground. Moreover, the organization and function of his Kokang troop in Mong Hsu are questionable. On one occasion, he acknowledged that the troop was a unit of ethnic Kokang forces under the leadership of Peng Jiasheng. In other words, it was not his troop. Because he was reluctant to reveal further details, I am unclear about the degree of order maintained by this troop. It may have been one of the forces competing for control of informal taxation in Mong Hsu. Despite lack of details, his history and narration illuminate how Shan State was divided into different groups, as well as the common motive among numerous militia leaders—the pursuit of power and leadership.

I was intrigued that he abruptly ended his story with his youngest son's accident. In contrast to his other heroic accounts, this brief revelation reveals his soft side as a caring father. A melancholic expression overtook him as he told me about it, and I felt awkward asking further questions. Yet I wondered why he did not keep this son working for him, and why this son wanted to join an ethnic militia group while his eldest brother had chosen another direction. Only later when talking to Guoguang about his youngest brother's accident did I learn a missing part to the story. Guoguang said the militia leader was a friend of his father, and it was his father's suggestion that his youngest son work for this leader as a bodyguard. Guoguang did not reveal more information about the connection between his father and this militia leader, but it is clear that Mr. Li regretted his earlier suggestion. He may have felt responsible for the accident. He had the power to control many things, but not fate, as many Yunnanese informants used to say.

Regarding the ruby excavation craze in Mong Hsu, it lasted only for a short period. By the end of the 1990s, it had started to decline. Although the government legalized gem trading and excavation in 1992, it was not able to control the security in all mining areas. Several informants said that between Taunggyi and Mong Hsu there were many robbers who targeted ruby traders and ambushed their cars. The situation around the mines in Mong Hsu was even worse. Different ethnic militias competed to profit from this lucrative enterprise. They demanded taxes from mining companies, traders, and local shops. Conflicts among these ethnic groups occurred frequently, causing great destruction to shops and houses as well as a heavy toll in personal injuries. Despite the great dangers, streams of people flocked to Mong Hsu in search of fortune, as opportunities for making a living in Burma are very limited. Even young children joined this risky trade. (Ae Maew also went there for a short period.)

After his venture in the ruby trade Mr. Li moved his family to Taunggyi. He has since been involved in a series of activities through various collaborations. In 2005, the family started mining metals in Loikaw, Kalaw, and Dawei (Tavoy), an enterprise in collaboration with ethnic militias and Chinese investors. Mr. Li has a gem company license. The Chinese investors provided capital, and ethnic militias supplied local connections. While Guoguang remains in Taunggyi, Mr. Li's three other sons are in charge of mining in three different places. Guoguang had helped with the application to obtain mining concessions from the government. This had required the payment of much money to various officials. "I carried bags of money with me for this application," he said. After completion of the first term of three years, they will have to rebid for the concessions if they want to continue mining.

The Son: 1987 Onward

Guoguang arrived in Taiwan in 1987 to start another chapter in his life. He said:

"When the airplane landed, it was another world. I was anxious again when going through customs. Although I have two uncles in Taiwan, I didn't go to stay with them. I wanted to be on my own. I had friends who had been to Taiwan, and they told me to take the airport bus to Wugu [an industrial area in New Taipei City]. After getting off the bus, I started to look for accommodations. I checked several hotels and finally chose a cheap one, 150 NT a night. It was still OK in comparison with several places I had stayed in Bangkok. There was a cafeteria next to the hotel. One meal cost twenty-five to twenty-seven NT. The next day, I started to look for work in the nearby area. I checked many factories that posted notices for workers. Finally, one factory was willing to take me. When the job interviewer asked me where I came from I said Thailand because I used a Thai passport. The pay was fifty NT an hour, and the factory provided board and lodging. It was an electroplating factory, very dirty and polluted. No Taiwanese wanted to do such work. All the workers there were illegal laborers from Thailand, totaling fifty-three people. At that time Taiwan had not legalized the entry of foreign laborers. I started to work in that factory on the fourth day after my arrival in Taiwan.

"I spoke both Chinese and Thai. So, one month later, the boss promoted me to the position of foreman, with one thousand NT extra pay each month. Six months later, my pay was upgraded to fifteen thousand NT a month. I supervised fifty-two Thai workers. The factory was very dirty, replete with ammonia, sulfuric acid, nitric acid, hydrochloric acid, and so on. We had to wear long rubber boots. The environment was really filthy, with an awful smell. After I had worked for three years in that factory, the Taiwanese government began tightening the search for illegal foreign laborers and encouraged voluntary reporting for expulsion that would exempt the illegal worker from a penalty. I then turned myself in at the police station and prepared to leave Taiwan. I had to pay for the procedure fees and air ticket that cost twenty-five thousand NT. On my arrival at the Bangkok airport, the customs officer didn't ask any questions. He looked at my passport and knew I was an expelled Thai worker from Taiwan. I went back to Burma through Mae Sai. It had been six years since I left home."

Actually, Guoguang did not go home alone but with his Taiwanese wife, Chunmei, who had worked at the same factory as an accountant. Before leaving Taiwan, they had registered for marriage. However, in order to stay legally in Taiwan as a spouse, Guoguang needed to go back to Burma to apply for the necessary documents. It took nearly a year to obtain these documents and another half a year to apply to Taiwan as a returned overseas Chinese through a marriage union. This status granted him Taiwanese citizenship after he had stayed for a year in the country. However, it also entailed an obligation of military service, so Guoguang served for two years. Afterward, he went through a few jobs, all in the field of producing computer components. He started as a low-level employee. With his accumulated experience and hard work, he was finally promoted to the position of manager in a company. He said:

"I was paid over sixty thousand NT a month. The company gave me a car. But after some years, I felt life had become more and more mechanical. The company often required employees to work overtime. To meet delivery deadlines, managers often had to help on the production lines. We worked overtime the whole night, went home to sleep for a few hours, and then returned to the company and continued to work. My wife was working too. She got forty thousand NT a month. We had everything—two condominiums and two cars—but not enough time to spend with our children. After paying mortgages for the condominiums and cars, children's educational fees, and our living expenses, we were not able to save much money. Also, I only had a high school education. Although I had been promoted to be a manager, I saw that I would someday be replaced by more qualified young people. The pressure of life in Taiwan was too great. We finally decided to come back to Burma. It had been nearly twenty years between the first time I went to Thailand [in 1985] and my family's return to Burma [in 2004]. It is hard to imagine that I, born in a mountain village in Burma, could have become a manager in a Taiwanese company."

Guoguang and his family seemed happy with their present life. Although the total income from the bookshop, his brokerage, and his wife's teaching was much lower than their income in Taiwan, they could afford to hire two workers to help in the shop and with the housework. They felt life was easier in Burma and their children were happier without the intense educational pressures. Their return, however, is an unusual move. It is far more common for Yunnanese from Burma to remain in Taiwan (like Zhang Dage and Ae Maew) once they find work. Guoguang's children are still young, one studying in high school and the other in primary school. What would they do in their lives? Would they stay in Burma or follow in their father's footsteps to Taiwan or other countries? It would be interesting to track them in the future.

A review of Mr. Li's and Guoguang's career evolution shows their courage in pursuit of their respective ambitions by engaging in a series of journeys. Despite their taking different paths in life, their narratives refer to two significant shared social values that have exerted much influence on the cultivation of Yunnanese/Kokang male subjectivity—exploring the world and enhancing social connections. Drawing on his family background, Mr. Li expanded alliances with a range of military groups—the KMT Third Army, the Burmese army, and other ethnic militias. His appropriation of connections was motivated by a search for power and leadership, and this resulted in his moving from his home place to many other places and even to Thailand. Though rejecting a military path, Guoguang has physically traveled farther than his father. Along the course of his ambitious pursuit, he has largely cultivated his own networks of connections and has crossed several national borders as well as the borders of social status and class—from a migrant worker first in Thailand and then Taiwan, to a company manager with Taiwanese citizenship. Interestingly, he decided to return to Burma after having established his own family and a good life in Taiwan. Both Guoguang's return and his father's persistent devotion to the affairs of Kokang associations underscore their rooted identification in Shan State, Burma.

Despite their somewhat strained relationship, the two social values analyzed above may constitute a common base of understanding between Mr. Li and Guoguang. Mr. Li told me in our last meeting: "On discovering Guoguang's departure, I immediately had my men trace his whereabouts. But I let him go and explore the outside world [*rang ta daowaimian chuang yi chuang*]." Maybe Mr. Li identified with Guoguang's will to establish his independence. Maybe this was what he himself had tried to demonstrate in his military activities from a very young age. After all, Yunnanese and Kokang men have been very mobile in history owing to a range of political or economic causes. The word *chuang* (to explore the world) is often used by male informants to refer to their passion for movement and overcoming challenges and frictions. Their engagement in long-distance traveling is often looked upon as heroic by their fellow men. Moreover, their social memory of ancestral migrations encourages them to continue in this trend of cross-border movement in the face of limited opportunities in Burma and its insecure and constraining environment. In the following chapters I will explore these ideas further.

4

Islamic Transnationalism

Yunnanese Muslims

> While in Burma, I was made to feel that I carried two sins. One was being Chinese, the other being Muslim.
> —Deputy Imam Bao in Taiwan, August 28, 2009

> Yunnanese Muslims have no homes. Burma is not our home. We are only guests here, even though we have obtained *hmatpontin*.
> —Grandma Ma in Mandalay, January 22, 2005

If the Yunnanese Han feel marginal in Burma, the Yunnanese Muslims sense their peripheral position even more. While the mainstream Burman-Buddhist majority constitutes Burma's core in terms of ethnicity and political power, the Muslims in the country have experienced acute social and religious discrimination imposed by the government, including random arrest, destruction of mosques, confiscation of property, closing of religious schools, and denial of citizenship (Aung Su Shin 2003; Berlie 2008; Priestley 2006; Selth 2003; Tagliacozzo 2014). In addition, since June 2012, ethno-religious violence organized by Buddhist fundamentalists against Muslim communities in Arakan State, Meikhtila, Lewei, Pegu, Yangon, and Lashio have caused grave damage to lives and properties. Among the four main Muslim groups in Burma—Muslims of South Asian origin (often referred to as Indian Muslims or Kala), Rohingyas, Burmese Muslims, and Chinese Muslims—the Rohingyas are especially marginalized and denied citizenship (Berlie 2008, 7; Leider 2012; Selth 2003; Yegar

1982).[1] There is no reliable record of the total Muslim population in Burma, but estimates range from two to eight million (Selth 2003). The Yunnanese Muslims account for only a very small portion of these—around twenty thousand, based on data provided by several Yunnanese Muslim mosques. The group is commonly known as Panthay, but in Chinese they refer to themselves as Chinese Muslims or Yunnanese Muslims or Hui. The use of multiple terms suggests the group's liminality.

The Yunnanese Muslims are as mobile as the Han, and can be found in many towns and cities in Burma, mostly concentrated in upper Burma. They also have fellow communities in Thailand, Taiwan, Japan, Singapore, and the Middle East, and a small number have even migrated from Burma to Western countries. These transnational nexuses have provided multiple functions, including economic support, information about migration, religious communication, and marriage partners. While carrying on their predecessors' peripatetic lifestyle in upper mainland Southeast Asia, their mobility also corresponds to the Islamic traveling tradition for the sake of trade, proselytization, Hajj, or war (cooke and Lawrence 2005; Cornell 2005; Ho 2006; Tagliacozzo 2013). In this chapter, based on several narrators' accounts of their personal experiences and social memory, I look into the migration history of contemporary Yunnanese Muslims of Burma and their Islamic transnationalism. The key question addressed is: What are the elements that connect diasporic Yunnanese Muslims across a wide range of places and distinguish them from Yunnanese Han and other Muslim groups? The findings point to their anchorage in both Islam and Chinese identity, which helps strengthen their communal and transnational Hui networks and also underscores their ethnic boundary vis-à-vis other Muslim groups. The narrators in the following sections are located in both Burma and Taiwan.

Ma Yeye in Kengtung

I took my first field trip to Kengtung, a scenic historic town, by air in December 2008. The small domestic airliner took off from the Yangon

---

1. Popular speculation points to conservative power within the Burmese military as the instigator behind the repeated riots in its effort to set back the Thein Sein government's democratic reforms (*Irrawaddy* 2013).

airport, with multiple stops in Naypyidaw, Mandalay, Heho, Tachileik, and finally Kengtung. As the plane approached eastern Shan State, I looked through the window and saw chains of high mountains below. I pondered that it must have been a challenge to navigate this rugged terrain by means of mule caravans, a traditional mode of transportation for centuries until vehicles gradually replaced them in the 1980s (chapter 5). Air travel has compressed traveling time and spared travelers all the hardship of land travel. Nevertheless, several passengers were vomiting by the time our flight finally landed in Kengtung.

Located in a far eastern corner of Shan State, Kengtung was for centuries a principality that enjoyed its political autonomy while maintaining a tributary relationship with China and Burma. It kept a close relationship through exchange of gifts and royal marriages with neighboring Tai principalities and kingdoms, reaching as far as Sipsong Panna (in southern Yunnan), Lan Na (in northern Thailand), and Lan Zhang (in Laos) (Hsieh 1995). The hereditary ruler was addressed as *saohpa*, meaning Lord of the Heaven, by his people, who were primarily Tai Khoen (also written as Khün) and Tai Lue.[2] The ruling tradition of chieftainship through a hereditary system was recognized by British rule and was continued by the parliamentary government after Burma's independence, until 1959 when the caretaker government led by Ne Win removed it.

Because of its geographical location, Kengtung has been an important trading center connecting with Yunnan to the north, Laos to the east, and Thailand to the south. Historically, the long-distance Yunnanese caravans moved back and forth within these trading networks, and the Yunnanese Muslims were a distinctive group of caravaneers in this region. However, because historical records are scarce, it is difficult to determine exactly when the Yunnanese Muslims began to take up economic activity here. Possibly, when the Mongols brought a large number of soldiers and craftsmen from Central Asia to settle in Yunnan, some of them started to explore these trade route circuits. Nevertheless, major settlement of Yunnanese Muslims in Burma did not take place until the failure of the Muslim Rebellion (1856–1873 CE) (Forbes 1986, 1987).[3]

---

2. For the history of Kengtung and Shan State see Conway (2006); Li (2003); Sai Aung Tun (2009); Sao Saimong Mangrai (1965); Scott (1901).

3. In 1868 Yunnanese Muslims constructed their first mosque in Burma on a piece of land bestowed by King Mindon in Mandalay, the capital of the kingdom. Many Yunnanese Muslims,

Figure 4–1. Panthay mosque in Mandalay

The Yunnanese Muslims are also called Yunnanese Hui or Huihui in China, and they belong to the Hanafi school of Sunni Islam (Suchart 2010, 111–14). The term *Hui* or *Huihui* became a popular name that referred to all Muslims since the Yuan period, and Islam was termed *Hui jiao* (religion of the Hui). But in 1954, the People's Republic of China created the Hui nationality (*huizu*) and limited its reference to "Sinicized" Muslims. The Hui are located in different parts of the country, and the Yunnanese Muslims are a part of that group. Over centuries, they have absorbed much of the dominant Han Chinese tradition in their everyday life as displayed in their language, dress, food, naming, and housing, among other things, while upholding their Islamic heritage. Apart from the Hui, there are Muslim groups whose members speak Turkic-Altaic and Indo-European Muslim languages in China—the Uighur, Kazakh, Dongxiang, Kirghiz, Salar, Tajik, Uzbek, Baoan, and Tatar (Gladney 1996, xv, 17–20; 2004, 101).

---

primarily traders, settled around the mosque (Figure 4–1) and formed a Panthay compound. The compound still exists, located on Eightieth Street, between Thirty-Fifth and Thirty-Sixth Streets; see Maung Maung Lay (1999, 97–100).

In 2008, there were about seventy households of Yunnanese Muslims (and more than seven hundred households of Yunnanese Han) in Kengtung.[4] Most of these Yunnanese Hui parents or grandparents migrated from Yunnan prior to 1949; some are descendants of earlier migrants who came to Burma more than one hundred years ago. Ma Yeye was a key person I intended to interview here.[5] During my former field trips in Mandalay, I had heard from other Yunnanese Muslims about the flight of Ma Yeye's ancestors to Burma after the Muslim Rebellion and their heroic resettlement afterward. I hoped to record Ma Yeye's narration about the history of his family line.

A Yunnanese Muslim friend in Mandalay had helped to arrange my visit. On the third day after my arrival in Kengtung, I walked from my guesthouse to Ma Yeye's house. On the way I passed four Shan temples, the tomb of the last Kengtung prince, Sao Sai Long, and then the Paleng Gate leading to the Chinese mosque a few hundred meters away. The military government has tried to repress the cultures of minority groups by destroying historical sites such as these, as well as by enforcing Burman education and encouraging official immigration of the Burman population to areas in which minority groups are concentrated. Nevertheless, these surviving structures and other cultural forms expressed through Shan language and religious beliefs still inscribe Kengtung's history into the everyday lives of the local inhabitants.

I found Ma Yeye's spacious wooden house situated in an alley near the mosque (Figure 4–2). Several framed posters of Quranic citations hung on the living room walls, along with a photo of the Kaaba centered and facing the garden.[6] "As-salaam alaikum" (peace be upon you), Ma Yeye greeted me in the traditional Islamic way. Though not a Muslim, I replied: "Wa alaikum assalaam" (may peace be upon you). After we sat down, a maid brought a cup of hot tea and a plate of dry dates. Ma Yeye said these dates were brought back by his eldest son from Saudi Arabia last Ramadan (about four months earlier).

---

4. There are about two hundred Indian Muslim families in Kengtung.

5. *Yeye* means grandpa in Chinese. "Ma" is the most popular surname among the Yunnanese Muslims.

6. Kaaba is the holiest place in Islam, a black cube structure inside the al-Masjid al-Haram Mosque in the center of Mecca.

Figure 4–2. Panthay mosque in Kengtung

"How many children do you have?" I asked.

"Six—two sons and four daughters. They are all married. My eldest son has been in Saudi Arabia since 1980. He is a construction contractor. He graduated from Yangon University, majoring in business. His wife is from Maymyo [Pyin U Lwin] and is also a Yunnanese Hui. They come back every year during the month of Ramadan. My second son and his family live in Yangon. I have a nephew who is a doctor in New York, another nephew, also a doctor, in Australia, two nieces in Singapore, and several relatives in Taiwan. They all come back from time to time."

Ma Yeye's transnational connections through family members' and relatives' emigrations were impressive. I had heard a number of similar cases. He went on to tell me the history of his origin. Ma Yeye was born in 1926 in Panglong, located below Kokang in the northern Wa region. Although no Yunnanese Muslims live there anymore, it was a significant place in the migration history of the Yunnanese Hui community in Burma. A Yunnanese Muslim scholar I interviewed a year earlier in Mandalay estimated that about 30 percent of Yunnanese Muslims in Burma today descend from Panglong.[7] Ma Yeye is the fourth generation, and after him there are three younger generations—seven generations in Burma. His great-grandfather, originally from Tengchong in Yunnan, led a group of fellow Muslims to Burma in the wake of the collapse of the Hui uprising. In 1875, they arrived in Panglong and founded their settlement. Ma Yeye related this migration history:

"Do you know about Du Wenxiu, the leader of the Hui Rebellion in Yunnan?[8] My great-grandfather was an officer under Du Wenxiu. His name was Ma Linyu.[9] He brought more than one hundred people with him from Tengchong, but only eighty-two survived to reach Panglong.[10] My great-grandfather requested the place, originally named Nanpha, for resettlement from a local Wa chief. The request was granted. He and his Hui fellows opened up the land and renamed it Panlong, meaning

---

7. However, Panglong Hui tend to give a higher estimate—50 percent.

8. Du established the Dali Sultanate in 1856 to fight against the Qing government. By foregrounding the multiethnic frictions plaguing Yunnanese in the nineteenth century, Atwill argues against the simplified explanation in former studies that attributed the Muslim Rebellion to mere Han-Hui conflict. He looks into the impact of massive waves of Han immigration to Yunnan and the bias and aggression of the imperial government and the new Han settlers toward the non-Han groups for control of socioeconomic resources (Atwill 2006). For a history of the Muslim Rebellion see also Huang (1976) and Yang et al. (1994).

9. A booklet about Panglong history (*Panglong booklet*), written by a descendant of Yunnanese Muslims from Panglong, records the name as Ma Lingji (Ming 1998). Forbes recorded it as Ma Yin-ang in his book (Forbes and Henley 1997, 120). But in *Yunnan huizushi* (History of the Yunnanese Muslims), which was published in Kunming, it is also recorded as Ma Linyu (Yang et al. 1994, 201).

10. The *Panglong booklet* recorded the arrival of thirty-six people in Panglong (Ming 1998, 4).

'moving to live together.'[11] Among the eighty-two people, there were three women. My great-grandfather married one of them. That was my great-grandmother; she later gave birth to two sons. One of them was my grandfather, Ma Meiting. Many other Hui men married women from Kokang or neighboring Wa and Shan villages. Within two years, more and more fellow Hui heard about the resettlement of my great-grandfather's group in Panglong and came to join them. The total number soon expanded to several hundred.

"We are Chinese Muslims [*zhongguo huijiao*],[12] Muslims of Han nationality [*hanzu huijiao*]. Possibly with a bit of Arabian blood, but we are different from those Muslims in Xingjiang, the Uighur. We are Han Muslims. During the *hongqi baiqi* [red flags versus white flags] incident,[13] 90 percent of the Yunnanese Hui were slaughtered. The original size of the Hui Muslim community was hundreds of thousands; after the massacre only a few thousand were left.

"Panglong belonged to the Wa territory. The Hui Muslims got along with the Wa very well. My grandfather married two women. My grandmother was the first wife. The minor wife was a daughter of a local Wa chief. After the marriage, my grandfather became a [Wa] prince."

"Was there also fighting with the Wa?" I asked.

"Well, the fighting, it was like this: We Chinese Muslims were culturally superior. We were talented at everything, especially business. But this incited jealousy from indigenous people and led to friction. Fighting occurred several times. Old people said a big one took place in 1926, the year I was born. The Wa chief wanted to chase us out of Panglong. But having established our households there, how could we leave? Consequently, we fought with them. Although the Wa outnumbered us, they were not as smart as we were. We had a trader, Wang Xuekai, who often traveled to Kengtung. He purchased modern weapons there—a kind of five-bullet

---

11. "Panlong" was later changed to "Panglong" and then "Pannong," but romanized, the place is mostly known as Panglong.

12. Grammatically it should be *zhongguo huijiaotu* (Chinese Muslims), but Yunnanese Muslims tend to simplify the term to *zhongguo huijiao* (Chinese Islam).

13. The Yunnanese Hui in Burma commonly use the term *hongqi baiqi* (red flag versus white flag) to refer to the Muslim uprising. The term was derived from the colors of the military flags used by the Mandurian troops (red) and Du Wenxiu's troops (white) (Jing 1991, 155; Yang et al. 1994, 129).

gun [*wuziqiang*]—and brought them back. You could insert five bullets into this kind of gun at one time. The fighting lasted for half a year.[14] We won in the end. The Wa had to apologize to us. These indigenous people were backward."

"What happened afterward?" I asked.

"After that, we had peace with the Wa. That was prior to the Second World War. But during the war, the situation changed. The Japanese invaded the region. They arrived in Kunlong, less than a day on foot from Panglong. The Chinese Nationalist government sent a delegate, surnamed Su, to organize a self-defense guard in Panglong. The guard leader was my fourth junior uncle, Ma Guanggui. My father was Ma Guanghua. The Japanese came and burned down our village. There were more than two hundred Hui households at that time. The guard was not able to beat them because the Japanese were regular forces. Panglong people were thus compelled to flee. Many escaped to Yunnan.

"It was 1942; I was sixteen years old. Our family fled to Kokang, then moved northward to Zhenkang and then arrived in Gengma. My parents sent me to Kunming to study. Some family members went to Baoshan, some to Dali and Shidian. One year after the Japanese surrendered, I set off on my way back to Burma. From Kunming I passed Baoshan, Mangshi, and then Wanding. I crossed the border and arrived in Kyugok and then made my way southward to Lashio and then eastward to Tangyan. My maternal grandmother was in Tangyan. Some family members also arrived in Tangyan, and we were reunited. I was married there in January 1952. Late that year my wife and I moved to Kengtung."

"Why didn't you go back to Panglong?" I asked.

"It had been raided by Li Wenhuan soon after the Second World War. You know of Li Wenhuan? He became the leader of the [KMT] Third Army later on; he was originally a bandit. After the war, many fellow Muslims had returned from Yunnan to Panglong, but before long they were dispersed to different places by the raid.[15] I was still in Kunming at that time.

---

14. According to the *Panglong booklet*, the war started on November 25, 1926, and ended in late March 1927, lasting about four months (Ming 1998, 23–41).

15. According to Mu Dadie (the following narrator), the Panglong Hui's flight after the Second World War was due to a series of inter-ethnic conflicts of which Li Wenhuan's raid was a final calamity.

Since then, Panglong people have scattered to Lashio, Tangyan, Taunggyi, and Kengtung. No more Yunnanese Hui live in Panglong today."

"What did you do while you were in Tangyan and Kengtung?" I asked.

"I transported goods back and forth between Tangyan and Mandalay. Meanwhile the family also made soy sauce to sell. After moving to Kengtung, I still worked transporting goods until 1963 or '64 when Ne Win confiscated all shops [*shoupuzi*]. Consequently, there were no goods for transport. We lived solely on soy sauce making. My niece is still running the business."

"I see. Business in food seems to be popular among Yunnanese," I said.

"Yes. We were refugees; most countrymen didn't have much capital for investment. The food business didn't require much capital. Many Yunnanese made noodles. Kala used to call us *Kauk-swei wala*."

"What does that mean?"

"Noodle men.[16] In return, we call the Kala *Kali wala*, meaning grooms."

"How about the term 'Panthay'? Do you call yourselves Panthay?" I asked.

"We are Chinese Muslims from Yunnan. 'Panthay' is the term used by the Burmese. We often call ourselves *musilin* [Muslim] or *huijiao* [believers of Islam]."

"What does 'Panthay' mean?"

"Don't know. It must have been a derogatory term."

"But young people [Yunnanese Muslims] have adopted it when speaking Burmese?"

"Yes."

"Do you intermarry with Han people?"

"No, no intermarriages."

"Why not?"

"Our beliefs are not the same. It is no good to have two religions in one family."

"How about with Kala?"

"No, no intermarriages with Kala either."

"Why not?"

"Our lifestyles [*shenghuo xiguan*] are different."

"No intermarriages at all?"

---

16. *Kauk-swei* is noodle in Burmese, and *wala* is people (mostly referring to laborers) in Hindi.

"Very few, very few cases. Also very few with the Han."

"Do you have social or business interactions with Han or Kala?"

"Yes, some people have more; others have less. It varies from person to person. We are Chinese Muslims. We observe Chinese culture [*zhonghua wenhua*] centered on Confucianism, such as filial piety, propriety, diligence, and thrift. Most Hui parents register their children at both Burmese and Chinese schools. In addition, they send them to learn Arabic at mosques or hire private tutors to do the teaching at home. Hui children therefore have to work harder than the Han, as they have one more language to learn. In comparison, we Chinese Muslims are more liberal and gentle than the Indian Muslims, who are religiously more conservative and fundamental and secularly more cunning, quarrelsome, and untrustworthy. You have to be careful. You go to a Kala mosque, you may not be able to find your shoes after you have finished your prayer."

I smiled at Ma Yeye's comment about the Indian Muslims. I had repeatedly heard similar remarks from other Hui informants. Finally I asked Ma Yeye if he has been on Hajj pilgrimage. He replied:

"Yes, twice, in 1984 and 1990. My belief has helped me strengthen my faith. Allah is the True Lord [*zhenzhu*]. Everything is predestined by him."

Ma Yeye's narration revealed an important part of Panglong history. Perhaps because of decades of chaotic situations and repeated migrations, only the generation over sixty years old knows the facts about Panglong history. Luckily, apart from oral transmission, a small booklet (*Panglong booklet*) written by a Panglong Hui outlining the history was printed in 1998 for distribution. This booklet records the founding of Panglong in 1875, the ambivalent relationship with the surrounding Wa that was characterized by reciprocity as well as warfare, the invasions by the British and Japanese, and the final flight of the Panglong people after the Second World War. Ma Yeye's narration and the *Panglong booklet* share a similar ethnocentric tone that renders heroic the ancestors' migration and resettlement experiences. Moreover, the booklet gives detailed accounts of several battles against the Wa that emphasize the remarkable prowess of the Panglong Hui.

The history of the Panglong Hui has seldom been explored. Yegar (1966) and Forbes (1986, 1988) are the two main scholars who have studied it. Their research was primarily drawn from colonial sources supplemented by a few interviews. Their works provide information on the layout of Panglong in its early days, its population growth, and the economic dynamism of Yunnanese Muslims.[17] Following the Burmese, they used the term "Panthay" to refer to the Yunnanese Hui, but pointed out that this migrant group neither liked the name nor used it among themselves.[18] The origin of "Panthay" is uncertain. One speculation is that the term is connected to an old Burmese word for Muslim, "Pathi," which was a corruption of "Parsi," meaning Persian. Another speculation suggests that it was derived from a name on stone inscriptions of Bagan—"Pansi." During the thirteenth century, the Mongols made three invasions from Yunnan to the Bagan Kingdom, and among the invading armies, some soldiers were Muslims from Central Asia (Maung Maung Lay 1999, 91–92). The term might have been used to refer to these troops.

With regard to the preferred name "Chinese Muslim," it indicates the Yunnanese Hui's double commitment to being Islamic and Chinese. In practice, they use the term to indicate their emigration origin and to differentiate themselves from other Islamic groups in Burma. Many senior Hui informants lay particular emphasis on their Chinese background by stating that they are Muslims of Han nationality (*hanzu huijiao*) or Muslims of the Han Empire (*hanchao huizi*). While the usage seems to suggest they have mixed up the ethnic classification created by the Chinese Communist government, it actually denotes a particular signification—their acknowledgment of the Hui's acculturation regarding many Han values, everyday practices, and language.[19] Most of the Hui informants I have talked to are aware of the origins of their male progenitors from Central Asia. (Ma Yeye's relation also admitted this historical fact.)

---

17. The number of houses in Panglong in the 1890s was recorded as over 300 (Harvey 1933, 5; Scott 1901, 740) and increased to 740 (with a population of seven thousand) in 1927 (Harvey 1933, 99).

18. Some scholars even use "Panthay Rebellion" to refer to the Muslim revolt in Yunnan (e.g., Atwill 2006), which sounds alienating to the Yunnanese Hui.

19. The absorption of Chinese culture by the Hui has been going on for more than a thousand years in China (Gladney 2004, 101). Distinctive articulation of Islam and Chinese traditions is particularly shown in the writing of the *Han kitab* (the Chinese Islamic canons) undertaken by some Muslim intellectuals during the Ming and Qing periods. These Islamic texts are written in Chinese. Several writers, such as Wang Daiyu and Liu Zhi, drew on neo-Confucian philosophy for explanation of Islam. Their language illustrates a grounding in Confucianism as well as the piety of Islamic religion (Lipman 1997, 72–85). The prefix of "Han" also appears among other minority groups in Yunnan that are considered to be sinicized, such as Han Baiyi, Han Lisu, and Han Jinghpaw.

In line with Ma Yeye, several Hui parents and grandparents also emphasized to me the value of Chinese culture. Despite their strong attachment to this culture, however, the religious difference represents a deep-seated boundary between them and the Han. While referring to the Han as *hanjiao* (believers of Han religion), they call themselves *huijiao*, often accompanied by emphasis on their dietary restrictions, especially pork and alcohol. In everyday life, they do not have much interaction with others, and intermarriages are rare.

Furthermore, Ma Yeye's narration reveals the importance of long-distance trade among the Panglong Hui, especially its critical role in the success of the battles against the Wa in 1926. Throughout history Yunnanese Muslims' economic prominence has been distinctive, although the Yunnanese Hui traders may not have been as numerous as the Han.[20] In addition to long-distance trade, Yunnanese Hui have engaged in transportation, food businesses, the gem trade, and hotels. While acknowledging the economic prominence of the migrant Yunnanese Muslims, Yegar and Forbes were pessimistic about the sustainability of the group's Islamic culture. Yegar claimed that the younger generation was withdrawing from the religion and traditions of their parents and wished to "assimilate with the Burmese Buddhist majority and to blur their peculiarities" (1966, 84). Forbes thought that "the Panthay community of Burma will disappear within one or two generations, either as a result of assimilation, or through migration to join the economically successful and culturally confident Yunnanese communities of northern Thailand" (1986, 392). However, their prediction has not come true. Despite the fact that a large number of

---

20. Based on Western travelogues and colonial surveys (e.g., Archer 1892; Colquhoun 1900; Hanna 1931; Sladen 1870), both Yegar and Forbes describe Hui predominance in the long-distance trade between Yunnan and upper mainland Southeast Asia since the Yuan period (1277–1367). However, this view is challenged by Hill (1998, 50), Sun (2000, 223), and Giersch (2006, 159–86), who refer to the Han Chinese as the primary trading group, grounding their argument on their historical findings from Chinese, Burmese, and Tai sources. My field research among the contemporary Yunnanese migrants in Burma and Thailand is also in line with Hill, Sun, and Giersch. In northern Thailand the Muslim population constitutes less than 10 percent of the Yunnanese migrants (Chang 1999, 113). Informants, both Han and Muslim, stressed the Han as the largest group in Thai-Burmese transborder trade. The finding thus contradicts many earlier Western travelogues and colonial surveys that maintained that the Yunnanese Muslim traders were the major group. My interpretation is that the Muslim traders could have been more noticeable in some of the borderlands, especially during the time when the Muslim revolt took place, as they controlled a major part of the Yunnanese border trade.

Muslim youth have migrated to other countries (especially Taiwan, Japan, Thailand, Singapore, and Malaysia), this outflow appears rather to provide the community with richer resources to found religious activities, as evidenced by initiatives providing free Islamic education in Burma and students sent to the Middle East for religious studies. The following narratives further explore this.

Mu Dadie in Pyin U Lwin

Pyin U Lwin was established as a military post by the colonial British government in 1896 and was named Maymyo after Colonel May. It was also a summer resort for the colonial officers. During this period, the British brought approximately ten thousand Indians and five thousand Gurkhas (from Nepal) there for service.[21] The population of South Asian origin remains large today, around forty to fifty thousand.[22] They are mostly Muslims spread throughout different neighborhoods centered around mosques; there are fifteen mosques in total, including one built by the Yunnanese Muslim community. A good number of colonial buildings still remain throughout the town. This colonial legacy, the cool weather, and attractive coffee and flower plantations have maintained its popularity for tourists. In addition, the town is an important military base, housing two military schools—the Defense Services Academy and the Defense Services Institute of Technology.

The Yunnanese Muslim community in Pyin U Lwin has grown notably since the 1970s (Figures 4–3 and 4–4). I met Mu Dadie by coincidence at the Yunnanese Muslim mosque in late December 2008. Learning of my research, he was happy to share with me the organization of the Hui community and introduced several fellow men to me. He is a successful businessman and also a pious Muslim, devoting much time and money to his community. He told me that his great-great-grandfather escaped

---

21. See Wikipedia "Pyin U Lwin"—http://en.wikipedia.org/wiki/Maymyo.
22. The figures were provided by Mu Dadie in 2008 (see following paragraphs). He said the total population of Pyin U Lwin is about 130,000.

Figure 4–3. Muslim graveyard in Pyin U Lwin

Figure 4–4. A Yunnanese Muslim's tomb in Pyin U Lwin

to Taunggyi after the Muslim revolt. He was born there in 1934, a fifth-generation Yunnanese Hui in Burma. He said that the Chinese mosque in Taunggyi, rebuilt in 1950, has a history of more than one hundred years. The Mus lived there for four or five generations before moving to Panglong during the Second World War because of the Japanese invasion. But before long the Japanese advanced to Panglong, and the family had to flee again. They escaped to Yunnan and stayed there for four years. After the war, the family moved back to Burma and first settled in Lashio. In 1949, they moved from Lashio to Pyin U Lwin—one of only four Yunnanese Muslim families there at the time, according to Mu Dadie—and remained there until 1954. After Pyin U Lwin, the family moved to Tangyan, where the Muslim community was much bigger. Mu Dadie got married there to a Panglong woman. Like Ma Yeye, he was engaged in transportation while living in Tangyan, but after the nationalization of the Burmese economy, he too was compelled to quit the business. In 1964, he and his family moved again to Pyin U Lwin and have stayed there ever since. In the late 1960s, the family took up machine knitting (*zhenzhi*) and is still in the business today. Between the 1970s and 1980s, Mu Dadie purchased twenty-five knitting machines from Taiwan that were smuggled into the country via Thailand, partly by mule caravans from northern Thai-Burmese border points, and partly by boats from Ranong (in southern Thailand) to Yangon. Between 1967 and 1978, he also traded jade stones, which brought him a sizable income.

Since the late 1960s, more and more Yunnanese Muslims have moved to Pyin U Lwin, especially from Tangyan.[23] There are now more than 130 Yunnanese Hui families in Pyin U Lwin (and about 1,200 Yunnanese Han families). Informants said that Pyin U Lwin's cool weather is a major attraction for settlement. Moreover, it is located on the principal road leading to northern Shan State and is only sixty-seven kilometers from Mandalay.

In several conversations in 2008 and 2010, Mu Dadie talked to me at the Yunnanese mosque and his home about the development of the

---

23. Because of increasing instability in the Tangyan area, many Yunnanese (both Hans and Muslims) moved out. An informant said that there were more than 400 Yunnanese Muslim families in Tangyan before 1970, but the number has now dropped to about 160.

Yunnanese Hui community in Pyin U Lwin and its religious life and education. He said:[24]

"Prior to 1972, we didn't have our own place for prayer and had to pray at Kala's mosques. In 1972, there were about forty Hui families.[25] We set up the Association of Mutual Help for Weddings and Funerals [*hunsang huzhuhui*], helping each other in the organization of these events, which took place at private homes. Every Friday some folks came to pray at my maternal uncle's towel factory. In 1975, I purchased my maternal uncle's place—one acre—and donated it for communal use. At that time my business was going quite well. We started to organize a basic Arabic class for our children there. I funded the class for the first ten years. However, we still didn't have our official mosque. Although we and the Indians [Muslims] follow the same religion, our cultures are different. We take on different habits in daily life. We and the Indians don't fit together well [*zongjuede gegeburu*]. It's better that we have our own mosque for prayer following our increased population. In 1986, our community bought another piece of land facing the main road where there was a two-story house. We finally had our own mosque. There were over eighty Chinese Muslim families at that time. Imam Zhang was our first Imam. A few years later we built another two-story building next to the mosque. This new building was used for Arabic class, weddings, and funerals."[26]

"My father-in-law was much concerned about the transmission of Islamic faith to the young generation and initiated the organization of a religious school. In 1990, the community founded Zhen Guang Awen-Xuexiao [The True Light Arabic School] at the two-story building [already used for Arabic class]. In the first year, there were only six or seven students and one teacher surnamed Ming, a graduate of a Muslim religious school in Yunnan. We registered the school as a student dormitory. Every month we have to report to the local government the number of students and pay one hundred kyat for each one. We use the second floor of the building for classes and the first floor for students' accommodations. The school is only

---

24. A space separates our different conversations in the excerpts that follow.
25. Another informant said there were ten Yunnanese Hui households in 1972.
26. A ceremonial hall was built in 1994 on the land that Mu Dadie donated to the Yunnanese Muslims' Association of Mutual Help. Weddings and funerals have been organized there ever since.

for boys, mostly from Tangyan and Lashio. We provide free education, food, and lodging."

"A complete education at the Pyin U Lwin School takes eight years. It was first sponsored by a Muslim businessman from Pyin U Lwin living in Taiwan, surnamed Zhao. Now it is funded by the Mings, who own the MK enterprise in Burma, which deals in the gem trade, cosmetics, textiles, clothing, plastic products, and electronic speakers.[27] The school has thirty-nine students and three full-time and two part-time teachers. The curriculum is composed of [Arabian] language learning and instruction of Islamic doctrines. We use textbooks from Saudi Arabia, Syria, and Egypt in order to prepare our students for further studies in these countries in the future. The classes take place from eight to ten in the morning and two to three in the afternoon. The students also go to Chinese school between six and eight in the morning."

"So far the school has had about thirty graduates in four years; not every year has seen new students or graduates. Around one-fourth of these graduates went abroad for further studies, the first batch in 1999, two to Syria and two to India. Later on we sent students to Saudi Arabia, Egypt, and Turkey. In Saudi Arabia we have a few Yunnanese Muslim folks living there. They pick up our students at the airport and provide other kinds of assistance during their stay. If the students abroad have financial difficulty, we help.

"Several students completed their studies and obtained a bachelor's degree at universities in the Middle East, but some dropped out and became guest workers. Most students who graduated in these countries have been recruited by mosques in Taiwan. So far only two students returned to Burma to teach. One is the current principal of our Zhen Guang School. He studied in Egypt for two or three years, went to Japan for a few years [as a guest worker], and then came back to Burma. The current chair of the Muslim Association in Taiwan, Ma Haolong, also a Chinese Muslim from Burma, once apologized to me for their recruitment of our graduates. I told him it is not a problem because we are still able to find teachers here. But the situation in Taiwan is different; they don't have local people devoted to Islamic studies and willing to serve at mosques."

---

27. Mu Dadie said that "MK" may be an abbreviation of the enterprise founder's name—Ming Shaokun.

According to Mu Dadie and other informants there are two other Islamic schools organized by the Chinese Muslims in Burma—one in Mogok, one in Tangyan. The one in Mogok has the longest history. It was founded before the Second World War. But during the war, the school was compelled to close down and was not reopened until 1954. The one in Tangyan was established in 1967. Its operation was interrupted a few times because of financial difficulty and lack of teachers. Originally it provided eight years of studies, but that has dropped to four. The Pyin U Lwin School is the newest, but it has become the best organized among the three.

Apart from these three Islamic schools organized by the Chinese, there are far more Islamic schools run by the Indian Muslims. Some Yunnanese youth attended these schools, especially the ones in Meiktila, Pyawbwe, and Yangon, and later served at Chinese mosques as imams or instructors. That is why Mu Dadie told Mr. Ma not to worry about recruiting their graduates. Actually, long before the Hui of Pyin U Lwin set up Zhen Guang Arabic School, they had sent students to the Middle East. In 1987 they sent four students to Egypt. Two of them completed their studies at Al-Azhar University, and both are serving as imams at mosques in Taiwan.

The active faith of the Hui community of Pyin U Lwin is demonstrated by their shared support of Islamic education and communal activities. Around the mid-1990s, the Hui in Pyin U Lwin started to plan a new mosque to be built on the location of the old one, but it took a long time to get their application approved by the government. In 2000, they tore down the old house and began the construction. However, policies can change abruptly in Burma, and the government called a halt to the work a year later. Informants said that, typical of discrimination against Muslims, they were not allowed to resume the construction for five or six years. In the interim, they had to use classrooms for communal worship. The new mosque was completed in late 2008.

During my two visits in 2008 and 2010, I observed the mosque packed with people (both young and old) for the noon prayer each Friday, except once when an old Hui passed away in Mandalay early one Friday morning. Upon receiving the information by phone, many Hui in Pyin U Lwin organized car pools and went together to the bereaved family. Informants told me later that it has been a tradition that Hui community members support one another whenever possible. By mutual participation in funerals, weddings, and religious activities, they have cultivated close ties among themselves. Moreover, widespread webs of kith and kin have further cemented their relationships via intra-marriage.

Hui informants in upper Burma and Yangon commonly remarked that the Chinese Muslims in the country are a small minority and that they need to be cohesive. While their religion has played an essential role in fostering this cohesion, the feature of being Chinese is another indivisible element in their community identity, as we can see from the narratives given by Ma Yeye and Mu Dadie. In practice, they alternately use features of "Chinese" and "Islam" to distinguish themselves from other Muslim groups and the Yunnanese Han. Specifically, they underline their Islamic belief when making reference to the Han, and they emphasize their Chinese culture in relation to the Indian and other Muslim groups.[28] While personal friendship across these socio-ethnic boundaries exists case by case, there is little interaction between the Yunnanese Hui and the other groups.

Being a migrant group with a religion that is discriminated against in Burma, the Yunnanese Hui are aware of their doubly marginalized status. Intriguingly, they have drawn on these two characteristics for expansion of their community connections with other Chinese societies and countries in the Middle East. Mu Dadie said that in the past thirty years or so, the Yunnanese Muslim communities have worked hard to build connections with Arab countries in order to open channels of religious studies for their youth. A distinctive example is the effort made by the main owner of the MK enterprise, Ming Shaokun, a successful Panglong Hui businessman who grew up in Tangyan, later moved to Pyin U Lwin, and then migrated to Thailand, where he has achieved economic success. Many of his siblings and relatives still live in Pyin U Lwin, Mandalay, and Yangon, and help to run the MK Corporation. The Mings have maintained good relationships with ambassadors of several countries of the Middle East, in Bangkok and Yangon, as well as with Burmese officials in these two capitals. Ming Shaokun himself was invited once by the royal family of Saudi Arabia to Mecca. Such relationships have facilitated the visa application of many Hui students to these countries.

---

28. In turn, the Han make the same distinction, often accompanied by negative remarks about the Hui as being troublesome and shrewd, which are the exact remarks that the Hui make about the Indians. This phenomenon of Han stereotyping the Hui also exists in China (see, e.g., Gillette 2000; Gladney 1996). I have not yet had an opportunity to learn about the Indian Muslims' perception of the Yunnanese Hui.

Yunnanese Hui in the Middle East and Taiwan

Several Hui religious specialists from Burma who finished their studies in the Middle East have been recruited to work in Taiwan. In order to gain a more comprehensive understanding of the transnational networks operated through the preaching of Islam (*Da'wah*) among the Yunnanese Hui from Burma, I conducted several interviews[29] between 2009 and 2010 in Taiwan with Imam Shan and Deputy Imam Bao at Taichung Mosque (in Taichung), Imam Liu at Lunggang Mosque (in Chungli), and Imam Ma[30] at the Cultural Mosque (in Taipei). Imam Shan and Imam Liu (both from Tangyan) completed their studies at Al-Azhar University in Egypt; Deputy Imam Bao (from Kengtung) graduated from the Islamic University of Medina in Saudi Arabia; and Imam Ma (from Pyin U Lwin) graduated from Ahmad Kaftaru University in Syria. I asked them to make comparisons between their experiences in Burma, the country of their studies abroad, and Taiwan. Their answers repeatedly underscore their core identification constituted by a Chinese background and Islamic faith. While devoting themselves to the propagation of Islam and acknowledging the origin of the religion in the Middle East, they stress their self-distinction—their Asian background and Chinese culture—from the people of the Middle East. Imam Shan's narrative given on August 28, 2009, is illustrative:

"[Imam Liu and I] went to Egypt, to the Al-Azhar University [in 1987] as students.[31] The elder generation [of our community back in Burma] thought that it was the best university for Islamic studies. We only went there for studies, not for migration. The country has its way of living that is different from ours. Although we and the people there share the same religion, we couldn't adapt to their lifestyle. We are Han, following Islam. We have been nourished by both Confucianism and Islam. Nevertheless, these two cultures share similar values. Confucianism emphasizes loyalty [*zhong*], filial piety [*xiao*], benevolence [*ren*], love [*ai*], trust [*xin*], justice [*yi*], peace [*he*], and harmony [*ping*], which are also emphasized in Islam.

---

29. Moreover, I have participated in their Ramadan activities since 2009 and interviewed several other Yunnanese Muslim migrants from Burma and Thailand who have settled in Taiwan.

30. Imam Ma worked in Lunggang Mosque as an instructor of Arabic prior to his promotion to be the imam of the Cultural Mosque (*wenhua qingzhensi*) in Taipei in 2010.

31. Actually they had to study at a high school for two years before entering the university.

Basically if you have learned Confucianism, you have no difficulty accepting Islam. Hence, we are better suited to go to Chinese societies to preach, such as Taiwan, China, Hong Kong, and Singapore. Burma has enough people for this task, but these Chinese-speaking societies are in need of such specialists. We have the obligation to carry out the work. Our students in Burma must learn Chinese, Arabic, and English in preparation for their future preaching abroad."

"Why do they have to learn English?" I asked.

"All international forums on religious studies are conducted in English. You must know the language in order to communicate with other people, exchange ideas, and build up international connections. I have attended such an occasion in Malaysia. That is my certificate." He pointed to a framed document on the wall.

"Is it necessary to go to the Middle East for Islamic studies? Or is it sufficient to do it in Burma?" I asked.

"You must go to the Middle East, to any of the orthodox universities in order to upgrade yourself to an international standard."

"With whom did you associate mostly while studying in Egypt?"

"Primarily with students from China, Thailand, Malaysia, and Indonesia. Egypt has its distinctive culture and tradition to which we cannot really assimilate. It's like countries of Africa; they have their particular cultures. But in order to learn the Arabic language, we also needed to mingle with local people," Imam Shan said.

The other three interviewees made similar remarks highlighting their Chinese and Islamic identification. Another recurrent point in their narratives dwells upon food preferences, which illustrate their difference from Arab Muslims while displaying an affinity with Chinese and other Asian people. On August 8, 2009, Imam Ma related his experience of having local food in Syria on the very first day of his and his friend's arrival:

"It was my first experience abroad. A friend in Japan had contacted a Muslim association to send people to pick us up at the airport. At the Damascus airport we were questioned for a couple of hours by the customs officials because they had never seen a Burmese passport. Luckily those Syrian friends who came to pick us up waited for us. We were very hungry, and they took us to eat at a restaurant. The first thing brought to us was a bowl of yogurt, pure yogurt, very sour, no sugar added. We couldn't take it on an empty stomach. I asked them: 'Rice, rice, where is rice?' They said: 'Wait a moment.' We waited and waited. I asked again: 'Rice, rice, where is rice?' Then they brought a dish with many small pieces, each wrapped in grape leaves. I asked again: 'Where is rice?' They said: 'Inside the leaves.' Such small pieces! What was inside was not rice."

After seven or eight months, Imam Ma and his friend decided to move out of the university dormitory. "We couldn't stand the food provided at the canteen anymore. It was too greasy for us. There was no rice. We rented a room and moved out. We started to cook our own food. But we didn't have a rice cooker and had to cook rice on the stove. The first time I burned the rice. Both the rice and the pot turned black. Luckily I learned the skill of gradually controlling the fire. Meanwhile we got to know more and more friends from China. They are from different provinces, including Yunnan. We visited each other. This made our lives more cheerful."

Although the pursuit of Islamic faith and knowledge was the main goal of these Yunnanese Hui in the Arab countries, they were conscious of cultural differences. The theme of food recurred in each of the four interviewees' narration. Imam Liu mentioned that the local people ate much more meat than vegetables, and that he and his Hui friends from Burma had difficulty finding varieties of green vegetables in Cairo. Deputy Imam Bao said there was no entertainment in Saudi Arabia, but he enjoyed making tea with his Chinese friends. Hence food became a key differentiating factor between them and the local people from the very beginning. At some point, they all sought to cook their own food in order to improve their lives. At their leisure, they explored connections, primarily with Chinese and other Asian students who all ate rice as a staple food. Gathering for meals became the major form of social activity that helped enhance their dull student lives. Although they also made contact with local people (mostly classmates), they confessed there was little interaction.

After their graduation, they were immediately recruited to work in Taiwan. Imam Shan arrived in Taiwan in 1996 and Imam Liu in 1997.[32] Since their arrival they have particularly stressed the importance in their religious work of providing Islamic education for the children of their communities. They and Imam Ma and Deputy Imam Bao work hard to address this task by organizing classes of Arabic learning and Islamic

---

32. The first Yunnanese imam coming from Burma to Taiwan was Imam Chen at Kaohsiung Mosque, who arrived in 1991. Deputy Imam Bao arrived in 2003 and Imam Ma in 2004.

doctrines for different age-groups at their mosques. Moreover, Imam Shan is keen to introduce Islam to non-Muslim young people at universities via invitational lectures and youth camps. A few Hui followers of Lunggang Mosque commented that prior to the arrival of these Hui religious specialists from Burma, the Islamic communities in Taiwan were declining because of the lack of Islamic education for the Hui children. The devotion of these religious experts has helped energize new development of the Islamic communities in this non-Islamic society.

While working in Taiwan, these Yunnanese Islamic experts have maintained close ties with the Hui communities in Burma via exchange of news. The Hui group in Burma has become the major source for Islamic experts in Taiwan. In turn, Taiwan has been an attractive immigration destination for many Yunnanese migrants in Burma. The Yunnanese Hui are a majority group among the Muslims in Taiwan. The community of Lunggang Mosque in Chungli is especially distinctive, composed of more than two hundred Muslim households that have migrated from Burma and Thailand during different periods since the 1950s.[33] Many Yunnanese men in Taiwan still look for marriage partners from Burma or Thailand.

In recent years the Yunnanese Muslims from Burma have extended their religious work to Singapore. One of Imam Ma's friends, also surnamed Ma, who was studying with him in Pyin U Lwin and Syria, also came to Taiwan as an instructor of Arabic after graduation. A few years later, he married a Yunnanese Muslim woman from Burma who was working in Singapore. After marriage they settled in Singapore, and Mr. Ma was recruited by an Islamic association to work among Chinese Muslims, especially those from Burma.

While aware of their doubly marginalized status as Chinese and Muslims in Burma, the Yunnanese Hui maintain a focus on foreign countries and have successfully extended their Hui networks abroad by emphasizing these two features. Applying Peter Mandaville's interpretation of Islamic

---

33. The Yunnanese Muslim community in Chungli, Taiwan, is a very interesting case for research on ethno-religious identity (Kimura 2006; Ma 2011). During the two KMT evacuations of 1953–1954 and 1961, over ten thousand Yunnanese arrived in Taiwan from Burma. Among them, a small minority were Muslims. In 1963 a mosque was built next to the military dependents' village of Chungchen in Chungli for the Yunnanese Muslims, a precursor of the present Lunggang Mosque.

transnationalism (2001), we can say that the diasporic Yunnanese Muslims' traveling has resulted in their translocality, characterized by repeated encounters with different cultural elements and groups of people, as well as by their ongoing reinterpretation and adherence to their Islamic faith and ethnic identity. Whether in Burma, countries of the Middle East, or Taiwan, the Yunnanese Muslims embrace their identification pertaining to Chinese and Islamic traditions, two cultures they see as separate yet compatible. It is interesting to note how these two traditions interact with each other in different places. While promoting their Islamic faith by studying in Arab countries, these Hui interviewees used their Chinese background to connect with ethnic Chinese and other Asian people in their social lives. Yet, while their arrival in Taiwan may be seen as deepening a connection with their Chinese roots, their religious work serves the propagation of Islam. Intriguingly, these two fundamental elements alternately display their prominence in different contexts and highlight the flexibility and dynamism of the Yunnanese Muslims of Burma while simultaneously showing their marginality and encountered frictions. Underlining what Homi Bhabha calls an in-between or interstitial subjectivity (1996), they see themselves, no matter where they are, as a minority group different from others. In particular, I observe that this marginal feeling is distinctive among the Yunnanese Hui guest workers (especially among the women) in non-Muslim countries. The story of Shuli in the following section illuminates this phenomenon.

Shuli in Japan

Economic immigration is another common means whereby connections are extended abroad among the Yunnanese Muslims of Burma. Taiwan has been a favored destination for both the Han and Muslims, as it is a Chinese society and relatively affluent.[34] The Yunnanese migratory movement

---

34. Whereas the earlier evacuees retreated from Burma to Taiwan (in 1953–1954 and 1961) for political reasons, the later arrivals are economic migrants. In the second half of the 1960s and early 1970s, there was a wave of Chinese migration from Burma to Taiwan to escape the repressive Ne Win regime, but most of these immigrants were Guangdong and Fujian descendants (Chai 2006). Meanwhile, a great number of Yunnanese migrants fled from upper Burma to northern Thailand (Chang 1999).

from Burma to Taiwan intensified between 1985 and 2005, a period when the Taiwanese economy was much in need of foreign laborers. Most of them arrived in Taiwan via Thailand, as Guoguang's story reveals (chapter 3). Prior to 1995, immigration to Taiwan for the Chinese overseas was not too difficult. The Yunnanese migrants who moved to Taiwan before 1995 were easily granted Taiwanese citizenship. After obtaining citizenship, many of them applied for their relatives in Burma or Thailand to join them. Apart from permanent emigrants, many Yunnanese in Burma went abroad as guest workers for short periods. Their major destinations include Taiwan, Japan, Thailand, Singapore, Malaysia, Hong Kong, Saudi Arabia, and Australia. Informants said that Taiwan and Japan were the most desired countries before 2005. The salary in Japan is especially attractive, but they can only work there clandestinely. The chance of obtaining legal residency there is very slim. Those who want to go there have to pay large service fees to the brokers who help arrange a tourist visa, and they either depart directly from Burma or indirectly from Thailand.[35] A cheaper way is to go to Taiwan first as a student and then apply for a Japanese tourist visa in Taiwan. Shuli used this strategy and worked in Tokyo for four years.[36]

The number of male Yunnanese working in Japan is much higher than that of their female counterparts. Japan is neither an Islamic nor a Chinese society. Moreover, it is farther away than Taiwan and other neighboring countries and is thus considered more risky for women to travel and work there. In Shuli's case, she had two elder brothers already working there who could assist her. While conducting fieldwork in Pyin U Lwin among the Yunnanese Hui, I noticed that almost every man between his late twenties and age fifty had worked in Japan. Several male informants confirmed that during the peak period from 1990 to 2000, nine male Hui out of ten went to Japan as illegal laborers. They said that in general the ratio of Yunnanese Muslim men venturing abroad as guest workers is higher than that of their Han counterparts because the former group has fewer business opportunities in Burma owing to their religion's ban on the practices of usury and alcohol making, both common sources of income for Yunnanese migrants.

---

35. The service fee could go as high as two hundred thousand baht in the mid-1990s, according to informants.

36. I got to know Shuli's fourth elder sister first through Ae Maew's introduction. She is settled in Taiwan and attended university with Ae Maew.

Moreover, Pyin U Lwin is a hill town with an agriculturally based economy. Men need to go outside the area for economic development.[37]

Shuli has three brothers and four sisters. All three brothers have had experience working abroad. Her eldest brother has been in Japan since 1986,[38] and the second elder brother was there for six years (1988–1994). Both worked in Bangkok for a few years before going to Japan. Brokers helped purchase Thai passports and Japanese visas for them. Shuli's third elder brother worked in Hong Kong for two years in the mid-1990s. Among the girls, only her fourth elder sister and Shuli herself have worked abroad. Both went to Taiwan as students, respectively in 2001 and 2002. This sister completed her university studies and then stayed on illegally for four years before obtaining legal status in 2009.[39] Shuli stayed in Taiwan for only half a year. She then used her student status to apply for a tourist visa to Japan, where she stayed for four years as an underground laborer. In our first meeting in late 2008 in the courtyard of her house, she told me about her experiences in Taiwan and Japan:

"After arriving in Taiwan, I felt very much discriminated against. Classmates looked down on me, like I was from some very backward place. I hated that kind of feeling. My family was not poor in Burma. My parents always provided for us. But in Taiwan, I encountered many difficulties. The first time I entered an elevator, I didn't know what to do. I didn't know how to take a bus, or where to find *qingzhen* food.[40] I could only eat vegetarian dishes at the beginning. Once I bought and ate a package

---

37. Geographical location also affects the decision of where to go for work abroad. For example, Kengtung is near Thailand, and many people there go to Thailand for work. Many people living in the northern border area go to China to seek their fortune. Those in Yangon and southern Burma first consider going to Singapore or Malaysia.

38. This eldest brother married a Yunnanese Hui woman in Japan. They have two children born there. The couple hired a lawyer to make a petition based on the fact that their children were born and raised in Japan. The children speak only Japanese and have been acculturated to the society, and therefore it would not be possible for the children to return to Burma. In 2009, all the family members finally were granted legal status based on humanitarian concerns.

39. A large number of ethnic Chinese from Burma stay in Taiwan illegally. In 2008, many of them requested that the Taiwanese government grant them citizenship based on their long residency in Taiwan and difficulty in returning to Burma. Most people claimed that they did not have Burmese citizenship and had purchased fake passports to come to Taiwan. A portion of the applicants were granted legal status in 2009.

40. *Qingzhen* food means purified Muslim dishes (halal food); for the concept of *qingzhen* see Gladney (1996, 7–14).

of instant noodles, only to discover it was flavored with pork. Everything was new to me.

"Classmates looked down on all the students from Burma. They saw me as Burmese. I couldn't stand them taking advantage of my compatriots from Burma [*miandian tongbao*] and once quarreled with them fiercely. I told them: 'We didn't come to Taiwan on foot, but by airplane. We are here to study, paying the same tuition fees as you do. We are poorer, but so what? Have we asked for money from you? If you don't apologize to me and my friends, I'll appeal to the military instructors.'[41] Finally they apologized to us Burmese [*xiang women miandianren daoqian*].

"I didn't like Taiwan and wanted to go back to Burma. But I didn't want to return with nothing. I didn't even have money to buy a plane ticket. My two elder brothers were working in Japan, so I decided to go there. With Burmese status, I needed to show my bank account when applying for a Japanese tourist visa. My eldest brother contacted one of his friends in Taiwan to lend me one hundred thousand NT. The money was put in my account book in order to show the Japanese consulate. After obtaining the visa, I immediately returned that money to my brother's friend.

"In Japan, I rented a room with two other Yunnanese Muslim roommates. The rent and the bills for water and electricity amounted to about one hundred thousand yen per month. We agreed that each of us would put fifty thousand yen toward a common fund for payment of the rent and other communal costs every month. Water and electricity fees were not much because we all worked outside the whole day and only returned for sleep. But some roommates appropriated the money from the common fund. We had agreed that it was only for common spending, not for personal usage. During those years some roommates took advantage of others, although not everyone did. When such a problem occurred, I couldn't say anything directly to the wrongdoer. I had to think about the consequences. Very often, I just had to swallow."

On another occasion, while we cooked together in the kitchen, Shuli said: "Going abroad was a big lesson for me. I was naive before I left Burma. I used to spend money carelessly. But while working in Japan, I learned how hard it is to make money. Most guest workers worked twelve

---

41. There are military instructors in each school above the junior high level in Taiwan. This has been a legacy from the Nationalist government since the reign of Chiang Kai-shek.

hours a day; I worked fifteen hours. I slept only three hours a day. I cut my hair short because I had no time to take care of it. After returning home from work, I quickly took a shower and washed my hair. I didn't even have time to dry it. I was always tired after work. I was very slim. Well, I wanted to make money. I knew that was my goal. I couldn't expect my family to support me while I was in Japan. . . .

"I worked at restaurants. I washed dishes. The pots were greasy with lard. I had to wash them. I washed, washed, washed. There was no other way to avoid touching pork and lard. The salary was 850 yen per hour at the beginning. Later on I worked as a waitress and cashier, and the salary was raised to 900 yen per hour, and then 1,000 yen. On Sunday the pay was higher, 1,200 yen per hour. . . .

"In the beginning I often ate plain rice mixed with butter. Gradually I also ate other kinds of food, except pork. It was too difficult to get strict *qingzhen* food. It was not possible to fast either. I had to work almost every day. I didn't go to the mosque, and I didn't pray each day. Under such circumstances, I realized the most important thing was my conscience. I didn't take advantage of other people or do bad things to anyone. My heart was clean.

"After four years, I was too tired to stay on. I thought it was time to go home. I reported myself to the police and then returned to Burma. Yet, I had great difficulty in readjusting to the lifestyle here at the beginning. I worked all day long in Japan, fifteen hours a day. But here in Pyin U Lwin, I had nothing to do. All I did was eat, sleep, and watch satellite television. I felt as if I were going crazy with this idle lifestyle. I told my family I wanted to go abroad again. But my family didn't allow it. They wanted me to get married and settle down. Finally, I managed to open this bakery. I hired one Indian baker and several Burmese workers. The business is OK. I no longer spend money carelessly. It is sad if you don't have money.

"I have to supervise the workers. Those Burmese workers give you a headache. They have been doing the same job for a long time. But still, you have to repeat the directions to them every day. They are like robots."

"Would you consider marrying a Burmese or Indian?" I asked.

"Definitely not. Our living standards and habits are very different. It would be too difficult to live together. Marriage is not only for me. I have to think of my parents and other siblings. It is sad for us Muslim girls, for our marriage circle is rather small. Muslim men can marry non-Muslim women and demand their wives convert to Islam. But we Muslim women could hardly do so. The Han men will not convert to Islam for their wives. That is why the number of non-married Chinese Muslim women is high.[42] Well, financially I'm independent. Whether I get married or not is not so much a problem. However, I know that an unmarried woman does not have a social footing in a Muslim community."

Shuli is certainly a capable businesswoman. She runs her shop efficiently. She still lives with her mother and third elder brother. This brother married a Han girl a few years ago; she converted to Islam before marriage. Shuli said this sister-in-law was very smart and mastered recitation of the Koran after studying Arabic for half a year with a tutor at home. However, this sister-in-law did not like the confinements imposed on a married woman in terms of social life, and she still liked going out with friends a lot. According to Shuli, although her mother was not strict, the sister-in-law did not feel she fit into the family, and she finally separated from her husband. "There are several similar cases of divorce. Islam is more conservative than other religions," Shuli remarked. Since returning from Japan, Shuli joins her mother for five prayers every day.

Despite her economic independence, Shuli acknowledged family pressure pushing her to get married. So far, Shuli and her fourth elder sister in Taiwan, both over thirty, are unmarried. Her sister in Taiwan confided to me that there have been several Han, Indian, and Burmese wooers for her and Shuli, but they have not accepted them. Among their own folk, they have not found suitable candidates either. While Shuli's story illustrates her economic agency, it also reflects her marginality as a Burmese national abroad, a Chinese migrant in Burma, and a Muslim woman wherever she is. Accordingly, multiple strands of influences and frictions generated from sociocultural, religious, and economic interactions affect the formation of her subjectivity and define her standing in different contexts. Her narratives illuminate how far she managed to resist various kinds of external demands and how she negotiated in order to hold on to her integrity as a Chinese Muslim woman in Burma and abroad. In the face of circumstances that compelled her to act against Islamic commands, she was able to locate herself in her conscience. This demonstrates a strong inner force that helps her combat her marginality when necessary.

---

42. I do not have the figure; however, most Yunnanese Muslim women I know are married.

On the other hand, her constant resistance to marrying ethnic others points to her desire to cling to her ethno-religious and gender marginality. She was aware that once she betrayed this marginality, she would likely also lose self-esteem and the esteem of her family and her community. She told me there are a few such cases of outside marriage among her relatives, and they are typically sources of shame for the family. Women who marry out of their community are not able to gain social recognition from either the Hui or their husbands' community. "Such marriages are tragedies. I prefer to live without getting married if I cannot find a suitable one," she lamented. Having interviewed Yunnanese Muslims in Mandalay, Yangon, Kengtung, Taunggyi, Pyin U Lwin, Lashio, and Tachileik, I find marriage endogamy steadfast among the group, an attitude that has been an essential factor contributing to the maintenance of their Yunnanese Hui identity.

The stories told by Ma Yeye, Mu Dadie, several Yunnanese Islamic specialists in Taiwan, and Shuli highlight the dynamism of the Yunnanese Hui of Burma. Being marginal does not mean being passive. Like the Yunnanese Han in Burma, the Yunnanese Hui have been very mobile and have successfully gained a measure of economic security and social stability. Their travels serve a range of purposes, including education, religious missions, employment, and marriages. Whatever the purpose, all their movement contributes to the expansion of the Yunnanese Hui's transnational nexuses. In effect, Islam, which is embedded in their beliefs and practices, has compounded the marginality of their allochthonous status while making their intra-interaction coherent. This positive-cum-negative phenomenon originating from a group's common religion is not seen among the Han. Moreover, the overlap of kinship, religious, and ethnic networks among the Hui is distinctive.

In sum, Islam, Chinese background, and intra-group marriages are fundamental elements that distinguish the Yunnanese Hui from other groups in different contexts. These elements have also facilitated their circulation across a wide range of places and interconnection with fellow members. Certainly, there are individual variations in terms of migration experiences and religious observance in daily life. Many young Hui confided to me that they do not observe five prayers a day, be they in Burma or abroad. I have also heard about drinking, gambling, and family violence problems. Nevertheless, the Yunnanese Muslim identity prevails among the group's members.

The Muslim Rebellion in Yunnan and subsequent waves of flight have been inscribed in the group members' social memory. Moreover, the Burmese government's discriminatory policies toward the Muslim minorities and a spate of anti-Muslim attacks since 2012 have fueled a feeling of persecution in this community. Although the Chinese Muslims were not directly targeted in these riots, many Yunnanese Muslims I came into contact with in Yangon, Mandalay, and Lashio in October 2013 expressed their deep fear that the situation might worsen. In the wake of these aggressive incidents, they have cautiously reduced their public religious visibility by avoiding Islamic greetings among themselves when they are outdoors and curtailing the call for prayers amplified over microphones from mosques.

In comparison, emigration among the Hui has been much more intensive than that of the Han. In the mid-1960s, the Hui population in Burma was about ten thousand to fifteen thousand (Yegar 1966, 83). The number has not increased much, possibly because of continuous migration abroad. Whether the current stream of sectarian violence will accelerate the emigration rate among the population remains to be seen. What can be discerned is that the group's cohesion has not been weakened despite its members' ongoing mobility. In contrast, it has assisted them to respond to "encounters across difference" (Tsing 2005) and to strengthen their feeling of displacement and ethnic identity. (Deputy Imam Bao's and Grandma Ma's words about having no home quoted at the beginning of the chapter reflect this sentiment.) Concretely, their double attachments as Muslims and as Chinese have contributed to the heterogeneity of Muslim culture in Burma as well as in the world. Such a phenomenon highlights the duality of the Islamic world, which is characterized by a religious universalism that pursues a global Muslim community (*umma*) and by numerous ethnocultural traits as asserted by scholars of Islamic studies (e.g., Gilmartin 2005; Launay 1992; Nasr 2002; Said and Sharify-Funk 2003; Zaman 2005). While this conjuncture of universalism and particulars has existed harmoniously among different Muslim communities in Burma for centuries, the society requires a greater degree of tolerance and understanding across today's ethno-religious boundaries.

Part II

(Transnational) Trade

5

Venturing into "Barbarous" Regions

Yunnanese Caravan Traders

> Mountainous societies have their own rules and knowledge to pass on.
> There's so much to learn. . . . Looking back upon my former experiences . . .
> living with nature, and coming and going around the forests and mountains,
> I feel that life was indeed exciting [*gou weidao*].
> —Zhang Dadie,[1] in Xincun, June 15, 2007

Economic ventures across borders have been a significant part of Yunnanese life, and the mule caravan trade, which lasted for more than two millennia, was, as noted in the introduction, the most distinctive commercial practice in the region. The ways in which the trade was carried out were connected to the mountainous environment, which obstructed fluid communication and contributed to arduous living conditions. Able to endure hard work, mules were central for the transportation of commodities to different corners of the region. With their help, the Yunnanese traversed upper mainland Southeast Asia. The accrued knowledge and ethos regarding this peripatetic engagement developed into what is called "mule caravan culture" (*mabang wenhua*) (Wang and Zhang 1993), especially in Yunnanese border towns. People who did not have the stomach for such work were labeled timid and mocked by other Yunnanese (Chang

---

1. Zhang Dadie is Zhang Dage's father.

2003; Fang 2003; Yin 1984). Drawing on the interpretation of migration culture given by Massey et al., it would appear that movement across borders is deeply entrenched in the behavior of the people in the border areas and has become a "rite of passage" for adult men (1993, 453).

Many elderly informants described making annual trips to upper Burma for the caravan trade before fleeing Yunnan, and continuing the business between Burma and Thailand after settling in these two countries. During the Burmese socialist period, it is estimated that black-market merchandise may have constituted over 80 percent of Burma's total consumption (Lintner 1988, 23; Mya Than 1996, 3). Market-dominated Thailand was the major partner in this illegal trade. According to informants, about 70 percent of the smuggled Thai goods entered the country through Shan State before 1980, mostly by means of mule caravans, and Yunnanese accounted for 70 to 80 percent of the Thai-Burmese cross-border traders.[2] Accordingly, the Yunnanese played a significant role in sustaining the Burmese *hmaungkho* (underground) economy during the socialist period.

Based on the narrative accounts of four key informants, in both oral and written forms, in this chapter I explore the factors that contributed to Yunnanese migrants' involvement in this contraband trade, reconstruct the trajectories of their movement, and look into their borderland knowledge and mercantile agency as they interacted with a range of political entities. Their stories illustrate the concrete and structured social history of migrant Yunnanese traders and demonstrate the cultural meanings of this economic practice during the Burmese socialist period.

Owing to practical constraints, I have so far been able to visit only a small number of the former caravan trading routes. Moreover, data from other ethnic communities are still lacking, a limitation of the present study. Nevertheless, current findings attest to the fact that borderlands are not passive geographical margins but active sites intertwined with different forces, constantly subject to tensions, struggles, and ongoing negotiations.

---

2. The rest were Shans, Karens, and other ethnic minorities. Among the Yunnanese merchants, 90 percent were Han Chinese and about 10 percent were Muslims.

Zhang Dage

On his former blog, Zhang Dage posted an essay about the long-distance mule caravan trade, which he had observed when living in Bianliang. He writes:

> Bianliang was a small village located in the lower range of a mountain. . . . There were about fifty families. It was a Chinese village; most villagers were dependents of the KMT troops that were stationed nearby. Villagers practiced Chinese customs and spoke [Yunnanese]. The village was distinguished from neighboring villages of other ethnic minorities by its housing style. . . . The highest building in the village was a two-story wooden house—the residence of Commander Luo. Bianliang was a vital point along a caravan trading route in [northern Shan State] providing connections to northern Thailand. All caravan traders passing by had to pay tolls. . . .
>
> The 1970s witnessed the heyday of the mule caravan trade in northern Burma. Owing to the Burmese government's ban on border trade, economic exchanges across international boundaries, including the trafficking of opium and jade stones, went underground. The KMT troops that were entrenched in the mountains of [Shan State and northern Thailand] became a dominant military corps engaging in this illicit activity.
>
> . . . Though located in the mountains, the [KMT stationed in Bianliang] had a wireless system. . . . Waiting [for the arrival of caravans] became the [most exciting] event [for the village kids]. When the first mule appeared in sight, the kids were elated.
>
> We children loved watching the adults unloading the packs off the mules with an efficient division of labor. They did this task in an empty space, arranging the unloaded packs in an orderly manner. Some muleteers arranged the unloaded packsaddles in rows on the ground . . . and covered them with pieces of tarpaulin. These then became warm caves for muleteers to sleep in. Some muleteers went up to the forest to cut bamboo poles for constructing fences and setting up tents. Some people busied themselves by building a fire for cooking. Usually a large caravan consisted of [many small teams] of seven to ten people with a leader. . . . The team members shared the work and looked after one another. The whole group was like a community.
>
> For food, the caravans usually carried dried meat and pickled vegetables. These types of food were easy to carry and remained unspoilt for a long time. When caravans reached a village, they supplemented their rations

with fresh vegetables and eggs, providing income for the villagers. The mules needed to be fed too. Some muleteers cut grass; others cooked yellow beans; both grass and beans served as feed for the mules. After arranging shelter and food, some muleteers and traders visited their friends or relatives in the village. The meetings were always hospitable and animated as they exchanged news about relatives living far away.

The size of a caravan often increased, with smaller mounted parties joining along the way. [Metaphorically] the journey between upper Burma and northern Thailand resembled the flow of a river with incessantly converging tributaries. The group required a military escort for its safety. Sometimes it encountered natural disasters, such as landslides or floods during the rainy season. Other times it faced attacks [from Burmese forces or other ethnic militias]. The traveling routes had to change from time to time.... Experienced groups reacted to danger with accumulated wisdom. What could not be controlled had to be entrusted to gods.

Our family also kept two mules. When caravans arrived in our village, Junior Uncle Fu would join them with the two packed mules. Father would write a note indicating the amount of goods [raw opium] and to whom these should be handed.... The trip concerned the economy of our family....

Zhang Dage's colorful essay portrays the intimate relationship between Yunnanese village life and the long-distance mule caravan trade. As he describes it, this risky economic activity excited the young boys from childhood. Having observed the arrival and departure of caravan merchants and muleteers, they were familiar with this traveling trade. It fired their imaginations, and they wanted to be a part of future journeys.

From 1961 to 1973, the remnant KMT forces (the Third and Fifth Armies) had several military bases along the Salween River to facilitate their caravan trade. Bianliang was one of them. The northernmost point was located in Mount Loijie, a four-hour walk southeast of Tangyan, or about half an hour by jeep; but their trading routes extended farther, to Kokang. The number of troops stationed at each post ranged from a few dozen to a few hundred. Each post had a wireless communication system, and the movement of caravans from post to post was reported by means of this system.

The region between Tangyan and Kokang was especially productive for opium cultivation. For the local people, growing poppies was a means of survival. Like Zhang Dage's family, they traded opium for other consumer goods. Zhang Dage's father, who stayed in the region for more than twenty years, said, "I've done different things, all for a living. In these mountainous areas, what could you grow? The land wasn't fertile enough for growing rice. If you didn't grow opium, you couldn't make a living." His words expressed the lamentable situation of the region, which had been observed earlier by a British commissioner in Shan State:

> The real point about opium in the Wa States and Kokang is that opium is the only thing produced which will pay for transport to a market where it can be sold. To suppress opium in Kokang and the Wa States without replacing it by a crop relatively valuable to its bulk, would be to reduce the people to the level of mere subsistence on what they could produce for food and wear themselves or to force them to migrate. (John S. Calgue, 1937, quoted in Maule 1992, 36)

Before the early 1970s, local people either sold their opium to the KMT forces or carried their produce to Thailand for sale, as Zhang Dage's family did, and then transported Thai commodities on the way back for sale on the black market.

In the foregoing story, Zhang Dage vividly described the performance of different tasks by the muleteers. Each one was assigned specific chores. In interviews and casual conversations, other informants also stressed the importance of caravan organization, which required strict observance of discipline, division of labor, and compliance with taboos (see also Ma 1985; Wang 1993; Wang and Zhang 1993). These were prerequisites for the efficiency of a caravan's movement and for coping with the perils of the long journey. A caravan comprised many small teams belonging to different traders. According to the usual way of classifying caravans, a small team consisted of five mules (*yiba*), and five small teams constituted a small caravan (*yidanbang/yixiaobang*) (Wang 1993, 310). The number of mules may have ranged from several hundred to more than a thousand. Every two to three mules required a muleteer in the long-distance caravan trade. A caravan formed a united body that was characterized by leadership and hierarchy. The group had a commander, usually from the escort troops, and each small team also had a leader. The cohesion among caravan members was reflected in the use of language. Each team organized its own meals; team members ate from the same pot (*guo*) of rice and referred to their team as *women shi tong guokou* (we are from the same pot). The team leader was traditionally called *guotou* (pot head), and the commander of the whole caravan *daguotou* or *maguotou* (big pot head / pot head of a mule caravan). Traditionally, the caravan commander had absolute authority. He was in charge of maintaining internal order and external relations and meted out punishments to those who broke the rules. Whenever emergencies occurred, he had to respond quickly.

Apart from transporting commodities, each team had a mule that carried food and kitchen utensils; this included "rice bowls, plates, soup basins, chopsticks, knives, chopping boards, fire-tongs, fire-forks, bronze teapots, bronze cooking pots, cooking oil, salt, soy sauce, vinegar, dried fish, dry meat, pickled vegetables, noodles, and rice" (Fang 2002, 25). This mule was referred to as *kongduo* (empty carrier) in Yunnanese (*kongtuo* in Mandarin). Usually it was an old mule that was not afraid of the clatter produced by the utensils while moving (ibid.). Each team had to calculate as accurately as possible how much food its members would need during the journey and where they could replenish it.

Caravans measured the distance of the journey using cooking metaphors. A half day distance, called *yi sao lu* (a journey that requires cooking one meal), was covered in about four hours. A break for cooking was termed *kai sao* (to cook outdoors). Most parts of the caravan routes wound through mountains and were full of dangers, such as wild animals and pestilential vapors (*zhangqi*), or flooding and landslides. Maintaining a peaceful relationship with nature has thus been an essential part of Yunnanese religious beliefs, demonstrated by their worship of mountain gods (*shan shen*) in most rituals.[3] Prior to departure on a long-distance journey and upon their return, travelers pay respects to the mountain gods by sacrificing chickens or pigs. Shrines and temples that house mountain gods are common in Yunnanese communities in northern Thailand and Burma. In addition, the Yunnanese interpret the overwhelming power of nature by strict adherence to taboos. A frequently cited taboo held that if rice was not well cooked during the caravan journey, serious misfortunes would occur. The caravan commander might halt the journey or even turn back. Other

---

3. This parallels the worship of the sea goddess, Mazu, among Fujianese in southeastern China and Taiwan, reflecting their engagement in fishing or marine trade.

taboos related to the use of language, the arrangement of dishes, and the appearance of certain animals (see Ma 1985, 154).

In addition to seeking harmony with nature, maintaining a good relationship with other communities was important. The KMT forces associated with the Shan, Kachin, and Kokang military groups for convenience of movement. Some of these groups were KKY forces. The KMT forces disguised themselves as KKY troops when entering the latter's territories in order to avoid attacks by the Burmese army. In exchange for this, the KMT provided a small number of weapons to these allied parties. Nevertheless, power conflicts occurred among them from time to time (as mentioned by Mr. Li in chapter 3).

Many informants related that before 1985, almost every village family kept a few mules at home, as Zhang Dage's family did. Villagers either engaged in cross-border trade with their own mules or rented out the mules to other traders. The caravans setting off from Thailand carried different types of consumer goods; among these, textiles were the major commodity. Mr. Tang, who was in charge of taxation in the KMT Third Army in Xincun, said that prior to caravan departure, all commodities had to be taxed (as payment for armed escort). The tax on one mule-load of textiles was eight hundred baht. After the tax was paid, the army issued a tax certificate. One load of textiles could be exchanged for four to eight *zuai* of raw opium in Burma (depending on the textile's quality). Apart from consumer goods, the troops and merchants also carried gold bars for the purchase of opium or for sale in Burma.[4] Informants said that at the beginning the gold bars were carried by porters. One person carried about twenty gold bars. Each bar weighed five *liang* and could be exchanged for eleven to fourteen *zuai* of opium.[5]

When the Burmese government decided to wipe out the KKY forces in 1973, it launched frequent attacks in the mountain areas in Shan and Kachin States, compelling many Yunnanese migrants to move to cities.

---

4. Several informants said that the gold bought in Thailand or Laos was imported from France or Switzerland. Merchants made good profits when selling smuggled gold brought from Thailand in Burma as it was not officially taxed. Part of the gold sold in Burma was further smuggled to India for sale. (Although Burma contains gold deposits, the mining zeal only started around 2000.)

5. One *liang* is about 37.5 grams. Porters who did not have to tend mules on the way could carry more gold bars. The highest number I have heard is thirty-two.

Around the same time, the CPB took control of the Wa Hills, east of the Salween River. Moreover, international pressure against drug trafficking grew more intense.[6] The KMT forces then withdrew southward inside Shan State. Consequently, the opium trafficking routes fell primarily into the hands of Khun Sa's army (Cowell 2005, 13). Nevertheless, the KMT remained active in their military-cum-economic engagement. The jade trade became the new enterprise for the KMT and for many other Yunnanese traders in Burma and Thailand. The trading routes led from northern Thailand to Taunggyi, Mandalay, and then up to Kachin State, where jade stones are found.[7]

Consequently, the movement of the migrant Yunnanese traders between Shan and Kachin States in Burma and northern Thailand formed a transnational configuration. Their trafficking was officially banned in Burma and denounced by the Thai government from time to time. They were dependent upon the protection of the armed ethnic groups (though these forces were a source of exploitation, too), and, in turn, the latter depended on the former for tax revenue. The composition of the ethnic forces was complex: some, like the KKY, were recognized by the Burmese government, while others, like the KMT, were tacitly accepted by the Thai government, and still others were rebels in the borderlands. They sometimes collaborated with one another to further their economic or political interests, and at other times they fought each other for the same reasons (a situation referred to by Mr. Li in chapter 3). The alliances and the power structures of these militias were in a constant state of flux, illustrating an ongoing process of what Leach calls fragmentation and inconsistency. Nevertheless, no matter how fragmented or inconsistent the power structure was, traders and ethnic forces observed self-regulated rules in relation to taxation, compensation, and meting out punishment as situations required, to ensure economic continuity.[8]

---

6. In 1972, the KMT forces made a deal with the US and Thai governments to give up the narcotics trade in exchange for $2 million in compensation. Informants confided that after the deal was negotiated, the armies abstained from openly engaging in the trade, but individual army members continued the business on a smaller scale.

7. The KMT troops that escorted caravans from Thailand only reached as far as Banbishan or Xunding in Shan State. But traders ventured to Taunggyi, Mandalay, or even Kachin State to buy jade stones (see the next section).

8. The best example is the underground trade of jade stones from Burma to Thailand (see Chang 2004, 2006b, 2011).

With regard to the sociocultural meaning of the caravan trade to the Yunnanese migrants, Zhang Dage's narration highlights several significant points. As a distinctive economic practice among the Yunnanese, it satisfied the consumption demands of people residing in much of the mountainous regions. Moreover, it resulted in webs of connection between different communities. Zhang Dage mentioned the exchange of news about kith and kin residing far away. Because of their mobility, the Yunnanese have relatives and friends in different places. Caravans conveyed not only goods but also information. In one conversation, Zhang Dage told me that in the days before electronic communication, the movement of caravans provided people with connections to faraway places. Oral messages were a common form of correspondence, but in case of urgent and important matters, the message sender would prepare a written note tied with a piece of dry chili, a chicken feather, and a piece of charcoal (objects that were associated with light and heat) to indicate its seriousness and urgency and hand it to a transmitter for delivery. This kind of "express mail" was especially utilized by the Shan armies in times of war.

Moreover, as Zhang Dage's story illustrates, the arrival of caravans always brought much excitement and expectation. The goods they supplied linked villagers' lives to distant places they had never been to. Elder sister Lin, now settled in Mae Salong in northern Thailand (Mae Fa Luang District, Chiang Rai Province), lived in northern Shan State in Burma from the 1950s to the 1960s. She once joyfully told me: "I love reading novels. I spoiled my eyesight by reading novels. I especially love the works written by Qiong Yao and Jin Yong. When I and my mother and brothers still lived in Burma and my father [a KMT officer] was in Thailand, our caravans used to bring novels of Taiwan and Hong Kong from Thailand to Burma. And also movie magazines, such as *Jiahe Magazine* [*jiahe dianying huabao*]. I was familiar with Mei Dai, Qing Shan, and other stars." Elder sister Zhou (a narrator in the next chapter), who taught dressmaking in Taunggyi from 1975 to 1980, said that she used the Japanese fashion magazine *Lady Boutique* as a textbook for teaching. Moreover, during our conversations Zhang Dage mentioned other interesting items transported by caravans to his village. These included Chinese dictionaries, copybooks for practicing Chinese calligraphy (*zitie*), Chinese painting books, Chinese almanacs, and so on. It is amazing to see how the Yunnanese migrants, while maintaining a Chinese lifestyle in these remote areas, were able to glean knowledge of famous movie stars and Japanese fashion through different types of cultural materials imported from abroad. Accordingly, the caravan trade played an essential role in the people's everyday lives by performing both economic and sociocultural functions.

Yue Dashu

Nineteen-year-old Yue Dashu[9] fled from Tengchong, a historical border entrepôt of Yunnan, to Burma with his bride in 1968 to escape the Cultural Revolution. His parents and other siblings fled separately to Burma in the 1950s. He said:

"I took the job of a muleteer for the first three years after my flight to Burma. It was arduous work. If the road conditions were good, one man could drive three to four mules for the short-distance trade. But for the long-distance trade, mostly walking on mountain tracks, one could only drive two to three mules. After walking a long day, muleteers still had to cut grass to feed the mules. But if the campsite was in a valley, mules were released to graze. Muleteers had to look for them the next morning. . . . After having saved some money from the job, I purchased two mules and became a small caravan trader. My number of mules increased year by year. By the late 1970s, I owned twenty mules and was able to hire a few muleteers."

In 1972, Yue Dashu moved his wife and three children to Xincun in northern Thailand. While he continued his transborder commerce, his wife sewed clothes and made Yunnanese pickled food to sell in the village market. While the KMT forces were still active along the Salween River, Yue Dashu used to go on trade trips to Tangyan. Sometimes the caravans left Thailand from Mae Sai and entered Tachileik. In Tachileik, the caravans entrusted their commodities to a KKY group for transportation by car to Kengtung. One load of goods was charged three hundred kyat. Traders and muleteers could join the KKY on the trip from Tachileik to Kengtung or make a separate trip. The traders reloaded their goods

---

9. *Dashu* (junior uncle), an address for male adults who are younger than one's father. I have known Yue Dashu since 1995. Over the years he has told me many stories of his former trading experiences at his general merchandise store in Xincun, northern Thailand.

on mules again on the outskirts of Kengtung. From there, they entered areas controlled by the ethnic rebels. "This is a region with big mountains. We had to walk up and down all the time.... There were dozens of tracks. Even though I traveled in this area for several years, I wasn't able to go through all of them. These places were very wild. The minorities lived in a very primitive way, except the Baiyi," Yue Dashu said.

One frequent direction the caravans took was northward on foot to Panghsang (also known as Pansam and Pangkang). This took five days from Kengtung. Continuing westward, they reached Pangyan, then passed the Salween River and arrived in Nakha (a military post of the KMT Third Army). They usually rested for one day in Nakha before going northward to Mount Loijie, the final stop for the caravans. This took two more days. Traders unloaded their goods at the villages of Mount Loijie and had them transported to Tangyan by vehicle. Two types of vehicles were widely used for the transportation of caravan goods: green jeeps and the Japanese Hino trucks. Prior to 2012, these vehicles still remained a common sight on the road. During the dry season, the entire journey took fifteen days; but during the rainy season, it could take more than a month.

Sometimes the caravans left Thailand from Piang Luang. After entering Burma, they moved northward until they reached a ferry port on the Salween River.[10] Yue Dashu said:

"Crossing a river took time. Both humans and goods were shipped by boats that were rowed manually. If there were several caravans, they were shipped according to their arrival order. This rule was commonly respected by caravaneers. The boats were carved from the trunks of big trees. One boat could ship eight loads of goods at a time, and it took one hour to cross the river. After all the goods had been shipped, the mules were driven to swim across the river. You had to use clubs to drive them. When swimming together, over a hundred at a time, the mules were not afraid of the river. Once mules started to swim, the people remaining on the departing bank had to keep silent and let those on the opposite side call the mules to swim across. If the mules heard noises from the departing side, they would be distracted and turn back."

---

10. Tamiao ferry was used frequently, but alternatives were sought when the situation required it.

After crossing the river, the caravans arrived at Nawan. Banbishan, a KMT military base, lay to the west, about four to five hours away on foot. They then carried on northward along the river until they arrived at Mount Loijie. The whole journey took about a month during the dry season.

Tangyan was the center of the *hmaungkho* trade in upper Burma before 1973. Most of the commodities that arrived in Tangyan were transported by car to Lashio and then to other main cities such as Taunggyi and Mandalay. These places constituted the first ring for distribution of *hmaungkho* goods. From these nodes the smuggled commodities were then conveyed to various parts of the country. Much of the transportation was undertaken by the KKY. Underground taxes were paid for the goods' passage to officials of various agencies including customs, the police, military intelligence, the migration department, the forestry department, and the military. Given their meager government salaries, the *hmaungkho* economy actually became these officials' main source of income. In other words, state agencies also participated in this underground trade and were in effect integrated into this informal economic mechanism, despite its illegality and denouncement by the government. Although confiscation by Burmese agents occurred from time to time, most confiscated goods were actually divided among the officials rather than handed over to the state. If the receipt of bribes was an affirmative way of participating in the *hmaungkho* economy, confiscation was the alternative. Yet neither method complied with the state-guided ideology—"the Burmese way to Socialism."

In 1975, Yue Dashu and many other Yunnanese caravan traders, following the steps of the KMT armies, which had withdrawn southward, shifted their trading routes. Sometimes they left Thailand from Piang Luang following the route described earlier, until they reached Nawan, then walked in the direction of Nansan to the north, then farther northwest to Xunding, a Shan village that was three to four hours on foot from Pinlong. Other times they left Thailand from Mae Aw (another KMT base in Ma Jang Bye District, Mae Hongson Province) and then crossed the border and walked northwest in the direction of Hsihseng, and then northward to the area near Banyin. (Caravans circumvented rather than entered these towns that were under the control of the Burmese government.) From the Banyin area, they continued westward and reached Kyawdalon (a Pa-O village). These two routes took from six to eight days during the dry season. Xunding and Kyawdalon were two major meeting points for caravans to and from Thailand; the former was in use from the late 1960s to the mid-1980s, and the latter from the late 1970s to early 1980s for a period of three to four years.[11] Thai merchandise was unloaded in these two places. Local villagers provided places for storage (*duizhan*) and received some extra income. The merchandise was further conveyed to Taunggyi, which became the hub of the *hmaungkho* trade after 1973.[12] From Taunggyi, the *hmaungkho* goods were distributed to different parts of the country.

Yue Dashu pointed out that caravans traveled primarily over mountain routes. Main roads, which they referred to as "public roads" (*gonglu*), were controlled by the Burmese army and had to be avoided. However, caravans sometimes needed to use public roads, and these occasions were said to be intense. Another informant said that caravans usually moved at night for safety. The escorting army had to block a part of the road to let the caravans quickly cross over. Sometimes they had to walk on the public roads for some distance before connecting to a mountain route. If they were unfortunate and encountered the Burmese army, fighting would take place.[13]

Before the early 1970s, Yue Dashu joined the armed caravans organized by the KMT forces once a year. He said: "The whole group often consisted of over one thousand mules. Four hours after the lead caravan had left a village, the rear one was just departing. Although guarded by troops, sometimes as many as seven hundred to eight hundred soldiers, big caravans incurred dangers because of their prominence." Afterward, he often led his caravan alone or joined small groups—totaling forty to fifty mules—that usually were not escorted by troops. He said: "The movement of small caravans was more dynamic than large-size caravans. They could

---

11. Kyawdalon was an alternative to Xunding when the latter was under Burmese control.

12. The goods from Xunding were first taken by mule to Pinlong (it took about four hours) prior to further transportation to Taunggyi by jeep (this took another five hours). Xunding was a major base of the Shan United Revolutionary Army referred to earlier. Its leader, Bo Moherng, usually stayed in the Thai headquarters in Piang Luang, where a troop of the KMT Third Army was also encamped. The two groups collaborated from 1969 to 1984. (Afterward, Bo Moherng began to work with Khun Sa.) Transporting the commodities from Kyawdalon to Taunggyi took about one hour by jeep. One jeep could carry seven mule loads.

13. From Nawan to Xunding, the caravans had to pass three public roads. The first was between Linke and Monpan; the second between Nansan and Kyusauk; and the third between Pinlong and Laikha.

switch routes immediately upon encountering dangerous conditions. Caravaneers were trained to listen to news [*ting xiaoxi*]. Upon arrival at a village, they would first visit the headman and inquire about the situation nearby. Headmen welcomed caravans and the goods they brought that villagers needed, and the caravans also purchased food from them, such as eggs, chickens, and rice. Transaction was often done with old silver coins [*laodun*—Indian rupees]." Within territories of ethnic insurgency, headmen were obliged to provide necessary information to traders, who in turn had to pay tolls to the ethnic armies. This was nothing new; it constituted continuity in the tradition of caravan trade in this ethnically diverse region that required collaboration between merchants and local political entities. In other words, different groups learned to live together symbiotically over generations in this area, developing their own political ecology. Knowledge of how to cope with emergent situations was transmitted.

In the early stages, Yue Dashu traded his Thai commodities for raw opium. Later on, he engaged in the jade trade for ten years. He left Taunggyi by car for Mandalay and then went northward by train to Mohnyin, which was one of the jade-trading places along the railway line. He said:

"There were several Yue households in Mohnyin that provided me with trading connections. I took my time to shop around, buy a few pieces one day and a few more another day. After buying jade stones, I stored them at the house of some local people. They were Shans. It is safer to store jade stones at the houses of local people, because the Burmese authorities were less likely to search their houses. Depending on our familiarity, I either gave presents to the house owner or paid him some money. Sometimes I stored my stones at a temple. I knew the monks there very well. I brought them the textiles used for monks' robes from Thailand. They were very happy with my gifts. Burmese people were very kind and friendly. I knew sufficient Burmese, and my Shan was fluent. I could travel easily with my purchased Burmese identity."

For a short time in 1981, Yue Dashu also traded British 555 cigarettes from Thailand to Burma. He said: "It was a very lucrative business. Each time I would purchase five thousand cartons that were then carried by ten mules. At that time, the exchange rate was two Thai baht to one Burmese kyat. I paid 88 or 89 baht for one carton and sold it for 280 kyat in Taunggyi. The price in Mandalay was even higher—360 kyat for one carton. But after four months of engagement in this business, the profits plummeted because of competition. What I had earned still allowed me to purchase sixteen *rai*[14] of land in Thailand."

Even though the profit margins were great, the caravan trade was highly risky, as mentioned earlier. Yue Dashu said: "I lost all of my caravan goods twice. Once the caravan was 'borrowed' [intercepted] by Khun Sa's troops. The other time, all caravan goods were bombarded at Banbishan by the Burmese air force. Fortunately, I escaped alive from that bombardment. But having lost the goods, I felt ashamed to go back home. Most goods were purchased on credit in Thailand. I then stayed in Burma and conducted local trade for two years. In this way, I managed to save thirty thousand to forty thousand kyat, and I used this money to buy jade stones that I took back to Thailand for sale. Subsequently, I cleared my formal debts and had enough money left over to build a house in Xincun."

Circumstances sometimes forced Yunnanese merchants on business trips in Burma to stay too long in one place. Yue Dashu related one such experience that occurred in the early 1980s; the episode reveals important information about interaction with local communities:

"Once I joined a large convoy of caravans composed of more than nine hundred mules, seven hundred to eight hundred traders and muleteers, and more than two hundred Wa escort troops. The caravans reached a village near Laikha [about nine hours north of Pinlong on foot]. The Wa troops assigned the traders and muleteers to different village houses for accommodation. The whole village was occupied by the caravans. Fighting between different Shan ethnic insurgents occurred on and off nearby and prevented the group from further movement. I and my hired muleteers, totaling ten people, stayed at a local family's house for nine months. The host was a Kala, and his wife was Shan. The latter was very friendly, but the former was not.[15] The husband was very strict with us; if we forgot to take off our shoes upon entering the house, we were scolded.

"This family had three daughters but no sons. They had a rice farm. That year, the father could not find enough laborers to transplant the seedlings that were already overgrown. I had been a farmer in Yunnan. After learning about the situation, I led my people to work on the farm. The Indian master was very happy with our help and changed his attitude. I

---

14. One *rai* (a Thai measurement for area) equals sixteen hundred square meters.
15. Shan hospitality was consistently praised by other informants.

often purchased food from the market and gave it to the mistress of the house for preparation. Yunnanese are not necessarily rich, but they spend generously.

"While I was there, I also did some short-distance trade. I purchased local tobacco wholesale and supplied it to other places. We were young at that time; we could endure harsh conditions. . . . Yunnanese often say you may die but you cannot be poor [*side qiongbude*]. If you die from trading, people will not laugh at you; but if you die from poverty, people will laugh at you."

Yue Dashu's words and his story demonstrate Yunnanese mercantile consciousness and their exceptional risk-taking spirit in this transnational enterprise. Although caravan trade was a lucrative business, unexpected situations, such as overstaying in Burma, required much spending. While stimulating the local village economy, it also resulted in the development of friendships based on reciprocity between traders and villagers. In Yue Dashu's case, the Indian master sought advice from him whenever he traded his cattle in Thailand thereafter.

Tangge

Tangge was Ae Maew's cousin.[16] In 1958, at age fourteen, he fled from Tengchong to Burma with many members of his extended family. Like many other fellow refugees who had originally belonged to the landlord class while in Yunnan, he was compelled to pick up whatever jobs were available to him. The most common occupations included farming, joining the KMT guerrillas, being muleteers or petty traders, and teaching at Chinese schools. In Tangge's case, he worked in a textile factory and then a tea factory in northern Shan State until 1970. Afterward, he took up trade in rotating markets (*zhuan gai/jie*),[17] a common engagement among

---

16. *Tangge* means senior cousin; he is of my parents' generation. However, I followed Ae Maew in addressing him as Tangge. I had interviews with Tangge in Ae Maew's house (Taunggyi) in 2005 and then at Tangge's home (Pinlong) in 2007.

17. Yunnanese pronounce it *zhuan gai* instead of *zhuan jie*, which is the Mandarin pronunciation.

migrant Yunnanese. He purchased goods from Pinlong or Taunggyi and sold them in the mountain villages of the Pinlong area. He explained:

"A mountain region was divided into several parts. Each part had a marketplace [*gai/jie*] that was open every five days. Traders went to a different market each day to sell their goods. I left around three o'clock in the morning; the market closed at noon. I returned home around three o'clock in the afternoon. . . . Every five days I went to Pinlong to replenish my stocks [which took two days round trip], and every fifteen days I traveled to Taunggyi to get larger stocks. . . . I used to go with three to five other traders with twenty to thirty mules. For short-distance trade, one person could lead five to ten mules. . . .[18] We left our mules in Pinlong and took a private jeep to Taunggyi, which took about five hours. Sometimes I stayed one night in Taunggyi; sometimes two nights; it depended on how the replenishment was processed. After returning to Pinlong by jeep again, I would load the goods on my mules and go back home."

Trading to areas of ethnic minorities was a popular undertaking among Yunnanese Chinese for centuries (Giersch 2006, 168–80; Hill 1998, 46–47, Skinner 1964). In this venture they became the middlemen for selling lowland commodities (such as textiles, needles, salt, salted fish, pots, and western medicines) to the highland, and hill products (such as hides, herbs, and opium) to the valley. Petty traders mostly traveled short distances with one or a few loaded mules, and rich merchants engaged in long-distance trips with organized caravans (Giersch 2006, 175). Traders of the former category often traded to several markets within a certain area, as Tangge described. These markets, called rotating markets, were held every five days by taking turns. This system may have started very early in southwestern China and upper mainland Southeast Asia.[19] Even today, rotating markets exist in rural Shan State in Burma.

Tangge said that prior to 1964, most wholesale merchandise in Taunggyi consisted of Burmese products, but afterward, smuggled Thai goods

---

18. Tangge's and Yue Dashu's references to the numbers of mules that one could lead for short-distance trade vary. This may be primarily due to different denotations of "short distance." The single trip mentioned by Tangge took only one day and was relatively short. Road and security conditions could be other factors.

19. There are records of rotating markets in the late-Ming *Xinanyi fengtuji* (You 1994, 366–67). Giersch suggests that they originated among the Tai (2006, 167).

predominated. In 1972, Tangge began to undertake long-distance trade to Thailand. He transported animal hides, raw opium, jade stones, and coffee beans to Thailand and carried Thai textiles back to Burma. In accordance with other informants, he confirmed that Thai textiles were popular in Burma. One meter of good cloth that cost about one hundred baht could be sold for three times the price in Burma. He said:

"Caravans gathered in Xunding before setting off to Thailand. . . . Sometimes there would be one hundred to two hundred mules in Xunding; sometimes the number was over one thousand; but most of the time it was around four to five hundred. . . .

"In the beginning, it was quite safe. There were not so many rebel groups. Traders only needed to pay regulated passage fees to them. But when the number of rebels increased, conflicts among them occurred from time to time. Some rebels were not disciplined and robbed traders. Consequently, traders needed to hire escort troops for safety. The most powerful ethnic military groups were the [KMT] Third and Fifth Armies and Khun Sa's forces. . . .

"Caravans did not have fixed places for rest at night. It depended on the situation. . . . There were different mountain routes. They had to ask for information all the time wherever they went [*yibian zou yibian tanlu*]. If there were Burmese troops, they had to take detours. . . . Only big traders rode horses; small traders had to walk. . . .

"Caravans engaged in trade all year round. During the rainy season, the economic benefits were much higher. Many self-employed porters who joined the trade during the dry season had to stop in the rainy season; this gave the caravan traders better margins [because of reduced competition]. Moreover, in the rainy season, the Burmese army was less active. . . . [Nevertheless,] it was very dangerous to cross rivers during the rainy season. Rafts capsized easily. Also, it was very difficult to climb up and down the mountain routes."

When caravans reached the border adjacent to Thailand, the Thai Border Patrol Police (BPP) would let them enter the country. There was an informal agreement between the BPP and the ethnic troops along the border to let the caravans through. Several KMT villages were entry bases for Yunnanese caravan traders from Burma. Many traders would go to Mae Aw, Piang Luang, Arunotai, Xincun / Ban Mai Nongbour, or Mae Salong and pretend to be village residents so they could apply for a permit from the BPP to go to Chiang Mai or Chiang Rai to purchase Thai merchandise.[20] Xincun was a major caravan post in the 1970s and 1980s. Old villagers described it as a bustling town where the lights were never turned off even during the night [*buyecheng*]. There were always hundreds of mules entering or leaving the village. Traders and muleteers frequented gambling houses, food shops, and general stores during their stay. The traders left their mules in the village and went to Chiang Mai by car.

Tangge was a small trader with three mules. Some of his goods from Thailand were given to his wife to sell in the Pinlong *hmaungkho* market; the rest were sold to other local traders. He said that he was not able to make a fortune from the trade. The goods taken on by his wife were confiscated by the Burmese local officials twice. Moreover, he and most traders were badly hit by repeated demonetization of the kyat during the socialist era.

By the mid-1980s, following the opening of the Chinese market, many Yunnanese migrants in Burma began smuggling between Burma and Yunnan. Chinese commodities were cheaper than Thai commodities. One informant pointed out that the price of Chinese textiles was only about one-third the price of Thai textiles, although the Thai merchandise was of better quality. While Chinese goods were imported secretly to Burma, Burmese natural resources, such as teak and jade stones, were smuggled to Yunnan. In 1986, Tangge switched his trading routes to Yunnan for the jade trade. He bought jade stones and entrusted them to private car drivers for transportation to Ruili, a Yunnanese border town. He then went to Ruili to pick up the stones and sold them there or farther north to Tengchong with the help of relatives. After being a closed economy for several decades, the Chinese welcomed the renewed importation of the much-beloved jade stones from Burma, often called *feicui*.[21] Tangge engaged in the trade for five years and was able to make a good profit. (However, most of his saved

---

20. Most Yunnanese refugees in Thailand did not obtain legal status until the mid-1980s. Prior to that, their movement was confined to the villages. Whenever they wanted to leave their villages, they had to apply for a permit.

21. Jade is a general term that indicates two different varieties: nephrite and jadeite. Scientifically speaking, the distinction is based on their respective chemical composition, density, and specific gravity (Hemrich 1966, 6). In terms of economic value and aesthetic preference, jadeite is usually more appreciated than nephrite for its rarity, more vivid green shades, and finer translucency. The jade procured in Burma is jadeite. The term *feicui* denotes the transparent green of high-quality jadeite.

money was wasted by his third son as mentioned in chapter 2.) Afterward, he retired and devoted himself to Chinese education.

Zhao Dashu

While the mule caravans provided the primary method for plying trade by land between northern Thailand and the Shan State of Burma during the Burmese socialist period, water shipment—by sea or river—was another way of trafficking. The accounts of Zhao Dashu[22] provide rich information about one major trafficking route by water, the manner of shipment, commodities traded, and the intriguing politics involved.

Zhao Dashu escaped from Yunnan to Burma in 1957 at age fifteen. After arriving there, he worked for several years as a muleteer for a maternal uncle based in Tangyan. The experience trained him in the organization of the long-distance trade between Burma and Thailand. Moreover, he managed to obtain both Burmese and Thai citizenship through connections with a Shan headman and the KMT Third Army respectively.[23] His legal status facilitated his transnational movement. From 1964 to 1969, he explored the trading possibilities at different points along the Thai-Burmese border, which led him to embark on trafficking between Mae Hongson (northern Thailand) and Loikaw (Kayah State, Burma) via water conveyance in 1970. Zhao Dashu was one of the pioneers on this trade route; trafficking via Mae Hongson was not popular until the mid-1970s. His good relationships with a Karenni (Kayah) militia group, the Kayah governor, and other local officials and policemen contributed to the success of his business, which lasted until 1986. His involvement was initiated by his visit to a Karenni insurgent group on the Thai border in Mae Hongson Province in 1969. He recounted the experience:

"I took two men with me to visit a Karenni insurgent base. Fortunately I was able to meet their chief military officer. He had been to university

---

22. I have known Zhao Dashu since 2009. The narratives quoted here were from several interviews given in 2009 and 2010 at his home in Taiwan.

23. The KMT armies that retreated to northern Thailand were in part recruited by the Thai government from the late 1960s to the early 1980s to fight against the Thai Communists. As reward for their military participation, the Thai government granted the troops and their dependents legal status. Many Yunnanese traders connected with the KMT armies took the opportunity to obtain a Thai identity card by reporting themselves as dependents of the troops.

and was a man of politics. He could speak Shan.[24] I told him my trade plan. He was sincere and gave me two guarantees. He said: 'Firstly, it is safe to trade in our area. Nobody will rob you even if you carry a bag of gold. Secondly, you need some connection with the Burmese authorities. The chief policeman in Loikaw is a good man. You can make friends with him.' I was very happy to receive these two guarantees and went to visit that chief policeman in Loikaw through the arrangement of a Karenni friend who had been an adjutant of the local chief of Loikaw during the colonial period. The chief policeman, that Karenni militia officer, and my Karenni friend had all worked for that chief. After independence, one [the chief policeman] chose to serve the government, one joined an insurgent group, and one became a businessman.

"The chief policeman had studied in Japan. He could also speak Shan. He was *kapya* [mixed blood]; his father was Karenni and mother Shan. His wife was also Shan. Later he became the acting governor of Kayah State until his retirement. He was not corrupt and helped my trade a great deal. During his incumbency, he only asked for one British-made jeep from me, which cost around twelve thousand kyat at that time [1975]. In addition, I also knew a military commander who was Karenni too. That commander had been stationed in Lashio earlier. His wife was Shan from Lashio. I had known them when they were living there."

Like Mr. Li's, Zhao Dashu's narration points to an intriguing picture of political division as well as connection. While politically the local authorities and ethnic rebels were against each other, they were connected in other respects, such as personal friendship from the past and economic interests in the present. Zhao Dashu's proposal to trade via Mae Hongson was warmly welcomed by that Karenni rebel officer, who was aware of the potential economic gain from levied taxes. Likewise, the chief policeman was willing to help. Burmese society was badly in need of smuggled goods from neighboring countries to satisfy people's basic consumption demands. Local authorities understood that the relaxation of the black-market trade was necessary in order to curb potential public riots (Kyaw 2001, 195). In addition, they obtained "extra" income from black marketeers. Whether

---

24. Like many Yunnanese traders, Zhao Dashu is fluent in Shan, which is the lingua franca in Shan State. He learned the language while staying in Tangyan. It was useful for his connections with several key persons in Kayah State.

they were state-recognized troops (the KKY), the Burmese army, local authorities, or ethnic insurgents, all participated in the contraband trade directly or indirectly.

The following narration by Zhao Dashu gave detailed information about the trade route he resorted to via Mae Hongson and the manner of water shipment:

"We purchased most of the merchandise in Chiang Mai and transported it to Mae Hongson for further smuggling across the border. In the early days, the road conditions were very bad. During the monsoon season, the road was not accessible, and we had to depend on air transport, which was more costly. This situation lasted for five or six years. Afterward, the roads were improved, but sometimes it still took more than three days to reach Mae Hongson during the rainy season. We bought the goods that Burma didn't have, such as sarongs, tin plates, monosodium glutamate, soap, and other consumer goods. The sarongs were mostly made in Indonesia, of better quality than the Thai. In Chiang Mai, I handed the commodities to two companies run by Chaozhou/Teochiu merchants for transport to Mae Hongson."

The goods were transported by cars to Huile, a river village three kilometers from downtown Mae Hongson. From there the goods were loaded on boats and transported via the Pai River. Transporters paid underground taxes to the Thai police before leaving Mae Hongson and then to the Karenni rebel group after reaching the border. In the first year, Zhao Dashu used long, narrow wooden boats for shipment. Each boat could be loaded with one thousand kilos of commodities and required seven to eight rowers. Usually, Zhao Dashu's goods needed two boats. From Mae Hongson, the boats flowed westward with the current and reached the border in two hours. Passing the border, it took another three hours continuing westward to reach the Salween River. The junction was Sopai, from where the boats went southward for two to three hours to Hpasawng. From there, the goods were transported by a big truck to Loikaw, which took about one day. On the way back, the boats went against the current and took six hours from Hpasawng to Sopai and ten hours from Sopai to Mae Hongson.[25]

---

25. An alternative route was to bring the goods from Sopai across the Salween River to Ywathit, where they were then loaded on oxen carts and transported to Bawlakhe and then to Loikaw. This land journey took two days in the dry season.

In 1971, the wooden boats were replaced by iron boats installed with motors, making the transport faster—one hour from Mae Hongson to Sopai and twenty minutes from Sopai to Hpasawng. On the way back, it took one hour from Hpasawng to Sopai and three hours from Sopai to Mae Hongson. However, the iron boats were too light and easily capsized. Zhao Dashu thus switched back to wooden boats that were installed with motors.

In Loikaw, Zhao Dashu opened a wholesale general merchandise store and hired his nephew to run it. There were about twenty households of Fujianese and Cantonese and ten households of Yunnanese in the town. They all ran general stores, but Zhao Dashu's store was the largest one, and it provided wholesale goods to the others. Apart from the commodities that were smuggled in from Thailand, the shop sold Burmese food products including rice, oil, salt, noodles, fish sauce, chilies, salted fish, and turmeric powder, which were purchased in Mandalay and Meiktila.

Zhao Dashu had four vehicles for transportation. From his shop he sold and delivered sundries and other Thai commodities to shops as far away as Mandalay, Meiktila, Taunggyi, Lashio, and Mawchi. The last point was famous as the largest tungsten site in the world (Steinberg 2010, 31). The mines employed thousands of miners who required a large amount of consumer goods. Zhao Dashu said that his store needed one large truckload of replenishments each month to satisfy the demands from the places listed.

Apart from trafficking via the Mae Hongson trade route, Zhao Dashu conducted business in other places. He purchased a fishing boat with 220,000 kyat that was used to transport gasoline and oxen (purchased in Yangon) to Mawlamyine (Moulmein). Zhao Dashu purchased gasoline from the government through his connection with an immigration officer in Yangon. The government gasoline was very cheap, but one needed connections for quantity purchases. The gasoline was resold to fishermen in Mawlamyine. The oxen were driven from Mawlamyine to two border posts—Myawaddy (connected to Mae Sot in Tak Province in Thailand) and Payathonsu (connected to Sangkhla Buri in Kanchanaburi Province in Thailand). Zhao Dashu's men paid taxes to the Karen and Mon ethnic insurgents in these two places. One big ox was taxed fifty baht, and a smaller one thirty baht. The animals were sold here or later in Bangkok.

Myawaddy–Mae Sot and Payathonsu–Sangkhla Buri were two trafficking access points during the Burmese socialist period. The former was used by porters, mostly Karens. Since the 1980s, many Yunnanese jade traders have also resorted to this route for the transportation of jade stones by hiring Karen porters. A male porter could carry as much as fifty kilos and a female as much as thirty kilos. At the height of the trading season, the number of porters passing through this route each day could reach one thousand (Boucaud and Boucaud 1992, 61). As for the second route, it is commonly known as the Three Pagodas Pass and has existed since ancient times for economic, cultural, and military exchanges. During the socialist period, traders, including Mon, Fujianese, Cantonese, and Yunnanese, transported goods purchased in Bangkok to Burma via this pass by car. Burmese commodities, such as oxen, antiques, teakwood, and goose feathers, were smuggled to Thailand via these two access points.[26]

It is obvious that Zhao Dashu's connections with different Thai and Burmese authorities and ethnic insurgents greatly facilitated the expansion of his trade to various locations. He said that going to a new place was like traveling for fun. He often made new friends through old friends' introductions, expanding his network. His pioneering status on the Mae Hongson–Loikaw route and active interactions with various political powers strengthened his politico-economic role. Since the late 1970s, General Li of the KMT Third Army and Khun Sa competed with each other for trade routes via Mae Hongson Province. Fighting flared up from time to time. In order to ensure the flow of border trade, the KMT and Khun Sa repeatedly engaged in negotiations. Zhao Dashu was proud to say that he was invited three times by both sides to act as a mediator. In short, the pursuit of economic interests in underground trade is split between intense confrontation and connection among involved parties. Informants' accounts repeatedly attest to the fact that there is no absolute line between friends and enemies. Zhao Dashu moved his family to Taiwan in 1980, but he continued his cross-border business and remained mostly in Burma and Thailand until the mid-1990s.

---

26. Zhao Dashu and a few other informants also mentioned the smuggling of large amounts of Thai consumer goods from Ranong to Kawthoung during the socialist era. The contraband goods were further shipped by sea or land to Mawlamyine and Yangon. The traders on this route include Fujianese, Cantonese, Mon, Burmese, and Yunnanese. I have not been to the south for fieldwork and cannot determine these traders' engagement. Their involvement may have been primarily linked to their geographical residency. The number of Yunnanese traders was said to be few.

A Transnational Popular Realm

While the large stretch of migrant Yunnanese trading territory discussed in this chapter was seen as an untamed frontier by the central states of both Thailand and Burma, it was in practice an economic core for the Yunnanese merchants and also the heart of the black market for Burmese society—in fact, its economic mainstay. Time and again, informants stressed that their engagement in the risky transborder trade was compelled by external circumstances. Their lives were at stake as they faced a desperate situation that pushed them to the edge of liminality. This arose initially from their marginal positioning as unrecognized refugees from abroad and later from the politically divided frontier in which they were situated. One way to confront the state of double liminality was to venture into this untamed region by taking up cross-border trade by mule caravans or by boats. By doing so, they not only retrieved the traditional knowledge related to this activity but also (unconsciously) broke away from their own ethnocentric perception of viewing the borderlands as "barbarous." Their economic participation required a reciprocal relationship with the ethnic forces and local people. There were rules to learn and respect, although the process was replete with fragmentation and unpredictable inconsistency. Zhang Dadie's words quoted at the beginning of the chapter best characterize this reflection.

With reference to Tsing's discussion of the Dayaks in forested southeastern Kalimantan (2005), the Indonesian government and international corporations, with their overwhelming political and economic control, jointly turned the land into a "savage frontier." A strategy they have applied is to promote the land as comparable to the American Wild West, waiting to be opened up, with resources to be exploited. In their operation, the indigenous are dehumanized and their tradition is erased. In contrast, the Thai-Burmese borderlands we have examined in the narratives above were not areas of complete deregulation, although the government and Yunnanese did perceive them as barbarous. Among a range of intersecting parties, the Burmese authorities made up only one entity, and not the predominant one. The other parties included many ethnic armed groups and civilian traders. All the involved parties were aware that none of them was powerful enough to lead and that complete chaos would benefit no one. Despite frictions and clashes among them, they tried to maintain some kind of a "middle ground" in the region in order to allow economic engagement.

Considering their liminality, the Yunnanese migrant traders' economic agency was outstanding. Regardless of the Burmese socialist regime's isolation from the international arena, the Yunnanese traders found their own way to reach out to the outside world. Neither borders nor national policies could absolutely bar them, physically or mentally. The prevalence of illegal trade opened the window of exchange and saved the country from acute deprivation resulting from the "Burmese Way to Socialism." By the early 1970s, illegal trade already dominated Burma's economy (Kyaw Yin Hlaing 2001, 205). It was tied to the everyday life of the nation—that of civilians as well as state officials.

Geographically speaking, the great majority of the Yunnanese migrants were located on the peripheral frontiers of Burma and Thailand. Yet, economically speaking, they transformed the region into a central area for transnational trade from which smuggled goods were further distributed to widespread locations. Their movements for migration and traveling commerce transgressed the national boundaries of China, Burma, and Thailand, while at the same time connecting them to a wider market economy. In consequence, this resulted in what Roger Rouse calls "transnational migrant circuits," which maintain "spatially extended relationships as actively and effectively as the ties that link them to their neighbors" (1991, 14, 13). The concerned borderlands therefore were not essentialized negatively as wastelands, backward and lawless in a conventional sense, but they embodied paradoxical features—peripheral and central, separate and connected.

In the case of the Yunnanese migrants, their mobility and links with faraway relatives, the KMT forces, other militias, and the state agencies of Burma and Thailand in effect constituted a transnational configuration. Taking the perspective from borderlanders at the "interstices of transnational and transcultural processes" (Thongchai 2003, 23), I suggest that the cross-border economic practices of the migrant Yunnanese constituted a *transnational popular realm* (*kuajing minjian*) that formed an informal oppositional power against national bureaucracies, while incorporating varied state agencies. The concept of "popular realm" (*minjian*) is derived from Mayfair Yang's work (1994), in which she applies the concept to the analysis of the production of *guanxi* (social connections) in everyday activities in China. She points out the emergence of an unofficial order, known in Chinese as *minjian*, that is generated through infinite weaving and spreading of personal connections and group formations and its social force vis-à-vis the Chinese central government. Dealing with a diasporic community, I adopt Yang's use of the concept, but I apply it to explicate the transnational rather than simply the national. The composition of *minjian* is thus predicated on the people's movement and their interconnection, instead of being truncated by the national boundary. This is in contrast to the viewpoint in the international arena that holds the nation-state as the most widely accepted political entity.

While this popular realm enjoyed informal power in comparison to the power exercised by the governments of Burma and Thailand, it also incorporated a range of official agencies in the course of its operations. Nevertheless, it was not a united popular realm, powerful enough to challenge the central states; rather, it was crisscrossed with factions and characterized by intense competition. Its strength was derived from economic force rather than political power. Alongside the government institutions of these two countries, the mercantile spirit of the Yunnanese migrants created its own civil mechanisms, composed of prevailing networks. As a result, their activity space was not defined by borders but by their transnational connectivity. Moreover, in politico-economic terms, it was not restricted to the fringes of the Thai-Burmese frontiers, but extended to comprise a wide territory within both countries. The interacting forces during the trading process embraced different scales of geopolitical and geo-social entities, ranging from local, regional, national, to transnational.

Seen from a long historical perspective, the long-distance trade, especially by mule caravans, supported the demand and supply of consumer goods in upper mainland Southeast Asia for centuries. Despite the vicissitudes of regional politics, the flow of commodities persisted across "natural and social landscapes" by means of both "regulated and subversive travel," in James Clifford's words (1992, 109). This persistence highlights the economic agency of borderland traders, which originated in their urge to earn a livelihood, and affirms the argument given by Michiel Baud and William van Schendel: "People will ignore borders whenever it suits them.... Local inhabitants cross them whenever services or products are cheaper or more attractive on the other side; and traders are quick to take advantage of price and tax differentials" (1997, 211). Relying on their economic tradition and local knowledge, the migrant Yunnanese traders handled with notable success the risky military-cum-economic engagement that played a major role in the Burmese economy during the socialist period.

6

Transcending Gendered Geographies

Yunnanese Women Traders

Do not cut grape vines for firewood. / Do not marry off your daughter to a muleteer. / Bride [of a muleteer] on the 30th eve, / her husband leaves at dawn of the first [the next day].

—quoted in Wang and Zhang 1993, 220–21[1]

Eldest sister came home, tears in her eyes. / Sullenly she related her stories to her parents. / Do not marry your daughter to a man of Heshun. / During a period of ten years, the couple is together for half a month.

—*Yangwentun xiaoyin*; quoted in Dong 2000, 30[2]

I call my son once again, / Listen to my words carefully. / It is hard to raise you; / Aged only seventeen, eighteen, or nineteen, / You are setting off on a long journey. / See you again perhaps in three or four years. (ibid.)[3]

---

1. This is a muleteer song (*ganmage*); the author is unknown. The Chinese lyrics are: "Kanchai mokan putaoteng / Yangnyu mojia ganmaren / Sanshi wanshang zuoxifu / Chuyi zaoshang tichumen." The lyrics vary slightly from place to place.

2. Heshun is a border township of Tengchong, famous for the exodus of its men to Burma for trade. *Yangwentun xiaoyin*, a manuscript compiled around the Xianfeng era (1850–1861 CE) during the Qing dynasty, was kept at the library of Heshun (Dong Ping 2000, 45). It records many local poems telling stories of separation of family members due to men's economic engagement. The Chinese lyrics of the quoted poem are: "Dajie huijia lei wangwang / Choumei kulian su dieniang / Younyu mojia heshunxiang / Shinian shougua banyueshuang."

3. The Chinese lyrics are: "Jiao yisheng wodeer / Xiting genyou / Feirongyi / Fuyangni / Shi qi ba jiu / Zong quyuan / Yizhike / Sinian sanqiu."

These are a few old songs and poems in Yunnan that vividly describe the stressful situation faced by women left behind by their husbands and sons for the sake of long-distance trade. In contrast to the mobility of Yunnanese men engaging in this type of trade, Yunnanese women[4] were traditionally confined to domestic life and restricted from the public sphere (*buke paotouloumian*). Men were considered the active participants in economic undertaking, although women (especially those in the lower class) in practice also contributed to the family income by weaving, making clothes, raising animals, and working on farms (Fei and Chang 1948; Hsu 1967; Johnson 1975; Topley 1975). While men were away, many of them also set up parallel homes in different places (Dong 2000). Many Yunnanese women were oftentimes separated from their husbands and sons and possibly in sole charge of household responsibilities. It is a pity that historical records do not leave us information about women's life stories. However, we may presume that married life was tough for them.

Differing from this conventional picture of restricted women's movement in Yunnan, migrant Yunnanese women in Burma have generally been compelled to be mobile as well as economically active in order to sustain everyday family life in the face of numerous vicissitudes. My field data show that in many cases women are the actual household managers, as their husbands are unable to provide economic support because of military engagement, loss in trade, or drug addiction. In contrast to the prominence of men's military activities and engagement in the large-scale mule caravan trade, the women's life experiences are less visible and easily overlooked. Nevertheless, these women have played an essential role in the maintenance of their families by participation in different types of economic activities, including long-distance trade, thereby breaking the conventional restraint on women's movement. These women straddle household and economic undertakings and the gap between restrictive gendered ideologies and economic responsibilities. While earning personal autonomy, their economic practices also generate familial tensions and feelings of ambivalence in their self-identity.

In line with the findings about women traders in a range of places in Asia, Africa, America, and Europe presented in the volume edited by Linda

---

4. In line with other chapters, I only refer to Yunnanese Han and Yunnanese Muslim women here.

J. Seligmann, the Yunnanese women traders in Burma are also situated "within complicated webs of social ties, institutional structures, and economic forces" (Seligmann 2001, 3) that embrace intricate factors ranging from kinship habitation, gendered ideologies, an oppressive political system, insecure socioeconomic conditions, and borderland location. Consistent with Tsing's interpretation (2005), interaction of these factors entails frictions that either facilitate or obstruct these women's participation in economic pursuit. Consequently, they lead to an ongoing process of shaping and reshaping "gendered geographies of power" (Mahler and Pessar 2001) that accommodate these women's business acumen, frustration, and pain.

How did the women carry out their economic undertakings during the grievous Ne Win regime? How have they been able to grasp new economic opportunities since 1988? How do they identify themselves as women traders and differentiate themselves from their male counterparts? And what are the tensions and creative forces involved in their mobility? The following stories highlight the economic lives of a few female traders and illuminate their agency in the face of multifarious ruptures—political, economic, and sociocultural. Their narratives not only provide insights into their lives but also into an important aspect of the social history of the Yunnanese migrants in Burma.

Qiu Dajie

In January 2006, after learning about my upcoming trip to northern Shan State's capital, Lashio, to study the border trade, a Yunnanese friend in Taiwan suggested I visit Qiu Dajie.[5] I took the same route from Mandalay to Lashio by bus as I had during my first visit in 2000. The bus was still full of passengers and goods, and the road was crowded with many trucks overloaded with import-export merchandise. Lashio is a bustling city located on the Burma Road, which leads northward to Muse, the border town adjacent to Ruili in Yunnan.[6] According to the Yunnanese

---

5. *Dajie* (senior sister) is an address for senior females of one's own generation.
6. Lashio had also been the final stop for foreigners traveling to northern Shan State until October 2013 when the government relaxed the restriction and allowed foreigners to go northward to Muse.

Association in Lashio, the total population there is around 300,000, and the Yunnanese (including the Kokang) account for 180,000 (data given in 2010). A great majority of them are involved in trade of varying scales, especially the import-export trade with China. Since the late 1980s Lashio has been the hub for the Sino-Burmese trade.

Partly inspired by the trading opportunities in Lashio, and partly pressured by her family's financial demands, Qiu Dajie has undertaken various economic activities since the mid-1980s. She was born in 1954. Her husband, originally a successful jade trader, is in jail for the second time because of his drug addiction. He was sentenced to eight years the first time, and now five years. Qiu Dajie has been the sole economic supporter of the family for more than twenty years. In early 2000, she spent a few million kyat to send her two sons to Great Britain. She did not see any future for them in Burma and was afraid that they might take on bad habits, especially drugs, if they stayed in the country. Using the pretext of further study, they went to London. All these years they have continually registered at language schools in order to stay in the UK, while working full time in restaurants and hotels. Qiu Dajie also has a daughter, who went to Taiwan for a university education. The daughter did not finish her studies but managed to obtain local residency. She now lives with her boyfriend, and they run a small breakfast shop. Coincidently, she brought her Taiwanese boyfriend back to Lashio for the Chinese New Year in 2006 while I was conducting fieldwork there. (It was only the second time she had returned home in her ten-year absence from Burma.) Over the years, I have occasionally visited the family and the daughter in Lashio and Taiwan.

Qiu Dajie now lives in a big house with a niece from a mountain village who studies at a Chinese junior high school and helps with the housework. The house is a one-story villa with a large front yard and palm trees that grow along two sides of an enclosing wall. Several kinds of herbs and vegetables commonly used in Yunnanese cuisine, such as fennel, coriander, white pepper, eggplants, and chili, grow there as well. During the Chinese New Year of 2006 the kitchen was filled with food—two big pieces of salted pork and several rows of sausages hung on a bamboo pole (Figure 6-1), and many jars of pickled vegetables and preserved soybean curd were placed on the ground—all made by Qiu Dajie. Since all her children are grown up and away from home, Qiu Dajie is relatively free. She often plays mahjong with friends, but from time to time she engages in buying

Figure 6–1. Salted pork and sausages made by Qiu Dajie

and selling crops, especially corn. In addition, she participates in many loan-bidding associations (*biaohui*) that earn much profit in interest.

Curious about Qiu Dajie's entrepreneurial spirit, whenever possible I requested that she tell me stories about her business engagement. At the beginning she often repeated the familiar statement that even three books are not enough to contain her story, but she did not reveal much content. I was hanging around nearly every day while she taught me Yunnanese cooking. Yunnanese delicacies contain varieties of ingredients, and the preparation is time-consuming. I wasn't able to remember the complex procedures, but I always enjoyed the simple tasks she handed me—peeling garlic, cutting vegetables, grinding spices, etc. Perhaps stimulated by my good appetite for her food, Qiu Dajie's narrations gradually grew richer, like the wonderful dishes she presented. She said:

"It was the external environment that pushed me to take up trade. Before getting married, I dared not go anywhere, and dared not speak to strangers. I didn't have to work. I didn't even know how to cook. My mother did everything for me. My life was easy. I met my husband when I was sixteen. We were in love for four years, but my parents didn't agree with our relationship. In the end, I eloped with him to Lashio. I was twenty years old at that time.

"My husband went to jade mines to buy jade stones. He was very capable and made a lot of money. He purchased this big house twenty-five years ago [in 1981]. He had started to take drugs at that time, but I didn't know. He was not even a cigarette smoker when I first met him." She sighed. "Drug addicts are all the same. Once they get the habit, everything goes wrong. They demand money all the time. I was only twenty-seven years old then. I still looked very young, but I already had three children. They needed my support; I couldn't abandon them.

"When my youngest child was three or four years old, I started to sell goods at the market while a maid took care of the children. I worked hard to earn money in order to raise my kids and also to meet my husband's monetary demands. I had no trading experience and was unfamiliar with the price fluctuation of *hmaungkho* goods. I began selling a small amount of commodities, such as monosodium glutamate, yarns, and some other daily consumer goods that were brought in from China and Thailand. I purchased the merchandise from wholesale dealers in Lashio. Every morning I got up around five o'clock to cook breakfast and work in the garden. I sold my goods at the market from seven o'clock in the morning until four or five o'clock in the afternoon. After returning home, I cooked again. I didn't play mahjong at that time. I had no leisure time. The children were too young.

"From the early 1990s, I started to go to Mong Hsu to buy rubies. The trade brought in a good profit in the first few years. I traveled to Mong Hsu [via Tangyan] by car—it was a small pickup truck with two benches attached to either side of the truck bed with a tarp overhead. Sometimes there were too many people in the truck; some people had no seats and had to grab hold of a bar and hang out the back. The road conditions were very bad, especially during the rainy season. Very often travelers had to hire motorcyclists to take them for some parts of the journey. When the road went downhill, it was frightening; I had to close my eyes. I was also afraid that the motorcyclist might rob me.

"After arriving in Mong Hsu, it still took one day to walk up to the ruby mines. The mountain was steep. On reaching the mines, I roamed from one pit to another to buy raw rubies. I normally purchased one to two million kyat of rubies in one trip. On the way back to Lashio, I gave my rubies wrapped in a piece of cloth to the driver who hid them in a secret place in the truck. The journey was fraught with danger. We were robbed several times. Once three armed robbers raided us. They took away the passengers' watches and money. Luckily they didn't find the rubies the driver had hidden.

"After returning to Lashio, I would wash the raw rubies and polish them with oil. I divided them into different small bags according to size. In the first two years, I sold my rubies only in Lashio to Chinese and local buyers. I earned two hundred thousand kyat after the first trip. I was very happy with the profit. Later on friends told me that the profit would be much higher if I took them to Ruili or Tachileik. The latter in particular was important for the ruby trade, as dealers came from Thailand. During the next two years I often traveled to Tachileik to sell rubies despite the long journey. Sometimes I went by airplane; other times by car. If I took the airplane, I would give my ruby package with my name on it to an airport staff member who would arrange its safe transportation. Of course, I paid for the arrangement. After the plane arrived in the Tachileik airport, a customs agent would pick up the package and deliver it to the address I had given in advance. If I went by car, I gave my rubies to the driver for safekeeping. It took a few days to reach Tachileik by vehicle. At night, passengers stayed at small hotels or villagers' houses. The cost was not much. The accommodation was rudimentary and dirty. Women slept together, separated from the men. The journey was harsh, really harsh [*leine zashilei*]."[7]

"Were female traders bothered by male traders during the journey?" I asked.

"No. Not if women behaved in a serious manner [*yiben zhengjing*] and did not joke with the men. Many women, including Shans, Burmans, Yunnanese, and other ethnic groups, participated in this venture regardless of how much danger was involved. I'm not afraid of death. I'm only afraid of not making enough money to support my children."

Qiu Dajie was in the ruby trade for four years. Afterward, for three or four years she was involved in carrying money for loans to the jade mines in Hpakant. This business is referred to as *zuo huishui*. Each time she carried from a few million to twenty or thirty million kyat packed in cartons. She said:

"I collaborated with my relatives in Mandalay in this business. They provided most of the capital, and I was in charge of carrying the money to the jade mines. It took one day and one night from Mandalay to Mogaung by train, and five to eight hours, depending on the road conditions, from Mogaung to Hpakant by car—it was a van with two passengers in the front seat and four other passengers at the back. Sometimes the car got stuck in mud during the rainy season. When encountering such a problem, the passengers had to find accommodation in a nearby village for a night. Every time I stayed in Hpakant four to five days, sometimes more than ten days. I only lent money to familiar traders and mining bosses, but I still encountered bad debts. Once I lent 470 million kyat to a mining boss referred to me by a friend. The borrower went bankrupt. I was unable to collect the debt and had to cover it alone."

"Where did you get the nerve for this risky business?" I asked.

"If you don't take risks, you starve [*nibuzuo yao efan*]," Qiu Dajie replied.

The interest rate was 20 percent at the beginning, and later reduced to 15 percent, then 10 percent, and then 5 percent, following the increasing

---

7. Qiu Dajie first traveled from Mong Hsu to Taunggyi by motorcycle and car and then to Tachileik by car or air.

number of creditors. Moreover, the Inwa Bank in Hpakant was established in 1999, which further hurt the business of underground lending (chapter 7). Qiu Dajie quit this business and started another venture—purchasing Chinese clothes in Ruili and selling them in Mandalay and Taunggyi. Since the late 1980s, the Burma-China border trade has been flourishing. Chinese consumer goods flow into Burma, while Burmese natural resources flow out to China. Before the Burmese government legalized border trade with China in 1988, the commerce between both sides operated underground. However, as informants point out, smuggling has remained rampant even since 1988, owing to arbitrary regulations and heavy taxation.[8]

In the last few years, Qiu Dajie has not traveled to Ruili as frequently as before—only about once a month. Instead, she spends more time playing mahjong, which has become a popular leisure activity among Yunnanese women in Burma since around 2000. Before that, only men, seen as the "official" breadwinners of their families, had the privilege of playing this game. This change indicates the women's growing economic power as well as their autonomy in arranging their lives.

Although Qiu Dajie no longer toils on business trips as much as before, she does not keep her money idle. She invests all her capital in loan-bidding associations, which are commonly referred to as *hui* (rotating credit). Such associations widely exist in Chinese societies to provide an informal mechanism for capital flow among the populace, whereas in Burma they function as an underground banking system.[9] Qiu Dajie participates in more than forty *hui*; half of them she organized herself. A *hui* is composed of a group of participants (mostly women) who contribute money periodically and wait for their turn to use the funds. The head of a *hui* (*huitou*) predetermines the minimal amount of interest in bidding and the interval for a bid. Qiu Dajie explains the mechanism using an example of a *hui* of 50,000 kyat and forty participants. Its minimal interest in bidding is 12,000 kyat, and the bid frequency is twice per month, on the first and fifteenth of every lunar month. There is no regulated limit for the maximal interest,

---

8. The major export commodities from China via Ruili include electronics, machinery, industrial and construction materials, textiles, cotton yarn, consumer goods, and fertilizers; those from Burma via Muse are agricultural produce, gems, fish, timber, minerals, and rubber. A large part of the traded merchandise has remained illegal (Chang 2013).

9. Similar mechanisms also exist in many other societies, especially in the developing world. F. J. A. Bouman refers to them as "rotating savings and credit associations" (1983).

but Qiu Dajie said that usually it does not go higher than 20,000 kyat with a *hui* of 50,000 kyat. The bidding targets the interest. Those who need capital for investment compete in bidding. The one who offers the highest amount of interest wins the bid and collects all the money contributed by the other members. After winning a bid, the participant cannot bid in the following rounds and has to contribute the full amount of *hui* money (*huiqian*), that is, 50,000 kyat, each time until the whole cycle of the *hui* completes. Those who have not collected the funds from their turns pay only a reduced amount. Take the tenth round of the *hui* of 50,000 kyat for an example. The offered amounts of interest in bidding range from 13,000 to 17,000 kyat. The one who offers 17,000 kyat wins the bid. Each of the previous bid-winners has to pay 50,000 kyat. The rest pay 33,000 kyat—the full amount of the *hui* money minus the highest amount of offered interest. The total collected amount is 50,000 kyat times eight[10] (people), plus 33,000 kyat times thirty-one (people), which amounts to 1,423,000 kyat.

The founding of a *hui* is based on trust. Usually the head of a *hui* invites only people who are familiar to her to participate. However, there is still the risk of bad debts, either from the head of a *hui* or other members. Qiu Dajie once encountered bad debts from a *hui* member who had collected the funds from her turn. That member claimed bankruptcy and disappeared. Being the head of the *hui*, Qiu Dajie had to cover the debts. Qiu Dajie commented: "Business contains risks. If you are afraid of risks, you can't make profits [yao zhuanqian jiuyou fengxian pafengxian jiu zhuanbuliaoqian]." Qiu Dajie participates in more than forty *hui* and sometimes bids for three *hui* a day.

What does Qiu Dajie's story tell? How do we interpret her business acumen and mobility in relation to her gender? In a paper tackling the issue of gender, transnationalism, and migration, Mahler and Pessar (2001) propose the concept "gendered geographies of power" to explore gender issues in migration. They advocate the analysis of people's social agency from both corporal and cognitive dimensions with reference to the

---

10. It is the tenth round, but the one who wins the bid does not pay, and the *hui* organizer pays a reduced amount. (The head of a *hui* collects the funds of the first round contributed by the other members with a full amount of *hui* money, but for later rounds she only pays the same reduced amount as that of those who have not collected their funds. In other words, the head enjoys the privilege of an interest-free loan.)

multiple hierarchies of power within which they are situated. They stress the need to see "gender . . . not as a set of static structures or roles but as an ongoing process that is experienced through an array of social institutions from the family to the state" (ibid., 442). Its operation involves "multiple *spatial* and *social* scales . . . across transnational terrains" (445). In another paper, Pessar and Mahler (2003) apply this concept to examine the role of the state and the social imaginary in gendering transnational processes. In the face of the low visibility of women in migration studies, the framework is a useful reference. It also corresponds to several authors' emphasis on a study of gender and space that examines how gender relations affect women's and men's movement and how movement reinforces or transforms the migrants' gendered ideology (e.g., Hayami 2007; Hondagneu-Sotelo 1994; Kaplan 1996; Massey 1994; Tsing 1993).

Drawing on Mahler and Pessar, we may ask: What are the cognitive changes underlying Qiu Dajie's corporal movement? How far does travel help her to break through the conventional hierarchies of power that are imposed upon women? How does she perceive her crossing not only geographical borders, but figuratively also over the borders originating from the female body, the family, and the Yunnanese community? Is there a new configuration of gender relations?

Without doubt, Qiu Dajie's experiences in trade demonstrate an entrepreneurial penchant that drives her to grasp different economic opportunities regardless of possible perils. Her repeated emphasis on risk-taking illustrates a daring spirit consistent with the trading ethos of the male merchants that characterizes the mule caravan trade. When encumbered with difficulties, she overcomes them and starts her business again and again. Her long-distance traveling in effect breaks through conventional spatial limitations on women. Nevertheless, instead of founding her economic practices on a desire for self-fulfillment, Qiu Dajie attributes her motivation to external causes resulting from unstable politico-economic conditions on the one hand and her husband's failure to provide sufficiently for the family's needs on the other. Once she said to me: "Women with good husbands do not need to venture out to make a living. The Cantonese and Fujianese came to Burma earlier and have built up their economic foundation. Most of them own shops, and their women do not have to travel for long distances to make a living, but help their husbands at home." Therefore, Qiu Dajie's workforce engagement is primarily based on familial obligations to be a good mother and a good wife. This phenomenon is consistent with Seligmann's observation: "Frequently, women will enter the market as an extension of household tasks they perform as well as to make possible the economic survival of those households and, particularly, to secure the survival of their children" (2001, 3). In the same vein, Johanna Lessinger (2001, 73) refers to the idea of "sacrificial motherhood" as the central cultural value that impels women's economic participation in south India, and Charles F. Keyes (1984), with reference to Buddhist texts, interprets Thai women's economic pursuit as predicated on the role of nurturing mother.

Regardless of Qiu Dajie's economic success, she laments her marriage and is aware of Yunnanese moral constraints on women. She said: "We Yunnanese are conservative. Even when women marry bad husbands, they don't divorce them. I don't like to stay in this house. I'm depressed with the relationship with my husband. I don't want to see him. Yet, I still visit him at the prison twice every month with cooked food. If I didn't go, my conscience would feel uneasy. But every time we meet we quarrel."

Paradoxically, although Qiu Dajie had the nerve to elope with her husband and risk her life to engage in trade, she will not divorce him for fear of transgressing Yunnanese tradition. Didn't elopement and economic pursuit via long-distance traveling also deviate from the Yunnanese tradition?

Several times Qiu Dajie expressed regret for her elopement. She said that because of it, her parents severed their relationship with her, and she did not visit her natal family until ten years after her marriage. Moreover, she sees her daughter repeating the same mistake. She does not approve of her daughter's relationship with her Taiwanese boyfriend, who has a ten-year-old daughter from his previous marriage. She is angry that this man does not intend to hold a public wedding with her daughter, and she considers him unreliable. She is much concerned about her daughter's reputation among the Yunnanese community. Accordingly, breaking away from the spatial confinement of women is acceptable when it is justified by familial demands; however, transgression against the gendered confinement of women for one's own sake is not. Despite the fact that women's economic pursuits indicate inner strength and creativity, their rationale is determined by the obligatory norms of being good daughters, wives, and mothers. (Ae Maew's story also attests to the same rationale.) In other words, their economic performance is not initiated by their desire for individual autonomy per se, but by a primary concern for familial stability and their family members' (especially their children's) well-being. The change in gendered geography has thus not really resulted in a new configuration of gender relations.

How then do women traders identify and differentiate themselves from their male counterparts? On one occasion, I asked Qiu Dajie what the differences are between men and women in business making. She answered:

"Generally we women are not as audacious as men. Men make quick decisions and aim for big trade. Men may go bankrupt quickly, but women are only able to obtain petty profits [*nande kuadekuai nyude zhangbudehao*]."

I pursued the subject: "Would you prefer to be a man or woman in your next life?"

"Of course—a man. A woman has to take care of children, do housework, as well as make money. Men don't care about their families. Most men don't."

"Is having menstruation inconvenient in traveling?"

"No, it's OK. When my period came, I still went for my trade. However, women are inconvenienced in other respects. If a mining boss comes to ask you to go with him to see rubies at night, do you dare go? I don't. But for men it is not a problem. Usually sellers do not sell high-price rubies to women. They think that only men dare to make quick decisions. Sometimes a deal requires secret negotiation or drinking, but this is not convenient for women."

Obviously, migrant Yunnanese women confront more obstacles in trade than the men do, not only because of the external politico-economic structure, but also because of the gendered discrimination imposed by patriarchal ideologies. Given these circumstances, the women's economic adventurism highlights their extraordinary courage and dynamism. Although their economic gain may not be comparable to men's in practice, it has greatly contributed to their household sustenance. One important factor that facilitates their economic activities is reciprocity originating from social networks, especially kinship connections that provide business information and capital loans. Qiu Dajie's account attests to this fact. The following story from two sisters who collaborate in trade provides another example.

Two Sisters

Dajie (eldest sister) and Erjie (second elder sister) are in their mid-fifties.[11] They grew up in a mountain village in northern Shan State and moved to Taunggyi in the late 1960s. The sisters have been very close since childhood. They are both married and had their houses built next to each other in 1998. They do many things together, such as shopping, visiting friends, making clothes, and engaging in economic ventures. Dajie's husband works as a van driver between Taunggyi and Yangon. Erjie's husband was a small boss in the jade mines from the early 1970s to the early 1990s. He was unable to accumulate wealth from this business and was compelled to leave the mines in 1992, as his capital limitations did not allow him to offer tender for mining concessions (see chapter 7). Since then he has been mostly idle at home.

From a young age, the two sisters had to contribute to the household economy by working on poppy farms. One afternoon, they recounted their memories of the opium harvest, which they called *hua yanbao*. Dajie said:

"Poppy pods are round. When scoring them, you have to use the right strength, neither incising too deep nor too shallow. The pods can be scored three times at intervals of a few days. The first incision is called *toujiangdao*, and the second incision *erjiangdao*. Before starting to work, an agreement [concerning the payment] is made with the farm owner. Usually the agreement is that the collected resin from the upper side of the blade belongs to the owner and that of the underside belongs to the worker. The first day you score the pods. The second day you use the upper side of a blade to scrape the resin from the pods and collect the drops of resin on the leaves with the underside of the blade. At the end of the day you give the resin from the upper side of the blade to the farm owner and keep the small amount from the underside for yourself. You may also sell the amount on the underside to the owner."

Erjie added: "Poppy flowers are very beautiful. They are red, purple, and white. The whole field is really beautiful. Poppy seeds are delicious too. They are small and white with a special fragrance. After the harvest, we would collect them when they had turned dry. They were delicious in soup."

---

11. I interviewed them in January 2005, January 2006, and June 2007 at their homes in Taunggyi.

Dajie had four years of education at a Burmese primary school. She said: "Life was difficult. I had to take care of the younger siblings, do housework, and also go to school." As for Erjie, unfortunately she did not have a chance to attend school. At age fifteen she went to Taunggyi to look for work. She was caught by the police for having no identity papers and was put in prison for five months. Interestingly, she learned Burmese from other inmates during this period. In their early twenties, both sisters were married in Taunggyi.

In the late 1970s, both sisters started a small business together by selling noodles and garden pea gruel (*xidoufen*) on a street corner near a school. Dajie said: "The business was very good. We bought five bowls to start with, and quickly added ten and then twenty. Many students came to eat at noon or after school. We didn't have time to wash the used bowls. After one student finished eating, we immediately filled that bowl with pea gruel for another student." Dajie and Erjie laughed at the memory.

In the late 1970s, women started participating in border trade by truck or car, a method that gradually became popular in the 1980s. People refer to this venture as *pao shengyi*, distinguishing it from the border trade conducted by men by means of mule caravans, referred to as *pao mabang*. Informants pointed out that the trucks of the Burmese government that transported supplies to the border areas adjacent to Thailand were often used for delivering contraband. Such a caravan often amounted to over one hundred vehicles. The drivers were paid to bring passengers and goods.[12] Informants estimated that the amount smuggled by vehicle may have accounted for 20 to 30 percent of the total underground transportation from the 1970s to the early 1980s and since then has rapidly come to predominate. While the mule caravan traders were mostly involved in smuggling large quantities of goods, the border traders by vehicle usually carried a smaller amount. At checkpoints, they bribed the Burmese officials in order to avoid confiscation. Nevertheless, bribery did not always work, especially when the offer was small.

In 1983 both sisters started to engage in border trade by going to Tachileik. Dajie said: "We saw people making money from the border trade by means of vehicle transportation, so we tried it too. Different ethnic groups

---

12. Very few private cars were used in business in these areas prior to the late 1980s because there were many ethnic rebels and bandits.

participated in this trade, including Shans, Burmans, Yunnanese, Kachins, Lisus, Benglongs, Karens, and Pa-Os. There were more women than men." Accordingly, while the mule caravan trade was dominated by male Yunnanese traders, the contraband trade by vehicle was undertaken by different ethnic groups, and especially by women.

Dajie and Erjie carried homemade food to Tachileik for sale. Dajie said: "When winter arrived, we spent two months making preserved meat, sausages, and pickled vegetables, and then we took them to Tachileik for sale. We had to carry our own bedding for the journey. After we sold the food in Tachileik, we crossed the border to Mae Sai to purchase Thai goods, such as monosodium glutamate, adults' clothes, children's clothes, and shoes. After shopping we took our commodities back to Tachileik and waited for a governmental truck to go back. It was safer to take a governmental vehicle in order to avoid robbery by ethnic rebels. Trucks had to climb up and down the mountains on very bad roads. Sometimes they overturned and passengers got killed. The dead bodies were lined next to each other on the side of the road. The rows of corpses were a frightful sight."

Erjie added: "When arriving at the checkpoints, I was always very nervous. My whole body sweated and shook. Sometimes the officials took away all of our goods. We had to kowtow to them and try to pull back our stuff. Sometimes they gave back our merchandise after we paid some money, but other times small bribery didn't work. We were petty traders and not able to pay too much."

By the mid-1980s, Dajie and Erjie also went to Ruili to buy Chinese merchandise. Dajie said: "The road was bumpy and winding. Whenever the drivers [transporting contraband goods] spotted a vehicle belonging to customs officials, they would speed up and wind around to look for a side road for hiding.[13] We lost our goods three times. Once we were on our way back to Taunggyi. Our car was intercepted by a customs vehicle from the Heho airport [one hour away from Taunggyi]. I was carrying fifteen packages of monosodium glutamate and fifteen pairs of shoes. They were all confiscated by the customs agents. I had a six-month-old child on my back and tried to pull the confiscated goods from a customs agent, but he took them back. I pulled them again, and he grabbed them back again.

---

13. Civilians' cars ran on this route because it was safer than the route between Taunggyi and Tachileik.

That agent shouted at me: 'If you still don't go, I will take you to prison.' I answered: 'I'm trying to make a living for my children. Why do you want to take me to prison?' In the end my goods were confiscated. Customs officials are licensed robbers! Thinking of those experiences I still feel frightened."

"You were scared of being caught by the officials, but you continued in this trade," I expressed in amazement.

"Teacher Chang, we were pushed by circumstances. If we didn't go out to trade, what did we eat? Children had to eat every day. Everything cost money. We had to look for money to raise our children," Dajie replied.

"How did you enter China? Did you have to pay taxes?" I asked.

Dajie said: "Each time we applied for a temporary pass. We tried to avoid taxes. It was easier to negotiate with the Chinese officials than the Burmese ones. Once a customs agent asked me: 'Why didn't you declare your goods at customs? Where are you from?' I said: 'We are from Burma. We bought these goods at companies. We don't need to pay a tax.' That customs agent said: 'Who told you that you don't need to pay a tax?' We then bargained with him and paid 150 RMB."

Like many Yunnanese women, Dajie and Erjie shouldered much of the responsibility for their household economy. They engaged in the border trade until 1990, when some of their children started to work. They said they toiled physically too much in the past and now suffer from joint and lower back pain. Even during their pregnancies they traveled until one month prior to delivery, and one month after giving birth they started to travel again. Even now they are not completely retired. Dajie still sells textiles in the market, while Erjie makes children's shoes at home. In one meeting with Erjie's husband, he acknowledged that his wife covered most of the family's expenses, for his jade-mining business did not bring him a stable income. Sometimes Erjie even had to obtain a loan to assist him in mining investments.

In another meeting I raised the question: "What is the difference between men and women in business making?"

Dajie and Erjie giggled at my question. Dajie said: "Men do not save money. During their trips, they spend too much on food and drink [*dachi dahe*]. Women are different. We save every penny. We pack food from home. Even when we have to spend money on board and lodging, we look for the cheapest."

Erjie added: "Women make money with whatever opportunities they find, even when the profit is petty. We are not choosy. Earlier when we took preserved meat and pickled vegetables to Tachileik for sale, some people questioned us and said: 'What can you earn from the food?' Well, we take whatever we can get."

Dajie's and Erjie's remarks on the gender differences in business are commonly echoed by other Yunnanese women. The idea of sacrificial motherhood is embedded in their practices. As Dajie said, women save every penny for their children. They also tend to feed and clothe them better. Another female informant in her fifties confirms this virtue. She said her late husband was the only son in his family and idle throughout his life. She thus had to shoulder the family finances throughout her marriage by participating in cross-border trade for nearly twenty years and then by opening a restaurant. Her mother-in-law helped look after her children when they were small. Despite being the breadwinner of the household, this female trader saved the better food for her children and husband. She said: "In the past, one sack of good white rice cost four hundred kyat and the coarse brown rice three hundred kyat. I purchased both types and cooked the good rice for my husband and children and the coarse rice for me and my mother-in-law."[14] Women's sacrificial behavior on the one hand illustrates their embracing love for their families, but on the other it also suggests an acceptance of the social perception of men's status as superior to women's. They are conscious of this gender inequality and often lament the multiple hardships they have to endure.

While the idea of sacrificial motherhood is essential to women, it is however circumscribed. In the past, the means of birth control were limited; women often resorted to abortion for unwanted births. A friend's mother (of a Yunnanese Muslim family) in her early sixties confided to me that she had four abortions after having given birth to eight children.[15] She said: "Every family used to have eight, ten, or twelve children. I know one family with eighteen children. After giving birth to my eighth child, I thought it was enough. My children were growing up; they needed to eat and study, and that required much money. Hence, I started to help my husband trade in rotating markets in the mountain areas of Tangyan.

---

14. Although the brown rice actually has better nutritional value than the white rice, Chinese in general consider the latter to have better quality.

15. Abortion was used among both Han and Muslim women, although the latter commonly deny this, saying that abortion violates their religion. However, the confession of this friend's mother disproves the general denial.

When I got pregnant again, abortion was the only way to curb the birth. I went to a Baiyi midwife and lay on a bamboo bed. That midwife touched my belly. After a while the fetus came out. In total, I had four abortions." The informant made light of the process, but another female informant told me that it was not touching but squeezing the belly, and that many women actually got infections or died from abortions.

In the face of numerous impediments to their economic efforts and private lives, female trading partners provide not only economic reciprocity but also emotional support for each other. They share family problems and are very willing to lend a hand in domestic work such as baby-sitting and cooking meals. While cheating takes place from time to time between male trading partners, especially in business collaboration involving large amounts of capital (Chang 2004), it occurs much less frequently among women traders.

As the "second sex" of a migrant group, largely located in peripheral areas (before the 1980s), Yunnanese women engaged in economic activities that resulted in the transgression of conventional Chinese gendered ideologies, national boundaries, and even their own bodies (especially in the case of abortion). Figuratively, we may regard this result as transgression of the ideological border, geographical border, and the corporal border. Apart from the various factors already examined—the demands of family finance, the politico-economic structure in Burma, Yunnanese networks and their geographical habitation—two other elements contribute to their economic pursuit. First, their experiences of fleeing transnationally and later repeatedly moving compelled them to break out of the traditional spatial confinement and tossed them into an unknown world with new problems and possibilities. The migration stories related by Ae Maew's mother shed light on this aspect. Second, the long trading history of indigenous women in Burma encourages them toward economic participation. It is a prevailing scene that indigenous women (Burmans and ethnic minorities) peddle on streets and in markets (Cochrane 1904, 55; Harriden 2012, 19).[16] Gender norms concerning division of labor in the host society are comparatively looser than those of the Han and Muslim Chinese in Yunnan. This situation in effect helps Yunnanese women to extend their household engagement to the market and long-distance trade.

---

16. In Southeast Asia women as traders in local markets have had a long history; see Andaya (2006, 123–24) and Reid (1988,162–64).

Several female informants frankly expressed having experienced a kind of happiness during their travels with women of various ethnic groups. They often used the Burmese word *byo* to describe any interesting, funny, or happy experiences during the journey. For example, they said traveling in groups to many places and seeing people of different ethnic groups is *zashi byo* (really interesting/happy). Although they did not refer directly to personal freedom and still stressed the sense of family responsibility as most fundamental for their engagement in trade, their happiness derived from the journey implies recognition of self-autonomy, and their borrowing of the Burmese word for such an expression indicates that the host society may have exerted some influence on their pursuit of independence and self-reliance.

However, some local norms or practices are also seen by the Yunnanese as markers of ethnic differentiation. Elopement is a distinctive example. Qiu Dajie eloped with her husband, who is also Yunnanese Han, and was compelled to sever connections with her natal family for ten years. One of Erjie's daughters eloped with a Pa-O boy. To save the family's honor, Erjie and her husband organized a wedding for the young couple after having located their whereabouts. Although elopement is an accepted practice in some areas by non-Han ethnic groups, the Yunnanese Chinese consider it shameful to the family, especially when it involves intermarriage with non-Chinese. To emphasize their sense of cultural superiority, Yunnanese often criticize the ethnic others as being loose or immoral in their sexual conduct and express their contempt toward the practice of elopement. Nevertheless, it occurs from time to time among the Yunnanese. Xue Dashen in the following account attests to this influence.

Xue Dashen

Xue Dashen's[17] first daughter-in-law, a Shan lady, was Ae Maew's best friend during high school.[18] Ae Maew took me to visit Xue Dashen for the first time in Mandalay in January 2005. In 1990 Xue Dashen's family

---

17. *Dashen* (junior aunt) is an address for female adults whose husbands are younger than one's father. I interviewed Xue Dashen at her home in Mandalay in January 2005 and January 2006.

18. Culturally, the Shan are recognized as a friendly ethnic group by the Yunnanese. While Yunnanese normally are not keen on intermarriages with ethnic others, some parents (but not all) accept their sons marrying Shan women.

moved from Mohnyin (in Kachin State) to Mandalay, Burma's second-largest city. The population of Mandalay totals about one million, according to the UN estimate in 2007.[19] During the 1970s and 1980s, many Yunnanese moved from rural areas to the city because of frequent fighting in the countryside. After 1990, following the opening of the Burmese market, far more Yunnanese from other towns and villages arrived to look for opportunities. Many of them have joined the jade trade (chapter 7). The registered Yunnanese households in the Yunnanese Association number around five thousand. Estimated figures, given by local Yunnanese, for their population (including the Kokang) in the city range between fifty thousand and one hundred thousand. However, outsiders tend to estimate much higher.[20]

Xue Dashen is in her early sixties and of the third generation in Burma. She grew up in Tarmoenye, a town in northern Shan State, and married at age fifteen. She said: "In our region when a boy sees a girl and likes her, he will steal her [*xihuan jiu qu toulai*]. Usually it is by mutual agreement. The boy tries to win the girl's heart by giving her presents, such as a bangle or a ring. They will set a date for elopement. In earlier days, there were three big fairs a year. While normally constrained in their movement, girls were allowed to go to these fairs. Boys would take these opportunities to look for their potential partners. That was how I met my husband [also a Yunnanese Han]. I was very young when I got married. I knew nothing and blindly accepted the courtship.

"After marriage, we lived in a mountain village named Mohau. We grew poppies, rice, corn, and raised pigs. Sometimes my husband went to Mogok for the ruby trade, but he didn't make money out of it. There were many ethnic insurgent groups around our region, and the living conditions were insecure. We therefore moved to Kutkai [north of Lashio]. I sewed clothes for five years with five or six hired workers there. The business was very good.

"I gave birth at twenty-one. Two years later, when I was pregnant with the second child, my husband went to Yangon and had a mistress. A

---

19. http://en.wikipedia.org/wiki/Mandalay

20. Wikipedia gives an estimate of 20 percent of the total population; that is around two hundred thousand. In addition, there are new immigrants from China. A report by the *Irrawaddy* in September 2009 says that more than two hundred thousand Chinese have entered Burma from Yunnan in the last ten years (Jagan 2009). Many of them move back and forth between China and Burma.

year later, he came back and asked me to forgive him. I then gave birth to another three children in Kutkai.

"While in Kutkai, my husband was jailed once for dealing drugs. The police came to search our house and took away everything. The children and I were starving. There was nothing left to eat. Finally, I managed to borrow one thousand kyat to bail him out. A few years later, we moved from Kutkai to Mohnyin. My husband then went to Hpakant to trade jade stones. He was home only three months a year. I raised pigs, made pickles, and distilled alcohol (*kaojiu*). I had to get up at one o'clock in the morning to steam sticky rice for later fermentation and to distill alcohol from the diluted solutions of ethanol that had been produced from fermented sticky rice. Distilling was an arduous process that required changing water time and again in a wok. I kept climbing up and down, up and down to change water. Around five o'clock I ended the work and cooked breakfast. After breakfast, I went to the market and then came back to do housework. I also had to feed the pigs and sew clothes to sell. I was still young and busy all day long. I gave birth to another four children in Mohnyin. Sometimes the Burmese army or Kachin rebels came to the village to demand money and crops and to dragoon people for military service. Life was difficult, really difficult. Whenever I felt too fretful or perturbed, I would go to temples to seek divine guidance by drawing lots [*qiuqian*]."

In contrast to Xue Dashen's sacrificial efforts to support the family, Xue Dashu (her husband), like most Yunnanese men, seemed to concentrate on economic speculation for his own sake. In my interviews with him his narration always centered on the gem trade, without reference to his family. He told me about different trade experiences and confided his repeated failures in business deals. He said: "In 1976 I went to jade mines and purchased three pieces of jade stone, which turned out to be imitations. I lost all my money and had to return home to look for money (*zhaoqian*). Later on, I went to the mines, but again I lost my money in bad deals. Such business failures were repeated seven times in the mines. Between 1984 and 1986, I collaborated with a few partners and entrusted our stones to the jade company of the Qius in Chiang Mai. But the partners in Thailand cheated me on the selling prices. Another time a partner took a jade stone to Hong Kong and sold it for forty-eight million Hong Kong dollars, but he told me it was sold for four million Hong Kong dollars."

The case of Xue Dashen and Xue Dashu reflects the common phenomenon of gender differences in familial devotion and economic involvement among the Yunnanese migrants in Burma. For women, the family's well-being remains the primary concern. Their accounts of economic engagement are always interwoven with those of domestic tasks and familial relationships. But for men, economic undertaking, especially in risky trade, is more a demonstration of manhood. Male informants speak a lot about their economic adventures but seldom make mention of their familial life. Although some men talk about education for their children, they avoid the subject of the husband-and-wife relationship.

By contrast, many female informants are expressive about their domestic life. They point out the fact that many Yunnanese men have mistresses or even set up a second family while away for business. Xue Dashen said: "My husband once had a mistress in Yangon. After he returned to me, that mistress came to Kutkai to look for him. I was furious. I took a rope to tie my *longyi* and thrust a package of salt and chili powder inside the *longyi* that I intended to stuff into that mistress's vagina [*yan tade sichu*]. I found that woman and my husband staying in a rented house. I beat that woman badly and grabbed back my watch and necklace that my husband had given to her. The onlookers cheered my action. I grabbed my husband and said: 'Time to go home.' He pleaded with me to calm down and went home with me.

"My husband and I seldom exchange good words. Our destinies are not compatible [*minggong buhe*]. I have been married to him for many years, and I tolerated his mischievous conduct for the sake of the children. Women are always at a disadvantage in marriage and have to endure the condition. Men may go out to gamble or look for mistresses [*zhao poniang*], but we women have to maintain the marriage. When men have the internal illness [*neibing*, meaning sexual urge] while away from home, they will seek doctors [meaning women]. If I don't see it, I let it go. But if it happens in front of my eyes, I will kill the woman who seduces my husband. I have many children and can't leave them behind. Baiyi women, they would have abandoned their children; but we Han women have to endure the condition [baiyi shi zhuai zhe hanren shi cheng zhe]. We cannot afford to make a mistake."

Xue Dashen's narration reflects her awareness of gender inequality, but like other Yunnanese women of her generation, she makes compromises to fit the Chinese patriarchal norms. No matter how much she contributes to the household finances, her husband officially represents the family. She knows that a divorced woman has no social position and is looked down upon. That is why she said that women cannot afford to make a mistake, and that despite her husband's disloyalty, her revenge target was the mistress, possibly a Baiyi or Burman woman, and not her husband. This shows Xue Dashen's strength and determination to protect herself and her children from a threat that might tear her family apart and to what extent this Yunnanese migrant society allows her to handle the situation. The onlookers represent the general public of the Yunnanese community. They cheered her victory in defeating the mistress and winning her husband back. But if Xue Dashen had also beaten her husband and divorced him, the onlookers may not have cheered for her, but blamed her for cruelty. Although divorce occurs nowadays among the younger generation, it is not socially sanctioned. In a few cases that I know, the divorced women are considered unfortunate, but not necessarily the men. The children, especially male progeny, normally remain with the husbands. Moreover, if their natal families are not supportive, divorced women are put in a dreadful situation.

These stories have examined the economic and familial experiences of a few small- and middle-scale women traders and highlighted their subjectivities characterized by dynamism in overcoming a range of challenges and adversities as well as their own frustration and ambivalence. Their economic tactics concentrate on interactions with the volatile and oppressive policies of the Burmese socialist period. The following narrator, Zhou Dajie, a successful entrepreneur, shares stories that illustrate her mercantile talents during both the socialist and post-socialist periods.

Zhou Dajie

I visited Zhou Dajie, an active businesswoman in her early fifties, in Taunggyi in 2005. She was born in Tangyan in 1954 and belongs to the second generation in Burma. Her father ran a shop, which burned down when she was three years old. The family then moved to a village in the Wa Hills, east of Tangyan, called Manxiang. Her father opened a new shop there, which was often patronized by the KMT guerrillas and indigenous Wa. That village had no school, so her father organized Chinese schooling for his and other Yunnanese children of the village. She said:

"When I was twelve years old, my father was killed on a business trip by gangsters. I had two younger brothers and one younger sister. My mother was compelled to take up the economic responsibility for the whole family. I remember unrest was growing in the area where we stayed at that time. There were different armed ethnic groups. Most Yunnanese didn't have legal status. We didn't know the Burmese language and dared not go to urban areas.

"When I was fourteen, my mother moved the family to Nongkang, which was nineteen kilometers from Manxiang. She started to sell goods at rotating markets. She alone led three mules, which were loaded with different kinds of pickled food and everyday consumer goods. With the profits, she purchased more mules and hired Baiyi muleteers to transport tobacco. A few years later, we had more than thirty mules. I took charge of the domestic work and looked after my younger siblings. But the region became more and more insecure. Our home was robbed once and burned down twice. My mother was tough. She tried to maintain a home for us in the face of adversity."

Zhou Dajie married at age seventeen. Her husband originally worked for a Taiwanese intelligence unit, Division 1920, under the command of the Intelligence Department in Taiwan. Its mission was to collect intelligence concerning Chinese Communists in Burma and Yunnan. Except for some cadre officials sent from Taiwan, most of its members were recruited from among the Yunnanese refugees in Burma. After marriage Zhou Dajie and her husband moved to Taunggyi for one year and then to Chiang Mai for another year. While living in Chiang Mai, she learned dressmaking, and after moving back to Taunggyi she opened a small dressmaking studio. Her husband joined another armed ethnic group and was away most of the time on military missions. Zhou Dajie essentially maintained the family finances. She said: "At that time, the fee for making a jacket was thirty-five kyat, which was enough for one day's living for a family of four people. However, you couldn't get rich by being a dressmaker. I taught dressmaking during the day and made dresses at night. I also had to breastfeed my babies." To improve the family's finances, Zhou Dajie started to run a breakfast shop with her eldest sister-in-law in 1981. She said:

"We saw that other people made money in the restaurant business; so we wanted to have a try. We began selling breakfast, including *monhinkha* [rice vermicelli in fish soup], *baozi* [steamed stuffed bun], *youtiao* [deep-fried breadstick], milk, and soy milk. We hired two cooks. Our food was good and we had many customers. Two years later we ended the breakfast business and opened a restaurant. We hired a chef from Yangon, who was narrow-minded and didn't allow me or my sister-in-law to enter the kitchen for fear we would steal his skills. However, he was unable to handle things alone in the kitchen. Clients were impatient waiting for their food. My sister-in-law and I had to keep apologizing to them. Finally he allowed us to help him cut vegetables in the kitchen. I secretly observed how he cooked, in addition to studying cookbooks and experimenting by cooking different dishes. Whenever I succeeded in making a dish, I would take the food to treat the chair of the Yunnanese Association and different shop owners with whom I had business and requested them to recommend our restaurant to their friends and customers.

"As our business became better and better, we hired the second chef. Unfortunately, 'a mountain cannot accommodate two tigers' [*yishan burong erhu*]. The first chef was looking for an opportunity to harm the second chef. Once when our restaurant was booked for a banquet, he saw the opportunity. He went out to drink the night before the banquet. Next day he said he didn't feel well and couldn't do the purchasing himself. The second chef had to do the job, but he was inexperienced. The purchased quantities were not enough. It was shameful that we were unable to provide a full bowl for each dish. Guests complained that they didn't have enough to eat. I thus had to apologize to all the guests. I humbled myself and said to the banquet host: 'We made a mistake in the purchase. You may pay whatever price you would like to. I will not ask for a full price.' After that, I learned to calculate the needed quantities for purchase and didn't rely on the first chef. Later on, when the restaurant was booked again for a banquet, I said to myself: 'I must save the restaurant's name in this deal. I will provide big full bowls of all dishes, even if I may not make money.' I calculated the needed quantities and supervised in the kitchen. It had to be more and not less [*keyi duo bukeyi shao*]. As a result, the guests were very satisfied with the food. I successfully recovered the name of our restaurant in one day. After that our restaurant had very good business. If I had not made some sacrifice in that deal, our business may not have been able to recover. My principle was: 'I must not let the customers down as I make money from them.'"

It is interesting to see how Zhou Dajie built up her business from small investment to larger investment. She had the courage to try new things and exerted herself to learn each step. She knew how to promote her restaurant through her connections and was willing to make short-term sacrifices for long-term development. Her interaction with government officials further illustrates her strategy. She said: "Many officials liked to eat at our restaurant. When they came alone or with their families, I would not charge them, but requested that they help our business. By doing so, I got many deals from the government."

Based on her wide connections, in 1992 Zhou Dajie and her sister-in-law opened a general store in Taunggyi and another one in Mong Hsu. Zhou Dajie hired a driver to transport goods from Taunggyi to Mong Hsu. She said: "There were more than thirty checkpoints on the road. The driver was a Shan, a trustworthy person. He made good contacts with all the Burmese officials. Whenever a new official arrived, my driver would inform me. We would send special presents to him. In addition, we paid tea money [bribery] at each checkpoint on each trip. If you do not maintain a good relationship with the officials at these checkpoints, your car will be assigned to deliver supplies for the Burmese army. We had very good business in Mong Hsu. The shop there required five to six replenishments a month. I could do all the arrangements by phone and had no need for long-distance travel."

Moreover, the two shops provided underground banking, which was a common service provided by big general stores in Burma. Traders or mine owners could deposit their money at Zhou Dajie's shop in Taunggyi before going to Mong Hsu. After arriving in Mong Hsu, they went to her shop there to collect the money. This service guaranteed the safety of the deposit, and big traders and mine owners resorted to it. Traders could also borrow money from the Mong Hsu shop and return the loan later to their Taunggyi location. With the returned debts, the Taunggyi shop ordered goods for the Mong Hsu shop. Consequently, their two connected locations facilitated the circulation of capital, commodities, and people between Taunggyi and Mong Hsu. The credit model resembles that of Hpakant.

In 1993, Zhou Dajie ended the restaurant business and embarked on a new venture by opening a distillery, an enterprise that required a lot of capital and good connections. She said:

"I got to know a Burmese general from my restaurant business. He asked me if I was interested in doing any new business. I heard alcohol distillation made a lot of money and told him that I would like to engage in it. A sister of that general also joined the business. The general helped us obtain a distillation license and a wholesale license. It took five months to build the distillery. We started selling liquor in 1994. At the beginning we only produced spirit liquors. But sales were not good. Only later I realized that most Burmese drink light liquors. Moreover, the wholesale license was regional and only allowed selling within a certain area and not the whole country. The market had already been dominated by a few brands, and it was difficult to break in. I tried to introduce our products to liquor agents, but most of them had already established deals with other distilleries and would not sell our products. In the end only a few agents were willing to work with us. We thus had to assign low prices for retailers in different places. Some agents and retailers disappeared, and we were not able to collect money from them. From 1994 to 1999, the business was in the red. That general's sister withdrew her share in 1996. It was very difficult to sustain the business alone, but I didn't want to give up.

"I bought books on spirits from Taiwan and China and different types of liquors from abroad. I studied them and experimented in mixing spirits. Originally I didn't drink alcohol at all. But I have a very good sense of smell and am now an expert in mixing spirits. I also surveyed the liquor market, which was dominated by different spheres of influence. I started to fight for my own domain without considering appearances [*sipolian de zheng*]. Only then did my business gain traction."

Zhou Dajie did not relate the details of her fight for the market, but she mentioned that she went to visit some *lukyi* (big men), meaning high-ranking officials, in Yangon. She said: "You need to obtain different types of licenses and tender for monopoly sale in different regions. At the beginning, I didn't fully understand the bidding process. I thought one would win a bid by offering a high price. But many bidders have private deals with the officials with a promise to give them a certain amount of tea money each year. Now I have certain agents who only sell our products, and I have obtained licenses for distillation, wholesale, producing white liquors, colored liquors, and glass bottles. Our brand is well accepted, and our volume is increasing. Every year I spend more than ten million kyat on Burmese officials."

Zhou Dajie is now a successful female entrepreneur. Apart from the distillery, she owns a sugar mill next to the factory and a hotel in Mengla. Both were set up in early 2000. Some relatives also hold small shares. (She closed the general stores in 1996 following the decline of ruby mining in

Mong Hsu.) The sugar industry complements the liquor making, because the molasses drained from raw sugar during the refining process is used in distillation. The hotel is a new undertaking. Mengla is a popular border town, eighty-five kilometers north of Kengtung. It is controlled by the armed ethnic Wa, and it is well known for casino games and active nightlife. Chinese tourists visit in large numbers, and Chinese currency is used there. The establishment of Zhou Dajie's hotel is partly attributed to her husband's connection with some Wa leaders who control the region's political economy. Zhou Dajie entrusts its management to a cousin and goes there once every other week.

In contrast to Zhou Dajie's active life, her husband remains much quieter. After leaving the army in 1975, he participated in long-distance trade for many years but without much success. In the past ten years, he has spent a lot of time playing mahjong and golf. Although his earlier military engagement did not bring about economic rewards, it has enlarged the family's social capital. Officially, he is still the head of the family, but its actual management is run by his wife.

In contrast with the previous cases, the prominence of Zhou Dajie's entrepreneurship is grounded on her well-established connections with multiple hierarchies of power that assist in her economic expansion. Although the post-socialist regime has issued various market-oriented policies since 1988, business opportunities are still based by and large on deals between the officials and businessmen under the table. The multiple hierarchies of power from the local to the central levels, plus the ethnic forces in different areas, simultaneously function as constraints and facilitators for economic operations, depending on the businessmen and women's interactions with them. Zhou Dajie's story illuminates her sensibility in cultivating political resources from a young age. She mentioned the KMT's patronage of her father's shop, her husband's political ties with the KMT and other ethnic military groups, and her networks with local Burmese officials cultivated while running the restaurant business, and later with the "big men" in Yangon who facilitated her distillation enterprise. The backing of these political powers, compounded by her willingness to take risks in large-scale business investment, demonstrates characteristics rarely seen among Yunnanese women.

What is the main factor that contributes to Zhou Dajie's business penchant? How does her gender affect her career development? In one conversation, Zhou Dajie attributed her economic keenness primarily to her mother's influence. She said: "My mother arrived in Burma to look for her father who had fled Yunnan a year before her. The political conditions were chaotic in rural Shan State. Ethnic troops fought against one another. My grandfather was an intellectual and didn't know how to trade at all. My mother worked on farms and made clothes and pickled food and snacks for sale. After marrying my father, she helped him run a shop. When my father passed away, she became the sole pillar of the family. I witnessed how she struggled in a very insecure environment to sustain the household economy by trading in rotating markets. She exerted herself to protect the family and suffered all her life."

Being the eldest daughter, Zhou Dajie learned from her mother to take responsibility for sustaining the family. She adhered to this role while her husband was away for a military career and later for long-distance trade. While the female traders of the previous cases also emphasize this virtue of self-sacrifice and caring for the family, Zhou Dajie explicitly attributes its practice to the mother-daughter identification,[21] meaning that the continuity of the female roles of daughter, wife, and mother anchors the principle of the household's well-being from generation to generation. Its realization is rooted in the mothers' upbringing of their daughters to always put consideration of the family before themselves. (This is very different from the upbringing of sons that encourages them to explore the world; see chapter 3.)

Although a patriarchal community, Yunnanese migrants commonly affirm that daughters look after the household better than sons (*nyuer bi erzi gujia*). This belief not only refers to women's devotion to their natal families before marriage, but also to their new families after marriage. In other words, concerns for the household are considered paramount for women; all other engagements are seen as extensions of these concerns. While the social expectation that women fulfill their household responsibilities propels them to be creative, it nevertheless also limits their development. This paradoxical situation entails an ongoing process of Yunnanese

---

21. The term "mother-daughter identification" is derived from Francis L. K. Hsu's "father-son identification" (1967), which refers to the mutual responsibility and privileges between the father and son for the continuity of patriliny. While studies on Chinese descent and family structure tend to focus on father-son identification, mother-daughter identification is often overlooked.

women's interplay with gendered politics characterized by a negotiable gap between the level of ideology and that of reality. This gap reveals their inner strength, with which they reinterpret the prescribed norms with or without betraying them, while it also shows how far the society tolerates the gap.

In line with Saba Mahmood's interpretation of female agency as a capacity for action (2001), Yunnanese women's breaking away from conventional constraints on movement cannot be seen as originating from a personal desire to resist the structure of male domination. Rather, it is centered on the embodied virtues of motherhood and household responsibilities, and their performance primarily aims for the "continuity, stasis, and stability" of these virtues (using Mahmood's words, 2001, 212). Instead of subverting the patriarchal system, they unanimously wish to be born as men in their next lives. (Since starting my research among the Yunnanese migrants in 1994, I have not heard any Yunnanese woman express the opposite wish.) Though the wish seems to be passive, it actually embraces their wisdom in knowing what may be changed and what may not be changed. Their bravery and devotion to their families illustrate their dynamism as well as frustration and pain in an ongoing process of shaping and reshaping their gendered roles. Consequently, the types of borders they have to cross during the course of their travels for economic engagements surpass those of their male counterparts.

7

Circulations of the Jade Trade

The Duans and the Pengs

> During 2007 and 2008, the transaction from an official auction of jade stones in Yangon was around three to four billion euros; in early 2010, the amount increased to seven to eight billion euros. For the last auction in March 2011, the amount doubled and reached sixteen billion euros. The value of jade stones is soaring, as traders foresee their resource will be exhausted someday. The demand is increasing.
> —Daqing, April 15, 2011, Taipei

In September 2006, I made my first field trip to Guangzhou via Hong Kong in order to extend my earlier research on the jade trade among the Yunnanese migrants of Thailand and Burma that I began in 2000. The purpose of my trip was to research the expansion of the Yunnanese trading networks of the jade business from Burma—where the most precious jadeite in the world is procured—to Guangzhou, current developments in state and non-state trading regulations, new forms of transaction, capital flows, and shipments of jade stones and products. My second field trip to Guangzhou took place the following year when I spent two weeks in Hong Kong, Guangzhou, and a few satellite trading nodes around Guangzhou. The Duans and the Pengs, families who were related through marriage and business collaborations, helped arrange interviews for me with other Yunnanese jade traders from Burma and Thailand and local dealers, as well as visits to three major jade companies founded by Yunnanese from Burma and Thailand. During my stay, I had the opportunity to observe the manufacturing of jade ware, including the cutting of jade stones, the making of designs on cut slates, and carving, plus the trading of jade in street markets, shops, and at organized auctions. Most importantly, the Duans and the Pengs related numerous stories about their lives and trading experiences in Burma, Thailand, Yunnan, Hong Kong, Guangzhou, and Taiwan. In 2009, through Mr. Peng's connections, I made an additional trip to Ruili, a border entrepôt of Yunnan, adjacent to Muse (Mujie) in northern Shan State in Burma, and then Kunming (the provincial capital) to observe the jade trade for a period of two weeks (Figures 7–1 and 7–2).

Initially, it was through the introduction of relatives of the Duans and the Pengs in Thailand and Burma that I came to know the two families. The meetings with these relatives began in Thailand in 1995. Between 2005 and 2009, I interviewed different members of the Duan and the Peng clans in Burma, Guangzhou, Hong Kong, Yunnan, and Taiwan. These meetings and interviews have helped me gain insights into the trading history of the two families. I learned of their ups and downs in relation to external challenges and personal luck, which are considered by traders to be two major determinants, among others, for success in this economic pursuit (Chang 2006b). Based on knowledge of their business developments, as well as of

Figure 7–1. A jade market in Guangzhou

Figure 7–2. A jade market in Ruili

the engagement of other informants in the same practice, I was able to build a detailed picture of this intriguing area of commerce, predicated on the extension of Yunnanese networks by land from Burma to Thailand from the 1960s to the mid-1990s, and from Burma to Yunnan since the mid-1980s, as well as by sea from Yangon to Guangzhou since 2000.

In this chapter, I look into the circulations that have evolved from the trade since 1962,[1] covering both the socialist period in Burma and afterward. After taking power in September 1988, the new junta partially opened the nation's economy for private trade and foreign investment. In 1992, it legalized the jade trade and opened the jade mines in Kachin State for private mining.[2] An exploration of two political periods helps to provide a comparative understanding of the structural changes over time.

---

1. In four other papers, I explore the trading networks and culture of the jade business during the period of the Burmese socialist regime (1962–1988) (Chang 2003, 2004, 2006b) and its historical contingency and continuity (Chang 2011).

2. Burmese jade (or, more specifically, jadeite) deposits are located in Kachin State in upper Burma, especially along the Uru River. Hpakant is the most famous area.

According to Markovits, Pouchepadass, and Subrahmanyam, "Circulation is different from simple mobility, inasmuch as it implies a double movement of going forth and coming back, which can be repeated indefinitely" (2003, 2–3); moreover, circulation refers to "more than the movement to and fro of men and goods. . . . Apart from men and goods, many other items circulate in a society (and between a given society and other societies): information, knowledge, ideas, techniques, skills, cultural productions (texts, songs), religious practices, even gods" (p. 2). They use the concept of circulation for analysis of the itinerant cultures in South Asia under colonial rule. In the same vein, this chapter attempts to study the back-and-forth movement of traded commodities (i.e., jade stones, jade products, and machinery), capital, people, information, and knowledge along the trade routes that are maintained through the circuits of Yunnanese connections that link by land and sea the various trading nodes located in Burma, Yunnan, Thailand, Hong Kong, Guangzhou, and Taiwan. Within this "circulatory regime," meaning the "totality of circulations" occurring in this large stretch of connected area (ibid., 3), we will discern that the flows are multidirectional. The back-and-forth circulation is not limited between two fixed destinations, but among many possible nodes supported by nexuses of trading that have the potential to shift and expand. I will use the trading history of the Duans and the Pengs as the core source of illumination, supplemented with data from other informants and material, to give a structural picture of the trade.

Transnational Business Bases of the Duans and the Pengs

"Once my husband [Mr. Duan] and brother-in-law [Mr. Peng] set off together for the jade mines in Hpakant. They had a radio with them. Before reaching their destination, they learned about the demonetization of the Burmese kyat [*dapiao bian*].[3] My husband then decided to return home, but my brother-in-law still wanted to try his luck in the jade mines and continued his journey alone. Later on he was kidnapped by rebels. The rebels sent a message back for ransom. He was released only after payment of the ransom. Undertaking the trade was very risky."

---

3. The regime demonetized banknotes respectively in 1964, 1985, and 1987. The event mentioned here is possibly in 1985.

The story was related by Mrs. Duan at a condominium located near the jade market (*yuqi jie*) in Guangzhou in 2006. Mrs. Duan and Mrs. Peng, who are sisters, bought the apartment together in 2002 and made it one of several bases for the families' transnational engagement in the jade trade. It housed the members of the families whenever they came from other bases to Guangzhou. Mrs. Duan and Mrs. Peng were the primary residents; other frequent visitors included their husbands, Daqing (the eldest son of the Duans), and Lifen (the eldest daughter of the Pengs). It was a bit crowded when several members of the two families were present.

I was a breakfast guest when Mrs. Duan told me the story of Mr. Peng's kidnapping. We had *babasi* (rice noodles) cooked Yunnanese-style with ground pork and tomatoes and several side dishes, including Yunnanese pickles. The breakfast was prepared by Axiang, a relative of the Duans from Yunnan whose mother had married a cousin of Mr. Duan. Axiang was nineteen years old. Both she and her younger brother had been recruited to work here. They slept in a nearby apartment that Mrs. Duan and Mrs. Peng rented as their working studio, and every morning Axiang cooked breakfast at the condominium. After breakfast, Mr. Duan made *pu-er* tea (*pu er cha*), a popular fermented tea from Yunnan. He and Mrs. Duan then recounted many stories about their life experiences in Burma, then in Taiwan, and now in Guangzhou. Lifen was present too. Born in Burma, she had moved to Taiwan with her family in 1988 at the age of seven. As she had grown up primarily in Taiwan, her aunt and uncle's stories seemed like amazing adventures to her.

Originally the Duans and the Pengs lived in Burma. The families moved via Thailand to Taiwan in 1988 when the political situation in Burma became unstable. They said that the main reason for moving was their children's education. The Burmese government closed down universities whenever there were strikes. Mr. Peng's parents and other siblings had already moved from Burma to Thailand in the late 1960s and then from Thailand to Taiwan in 1974. Both Mr. Duan and Mr. Peng had visited Taiwan a few times for business, as Taiwan has consistently been a primary consumer society for jade. From 1988 to 1992, the period when the Taiwanese stock market was booming, its rate of jade purchase was the highest among all Chinese societies. It was not difficult for overseas Chinese businessmen to apply for immigration to Taiwan at that time. The Duans and the Pengs purchased condominiums in central Taipei soon after their arrival. Most of their children still live in Taipei.

Mr. Duan's main investment is in jade mining. He owns the mining rights to about one hundred acres in Kachin State (in 2011).[4] He entrusts its management to a nephew (a son of his fourth elder brother) and the husband of a niece (the daughter of his third elder brother). Excavated stones are transported to Mandalay for storage under the purview of another niece (the daughter of his fourth elder brother) who resides in that city. These stones are later transported to Yangon and Naypyidaw (the latter since 2011) for auctions organized by the Burmese government before they are allowed to be exported. The husband of the niece in Mandalay is sent to Yangon to be in charge of the stones. Mr. Duan extended his business to Guangzhou in 2001, around the time many Yunnanese jade traders (mostly from Burma) arrived there. After coming to Guangzhou, he also began a business making jade products. He rents a four-story house in the jade market of Pingzhou. Originally an agricultural village, since 2000 Pingzhou has been transformed into an important town for the auction of jade stones and commerce in jade products, especially bangles. The town is only twenty minutes' drive from Guangzhou; it offers space for the expansion of the jade market and is thus considered a strategic place for developing the jade trade. The local government has built many shops in the market on communal land in the last few years. Many jade companies have been established here since 2005, the major ones founded by the Yunnanese from Burma and Thailand with bases back in Mandalay and Yangon. They organize auctions of jade stones almost once a month. The house Mr. Duan rents is used primarily as a storehouse for the jade stones shipped from Burma that are mostly excavated from his mines in Hpakant. The stones stored in the house are in part entrusted to jade companies for local auctions and in part reserved for making jade products for further sale. There are a few machines in the house for cutting the stones.

As for Mr. Peng, his main focus is on purchasing jade stones and making high-quality jade products for sale. Since 2004, he has been renting a ground-floor shop in a row of buildings in the jade market of Pingzhou, not far from Mr. Duan's storehouse. In it he sells both his products and those of other traders, items such as rings, earrings, pendants, brooches, bead necklaces, and bangles. The sale of other merchants' products earns 5 percent commission. He also rents the fourth floor of the same building for storing purchased stones. His first younger brother, who has a university degree in

---

4. He does not excavate all his mines but rents out a portion of them to other mining bosses.

mining and oil engineering from a Taiwanese university, takes care of the shop with a local friend. This brother joined the business in 1987 and was in charge of a base in Yingjiang, a booming border town in Yunnan, until 2000. He then commuted between Taiwan, Hong Kong, Yunnan, and Guangzhou for several years, partly for joint trade with his brother and partly for his own business, until he was entrusted with the shop in Pingzhou.

Mr. Peng was one of the few Yunnanese who extended business to Hong Kong prior to 1990. He has a firm located in the jade market of Guangdongdao in Hong Kong that was established with two Hong Kong partners in 1988. Since 2006, he has also been involved in the shipment of jade stones and in providing money transfer services for fellow Yunnanese. Lifen, his eldest daughter, who is in her mid-twenties with a bachelor's degree in hotel management from a college in Switzerland, helps to take care of the shipments and money transfers. The Pengs also have a residential unit in a condominium in Hong Kong. (While referring to Taiwan as the place where their homes are based, the Pengs and Duans travel between Taiwan, Hong Kong, Guangzhou, and Yangon for the jade trade.)

Mrs. Duan and Mrs. Peng started their business collaboration in Guangzhou in 2002 with the encouragement of their husbands. Although they were housewives before this undertaking, through the years they had acquired a great deal of knowledge about the trade. They had heard many trade stories from their husbands and had seen the alternations of good and bad fortunes that their husbands and other relatives had endured. As their children grew up, they thought of starting their own business in this already familiar trade. They purchase small sliced pieces of jade stones (*bianjiaoshi*), "leftovers" from larger pieces that have been used for making bangles or other larger pieces, from their husbands at less than market prices, and use them for making small ornaments.

The Duans' eldest son, Daqing, who is in his early thirties, began participating in the trade in 2002 after receiving a master's degree in architecture in Taiwan.[5] His father noted Daqing's interest in the jade business and his talent for evaluating jade stones quickly. While studying at university, Daqing

---

5. Although a few former classmates and he opened an office for architecture design after graduation, his main involvement has been with the jade trade. Lifen's and his higher education differentiates them from most jade traders of their parents' generation, who did not receive much education during a time of instability.

made close friends with Chinese overseas students from Burma. From them he again picked up the Burmese language, which he had stopped using after moving to Taiwan at the age of thirteen. During summer vacations, he would visit his father's jade mines. At first he sold jade products provided by his mother and aunt through a website that he set up for that purpose. The net profit was high, around the same amount he paid for the products. His wife, who has a background in painting, took classes in gem design and soon joined the trade by designing jade products in a modern style that is easily distinguished from conventional bangles and statuettes of Buddha and the goddess Guanyin. Moreover, with the guarantee of genuine and untreated jade stones from the family's jade mines, Daqing and his wife quickly built up their own brand in Taiwan using the latter's English name. In 2006, Daqing opened a gem shop in the bustling shopping area of eastern Taipei that has gone on to do very well. He hired two nieces, also from Burma, to work at the shop. They originally went to Taiwan for further studies, a popular option among ethnic Chinese students in Burma (like Zhang Dage and Ae Maew). Both nieces had completed their undergraduate studies and had acquired several years of work experience elsewhere before being asked to work at the shop. Daqing goes to Hong Kong and Guangzhou regularly to replenish his commodities; he still buys most of the products and semi-finished products from his father, mother, and aunt. Every year he also visits his father's jade mines in upper Burma.

It is clear that the Duans and the Pengs ground their transnational jade business primarily on kinship ties, especially among their own family members and close relatives. This is a common phenomenon in the jade trade, where the expansion of the enterprise draws in increasing numbers of kith and kin. In the case of the Duans and Pengs, their businesses are supported by the movement of participating members at different points. Even the workers who help in the houses and shops in Guangzhou and Pingzhou are recruited from among relatives in Yunnan.[6] Through the business networks, the traded jade stones and products are transported from one node to another. Their transportation is tied to the circulation of trade knowledge with value added at different stages, from excavated rough stones, to polished and cut stones at an auction, to finished products.

---

6. In 2006, only Axiang and her brother were recruited from Yunnan, but in the following year, two more relatives from Yunnan were brought in to work there.

This process accords with Arjun Appadurai's interpretation of the "social lives of things." He claims that "commodities, like persons, have social lives" (1986, 3), and they move in and out of different "regimes of value in space and time" (ibid., 4).

Daqing and his wife are keen to develop, disseminate, and demonstrate their expertise in the jade trade and jade production—the entire process of turning jade stones into finished products, from excavation to production. Daqing does more than simply buy ready-made products from his mother and aunt. He visits jade mines in Hpakant, auctions of jade stones in Yangon, Naypyidaw, and Pingzhou, and auctions of jade products by Christie's and Sotheby's in Hong Kong. His activities resemble those of his predecessors who traveled to various places in order to acquire jade knowledge. In Taipei, he passes on part of his knowledge to his nieces for explanation to clients. In addition, his wife's participation in design contributes to the completion of the final product. To gain an edge over their competitors, Daqing and his wife describe the "social lives" of their commodities—his family's mining sites, procuring process, auctions, and transportation of jade stones and production of jade ware—to their clients both on the website and in the shop. Daqing told me that his shop is the only one in Taiwan that sells products made from family-mined stones.

Although the jade trade is primarily based on kinship ties, it requires local links as well. Earlier I referred to Mr. Peng's firm, cofounded with two local partners in Hong Kong who had previously purchased jade stones he had taken to Thailand. They not only contributed capital, but their local status also helped to facilitate the registration procedures required to set up the firm. Other informants also point out that all the jade companies in Pingzhou that are primarily funded by the Yunnanese from Burma are registered under the names of local partners. Not only is it difficult to use Burmese status for registration in China, but applying for official papers in Burma for business investment abroad is far too troublesome.[7]

Following the introduction of the Duans' and the Pengs' transnational bases for their jade trade, the next section looks into the specific stories of members of the two families, in particular those of Mr. Duan and Mr. Peng, which reveal how they repeatedly encountered external constraints arising

---

7. Local partners' shares tend to be small. The strategy of using their names for registration implies legal risks; but so far I have not heard of actual problems.

from different power structures prior to 1992. The economic activities of these two families break through these restrictions and lead to configurations in their transnational trading enterprises that ensure the fluidity of people, capital, commodities, and trade knowledge and information.

Prior to 1992

Mr. Duan

Mr. Duan was born in 1947 to a family of the landlord class in Tengchong, Yunnan. In 1951, most of the members of the extended Duan family fled to Burma in order to avoid the Communist class struggle. Some family members joined the KMT guerrillas to continue military campaigns for fighting back in Yunnan. In 1971, Mr. Duan's parents and the family moved from a village in northern Shan State to Taunggyi to avoid the incessant fighting among different ethnic military groups and with the Burmese army. Other members of the extended family were scattered through other parts of Shan State.

In 1972, Mr. Duan started his venture in the Thai-Burmese underground trade by transporting Thai textiles to Burma. In 1973, he went to Mogaung for the first time to buy jade stones. Mogaung was a town located on the railway line joining Myitkyina and Mandalay. Many excavated jade stones were secretly brought here for sale. After General Ne Win took control of the country through a military coup and implemented a series of economic measures to nationalize trade and industry, gemstones were categorized as national properties and banned from private excavation and trade. However, the jade mining area was primarily under the control of the Kachin Independence Army (KIA). They supervised jade mining by levying and collecting taxes. Mr. Duan said:

"Prior to 1980, the KIA allowed only indigenous Kachins and Shans to mine while barring Chinese from the venture. Some daring Yunnanese disguised themselves as Shans or Kachins and tried their luck in mining. They had to hide themselves from the KIA as well as the Burmese troops. Most Yunnanese only bought excavated stones in the outlying towns, like Mogaung, Hopin, and Mohnyin. In 1977, I went to the jade mines for the first time to buy jade stones. Carrying some food and merchandise, I pretended to be a Shan peddler. However, before I reached the mines, two KIA soldiers stopped to question me. Though I was able to speak Shan fluently, having grown up in Shan State, the soldiers were not convinced that I was really Shan. They pointed out my fair complexion. I was in great fear. Fortunately, the soldiers were more interested in the goods I carried than my identity. They took some of my food and let me go. I stayed in Hpakant for six months that time. During the stay, I roamed around the mines to find good jade stones for sale. On my way back, I was unlucky and encountered a fight between the KIA and Burmese troops. I was sitting in a truck at that point, and the passenger next to me was hit in the eye by a bullet. I immediately jumped out of the truck and hid in nearby bushes until the fight stopped. Although it was very risky, I made my way to Mogaung or Hpakant once or twice every year in the late 1970s. Sometimes, I went with my brother-in-law [Mr. Peng] and other friends from Taunggyi."

One of Mr. Duan's stepbrothers was a high-ranking officer of the KMT Third Army that had retreated to Thailand. The army often collaborated in the jade trade. Mr. Duan was responsible for buying jade stones in Burma and arranging for their transportation to Thailand, and his stepbrother took charge of contact with the jade companies in Chiang Mai and, later, price negotiations with buyers at the companies. Due to this connection with his stepbrother, Mr. Duan obtained Thai legal status (as Zhao Dashu in chapter 5 did) and was able to move freely in Thailand whenever he entered the country. Prior to 1980, although jade mining was largely undertaken by Kachins and Shans, the jade trade to Thailand was primarily controlled by the Yunnanese because of the extension of their trading networks to Thailand and connections with the KMT troops. Moreover, the jade trade was essentially exclusive to the Chinese; most buyers were from Hong Kong and Taiwan. Without knowledge of the language and Chinese business connections, it was difficult for non-Chinese to enter the trade.[8]

In the 1980s, the KIA relaxed mining controls and allowed the Chinese to mine jade stones, possibly with the recognition that the opening would increase their tax income. Mr. Duan said:

"Many Yunnanese flooded the jade mines as mining bosses or miners in the 1980s. The ethnic Chinese from Guangdong and Fujian were

---

8. In Ruili there are a small number of Burmese Indians who engage in jade trade. Some have stayed in the city for more than ten years and speak Chinese fluently (Egreteau 2011).

largely concentrated in lower Burma. Most of them ran shops and were not involved in the jade trade, which they considered very risky. Soon the number of Yunnanese overtook that of the Kachins and Shans in the jade mines. In 1986, I launched my mining business. In the 1980s, excavation was still purely dependent on human labor, and the mining population increased rapidly. Every evening the center of Hpakant was jammed with miners and traders from nearby mines who came to look for food and fun after the day's labor. However, military conflicts between the KIA and the Burmese army still occurred from time to time. The mining bosses and jade traders had to pay both sides in order to get informal permission to work in the mines. Even then, unexpected dangers arose and sometimes robbed one of life and fortune."

Mr. Peng

Mr. Peng was born in 1950 in a border village in northern Shan State. Yunnanese called the place Pengxian, and it was composed of several Kachin and a couple of Yunnanese villages.[9] Mr. Peng was a member of the fourth generation born there. His father was the headman (*huotou*) of a Yunnanese village. One of his maternal uncles, the headman of another village, went to Taiwan for military training in the 1950s and was later assigned to lead a troop of sixty soldiers to collect intelligence in northern Burma for the Taiwanese government. Apart from this official assignment, he also engaged in the escort of caravans between Thailand and Burma. A large portion of the caravans from Burma transported jade stones. Mr. Peng joined this uncle's troop briefly in the late 1960s and learned to trade jade stones. Having knowledge of the Kachin language, Mr. Peng purchased jade stones directly from the mines. He explained:

"I went to the jade mines in Hpakant for the first time in 1970. By the early 1970s, I had already built up a name in jade trade circles, as I was able to purchase high-quality stones. The traded stones were uncut; one had to learn to estimate the quality of a stone by evaluating the appearance of its outer crust, such as the colored spots, defects, and texture of the sand of the skin. The lack of guarantee made the trading of jade stones akin to gambling. In 1973, I made a fortune from a deal and bought a house in

---

9. Pengxian is located one and a half days' walk east of Kyugok.

Taunggyi. At that time, we smuggled jade stones to Thailand via Taunggyi. I made good profits in the 1970s, but afterward, I lost heavily in deals for many years. Friends lent me money to keep on going; they trusted me, as I had a good reputation in the trade. . . . In 1987, luck finally knocked on my door again. I purchased a stone with a few friends at the price of 2.4 million kyat. I cut the stone and found it to be of outstanding quality. The piece was not big, but in full green. I took it to Hong Kong the following year and sold it for 19.88 million Hong Kong dollars. I moved my family to Taiwan that year and also established a jade company in Hong Kong with two local partners."

As the trade was illegal and constrained by the struggle between the government and the KIA, not only did traders gamble on the economic value of jade stones, but also on their own lives in the pursuit of the trade. Apart from his abduction by rebels, Mr. Peng was also jailed twice by the Burmese government for short terms, and was robbed several times while on business trips. He said:

"I was jailed the first time in 1978 with a sentence of six months. . . . On entering the prison, I made myself the big brother [*laoda*]. More than one hundred people were locked in the same room, very crowded. I told the original big brother and his two followers: 'You follow me from now on. I will have someone deliver half *zuai* of meat every day. You cook for me. We eat together.' If you had money, life would be OK. If not, your life would be miserable. Those who came before you would bully you, and you wouldn't even get space to sleep. . . .

"In 1981, I was jailed again. I was already married then. Before being locked up, I was told to spend my money. I bought fifteen hundred cheroots. I planned to use them as presents for the inmates. But then I was put in a cell alone. When a jailer delivered meals, I asked him for a match to light up a cheroot. I then kept on smoking one cheroot after another for twenty-five days. There were many rats in the cell. I had to use the smoke to chase them away. . . .

"A Burmese warden constantly walked back and forth in the corridor outside my cell. He was chanting sutras with a Buddhist rosary in his hand. Once while walking, he asked me: 'Are you from Taunggyi?' I replied: 'Yes.' He said: 'Do you know officer Thin Maung?' I replied: 'Yes, I know him.' I told him that that official had been transferred to another place. We then started to chat, and later on we became friends. . . .

"One has to live. In the past, one's life was not worth much. There's not much you could do in that environment. You had to risk your life. In that country, selling rice was illegal; selling oil was also illegal. Everything belonged to the government. Jade stones were labeled the nation's property; it was certainly forbidden to trade them. But how could we survive if we did not break the law?"

Engrossed by Mr. Peng's narration, I asked: "Were you in fear at all in those difficult days?"

"It was not that I was without fear. Fear was part of your life. You simply had to cope with it." His words correspond to those of the women traders. But like most male traders, in his narration he laid emphasis only on his boldness.

In the mid-1980s, migrant Yunnanese traders started to smuggle jade stones from Kachin State to Yunnan, but the major business remained in Thailand prior to 1995. In 1987, Mr. Peng set up a company in the Yunnanese border town of Yingjiang, despite having little financial leeway at the time. He sent his first younger brother to take care of the business as mentioned earlier, while he himself focused on the trade between Burma and Thailand. His company in Yingjiang sold smuggled stones to local Yunnanese merchants and some from Guangdong. Several informants (including Tangge in chapter 5) pointed out that the trade to Yunnan was an immediate success. Before the Chinese government closed down the border trade in 1949, Yunnan had had a long history of importing Burmese jadeite (Sun 2011). After the Chinese government relaxed economic control in the 1980s, several border towns recovered the jade trade with Burma. However, owing to an interruption of a few decades, local traders did not have sufficient knowledge for the evaluation of jade stones. This resulted in easy sales for the Yunnanese traders from Burma. Informants remarked that in the initial stage (the second half of the 1980s), jade stones with varying degrees of quality could find their market in Yunnan.

Mrs. Duan and Mrs. Peng

The sisters Mrs. Duan and Mrs. Peng are from a Yang family in Kokang. Their parents had nine children, two boys and seven girls. Mrs. Duan is the fourth daughter and Mrs. Peng the fifth. Because of the warring situation in Kokang, the Yangs moved from place to place before finally settling in Taunggyi in 1970. Mrs. Duan and Mrs. Peng were married there in 1976 and 1979 respectively.

Prior to marriage, Mrs. Duan and Mrs. Peng had been unfamiliar with the jade trade. Their father ran a brewery in Kokang; the livelihood of the family was well established before the mid-1960s. They found that life was much simpler in their maiden days; after marriage, their husbands were often away for trade. Each trip took at least two to three months, sometimes half a year or even longer. They were always worried for their husbands' safety and feared irregular checks by official agents at home. The Intelligence Department arranged spies to detect illegal trade in many places, and unannounced checks and interrogations became part of daily life for civilians. In a meeting with Mrs. Duan and Mrs. Peng in Pingzhou during my second trip there, they told of their life in Burma. Mrs. Duan said:

"Every time after my husband left home, I was very anxious for his safety. There was no means of direct communication, but from time to time there would be news about traders being kidnapped or killed on the way. I was so frightened whenever I heard such news; I often went to temples to pray. Once right after the departure of my husband and a few friends for trade, several agents of the Intelligence Department came to my house and inquired about the whereabouts of my husband. I was scared to death. My legs kept shaking. Fortunately, they didn't do anything. . . .

"Another time, my sister [Mrs. Peng] was sent for by the Intelligence Department for questioning. She was scared to death. Luckily she had a former Burmese classmate working there who told her not to be afraid."

Mrs. Peng added: "It was a frightful experience. An officer asked me if I knew my husband's whereabouts. I said: 'I don't know. He didn't tell me before leaving.' He said: 'You are his wife. How come you don't know where he is?' I said: 'I know he's away for trade. He goes to Mandalay first, but I don't know where else.' 'What merchandise was your husband dealing with?' he further asked. I replied: 'Whatever he can buy. Sometimes rice, sometimes textiles.' 'How long do his business trips take?' 'Two to three months.' 'Where does he go?' 'I don't know.' 'From whom does he purchase his goods?' 'I don't know. I'm just a housewife.' They kept asking me these questions for many hours."

Apart from emotional anxiety, women left behind often suffer economic instability. Mrs. Peng said: "Soon after marriage I was pregnant. Four months into my pregnancy, my husband left for Thailand to sell his jade stones. When he came back, Lifen was already three months old. During my three deliveries, my husband was absent. I had only my sister to attend me. Many times I also endured economic instability. On numerous occasions during our marriage, my husband lost large amounts of money in the jade business. I had to borrow money from my sister, who was the essential support for me."

Mrs. Duan concluded: "The repressive living conditions in Burma have trained Yunnanese people to be resilient. I still can endure the same hardships if the situation requires."

Comparatively, while most men tend to emphasize their heroic deeds in the face of austere circumstances, women are more open in revealing their feelings. Mrs. Duan's and Mrs. Peng's narrations echo the supportive sisterhood of the two Taunggyi sisters (chapter 6) and disclose an ongoing transformation of their inner life processes from carefree single women to married wives and mothers who not only had to shoulder household responsibilities alone during their husbands' absence, but also to confront institutional violence that generated overwhelming fear. Their accounts have reconstructed the social dramas in connection with their lived experiences, and they have delineated their agency and affects in response to patriarchal dominance as well as the political hegemony of the ruling junta.

After 1992

The Burmese government opened up jade mining and trading in 1992 when it was able to control the mining area, although the Kachin Independence Organization (KIO, the political organization of the KIA) did not sign a truce with the government until 1994.[10] The KIA's influence in mining has since become nominal. Informants said that prior to 1998, mining bosses still paid the KIA small annual fees, but thereafter, they only paid gift money occasionally.

In 1992, the government began to sell mining concessions. Each concession was valid for only two years but could be extended annually. The basic unit of a mining area was an acre; its bid started at two thousand euros, and

---

10. The cease-fire talks started in 1991. By then the area was becoming more peaceful (Lemere and West 2011, 150).

only Burmese citizens were entitled to participate in the bidding. Between 1992 and 1995, the government owned 25 percent of the value of excavated stones.[11] In 1996, each concession was changed to three years but without the possibility of extension. If the original mining boss wanted to continue to mine on the same piece of land, he had to submit a new bid. In 2000, the government changed this rule to the current one of giving priority to the existing mining boss. This means that if a competitor offers a higher bid for the new concession term, the government has to inform the current boss and ask him if he is willing to match the rival bid. After excavation, jade stones have to be carried to a nearby customs post for payment of *changkoushui* (tax at the mines), an ad valorem duty of 20 percent, prior to their further circulation. Since the stones are not yet cut, the appraised value tends to be low.

According to informants, the Yunnanese account for about 90 percent of all mining bosses. In 1992, Mr. Duan won the mining bid in three places, totaling more than twenty acres. He hired more than one thousand miners, recruited mostly from southern Burma. One of his relatives noted that local workers have better connections with local political power; it is thus better to hire laborers from faraway places who are comparatively more obedient. By the mid-1990s, the use of excavators, imported mostly from Japan, became popular. The price of a brand new excavator was around US$160,000 before 2012. With the increased use of machinery, the number of laborers has been greatly reduced. In 2007, Mr. Duan excavated more than thirty acres using only twenty-five excavators and about two hundred workers. Daqing said that his father's mines produce about two hundred tons of rough stones a year, which yield up to five thousand kilos of jade for product making. However, it is the quality of the stones that matters more than the quantity. Apart from the use of machinery, dynamite is applied in mining as well. Every boss wants to excavate as many jade stones as possible during his concession term, so mining takes place both day and night to maximize profit. The environment surrounding the mines is, however, badly affected. The first younger brother of Mr. Peng, who has a degree in mining and oil extraction, said that some places have been dug four

---

11. Later on the government's ownership ceased, but then resumed again. It accounts for 40 to 50 percent.

hundred to five hundred meters deep, resulting in the removal of mountains and diversion of rivers.[12]

The opening of the jade trade in Burma also contributed to a structural shift of the jade market from Chiang Mai to Mandalay. The opportunity to buy jade stones directly in Burma drew increasing numbers of dealers from Hong Kong, Taiwan, and China. Some Yunnanese traders in Burma started to provide brokerage services and to arrange deals between sellers and buyers and the shipment of purchased stones for the buyers. In 1995, the Burmese government issued permission for the establishment of jade companies to take charge of the brokerage. Mining bosses entrusted their stones to the jade companies for sale. At that point because of this law, the jade business in Chiang Mai more or less ended.

From the mid-1960s to the first half of the 1990s, jade companies in Thailand, which were founded on a strong monetary base and connections with different political agencies in Thailand and Burma, played an institutional role that supported the operation of the trade. Specifically, they handled negotiations between traders whenever disputes emerged, regulated informal tax rates, and meted out penalties to those who abused or broke trading agreements. Moreover, because of intense competition, jade companies sometimes had to resolve conflicts among themselves by seeking assistance from the higher levels of the political hierarchy, usually high-ranking Thai officers (see Chang 2004). During a period when the trade was predicated on underground trafficking, such an institutional role was fundamental to facilitate the operation of the jade trade. With the opening of the trade in Burma, the jade market then shifted to Burma, and new jade companies were established in Mandalay, leading to some notable changes. While the jade companies in Thailand were mostly owned by Yunnanese or other ethnic Chinese groups in the country, the new companies are primarily owned by Yunnanese in Burma, who have the advantage of local status and better local knowledge and connections. To a great extent, these companies maintain an institutional role in providing

---

12. A worker in Hpakant confided: "One of the biggest problems in Hpakant is where to throw the sediment from the mining. They destroy a 10,000-feet high mountain and dig 500 feet into the ground, and the question is where to throw the soil? They throw it into the Uru River which raises the floor of the river making the river bank narrow and causing floods" (quoted from http://www.burmalibrary.org/docs5/bloodjade-red.pdf).

brokerage services, in terms of adjustments to the tax rates for commission payments and assistance in negotiations when disputes occur between sellers and buyers. However, the former authoritative power of jade companies no longer exists.

Since 1995 there have been five major jade companies (first in Mandalay, then Yangon)—Fuji, Changlong, Jingu, Wenna, and Meiman. All of the bosses are local Yunnanese, except the boss of Jingu, who is Yunnanese from Thailand (but his wife is Yunnanese from Burma). However, whether these Yunnanese have their origins in Burma or Thailand, both sides are actually closely connected through kinship ties, as in the case of the Duans and the Pengs. Apart from these major companies, there have been hundreds of small companies that are mostly run by the Burmese to take care of local transactions. In Mandalay there is also a big jade marketplace (Figures 7–3 and 7–4), which was established by the government around 1998, located on Eighty-Seventh Street between Thirty-Third and Thirty-Fourth Streets, where a large number of Burmese traders composed of different ethnic groups congregate every day. However, informants estimated that local transactions among the Burmese constitute only about 10 to 20 percent of the total jade business; the other 80 to 90 percent is controlled by Yunnanese.

Before 2005, the major jade companies were located on the outskirts of Mandalay. Each one occupied a large piece of land with an imposing building and a big yard that served as storage for jade stones.[13] Each major jade company was backed by strong capital and helped sell jade stones from different owners for 5 percent commission. (Some jade companies were involved in mining as well.) The companies also provided loans to familiar mining bosses with the tacit agreement that when good stones were procured they had to be sold through the lending company. The loans were later repaid at an interest rate of 1.5 percent. In order to attract buyers from abroad, each jade company provided a range of useful services, including the booking of airline tickets, local transportation, hotel reservations, shopping trips for jade stones at different companies (not only its own), arrangements for paying taxes, and the shipment of purchased stones. Both

---

13. Take Changlong as an illustration. The company space is 150 feet by 320 feet. The stones placed in the yard are large pieces with a lower grade; those of high quality are deposited inside the building.

Figure 7–3. The jade market in Mandalay

Circulations of the Jade Trade 227

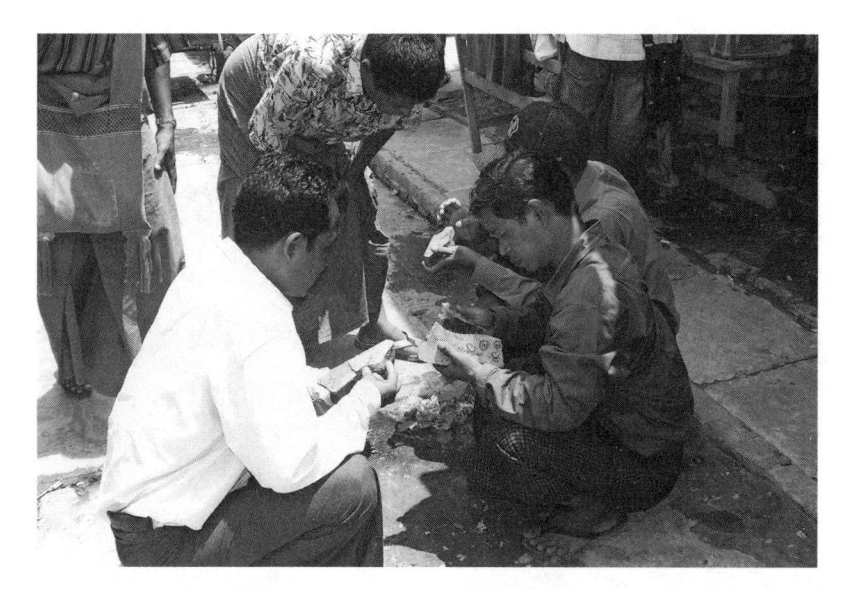

Figure 7-4. The jade market in Mandalay

jade stone sellers and buyers could visit a company at any time, not necessarily for business, often just to pass the time by chatting, smoking, playing mahjong, and eating. Local Yunnanese traders and those from Thailand were especially keen to play golf as a means of gambling. One day's stake for a player could amount to several million kyat. These leisurely pursuits contributed, in effect, to capital circulation; moreover, they were useful occasions for learning trading information and meeting potential trading partners, especially when one was interested in buying a high-priced piece but lacked sufficient capital. In 2005, the Burmese government issued a new regulation demanding that all export stones be sold first at public auctions (*gongpan*) in Yangon (Figure 7-5). As a result, the major jade companies moved from Mandalay to Yangon, and naturally the trade shifted there. Nonetheless, their services have remained by and large the same. (In October 2010, the Burmese government moved the auction venue again to its new capital, Naypyidaw. Consequently, several jade companies have established offices there.)

In the past, while the jade stones sold in Chiang Mai were often uncut, the stones sold in Burma now have mostly been cut through (*minghuo*). This is related to the fact that prior to 1992, both the mining and trafficking

Figure 7-5. A jade stone auction in Yangon

of jade stones in Burma were illegal. The high risk of engaging in the jade business consequently contributed to increased gambling on the trade. Both sellers and buyers staked their luck on the small quantity of jade stones safely brought to Thailand. However, following the opening of the trade, jade stones have been procured more easily, thanks also to the use of machinery. The large quantity of jade produced thus reduces the former emphasis on gambling. Foreign dealers are able to fly to Burma to buy jade stones, and they prefer to see cut stones before making purchases. However, among the Yunnanese, the trade in uncut stones still exists.

The Burmese government and the Union of Myanmar Economic Holding Company Ltd. (a Burmese military corporation) alternately organize three auctions annually, where they sell the stones for foreign currency.[14]

---

14. Prior to 2004, the currency used at the auction was American dollars; but following the American sanctions on Burma imposed in 2004 (based on the Burmese Freedom and Democracy Act of 2003), the currency has changed to euros.

Almost all of them have been cut, and one can easily evaluate their quality. According to a state regulation in Burma, only the stones purchased or bid upon by foreign buyers with foreign currency are allowed to be taken abroad after payment of a tax (also in foreign currency). However, many Yunnanese traders, like Mr. Duan and Mr. Peng, hold various nationalities, including Burmese, Thai, and Taiwanese, that allow them to export their stones from Burma and move in these countries (as well as to China) freely. (Those who do not hold a foreign identity usually ask for help from qualified relatives or friends or China / Hong Kong traders.)

In terms of tax payment, those who purchased stones at jade companies before 2005 had to pay an additional levy of 10 percent of the selling price at the customs house in Yangon prior to their exportation. The jade companies took care of the tax and shipment. In order to pay a lower tax, all jade companies under-declared the sold price. After the Burmese government issued the regulation stipulating that only stones sold at public auctions can be exported, the purchased stones have been taxed at 10 percent of the auctioned price without the possibility of negotiation. In this way, greater revenue income is guaranteed.[15] Despite strict regulations, underground trafficking of jade stones and products continues via the Burma-Yunnan border. It is difficult to ascertain the proportion of smuggled goods, but Mr. Peng estimated that it may constitute 20 percent of total jade sales.[16]

The sudden regulation change in 2005 at first had a strong impact on many other traders' enterprises. Foreign dealers could no longer buy jade stones at the jade companies, and mining bosses could not ship their stones directly to Guangzhou. Their goods were thus held up in Burma and they

---

15. The procedure for payment is as follows: After winning a bid at the auction, the buyer has to transfer the total amount of the bid price to the government's account. After the deduction of 10 percent for tax payment, the government then transfers equivalent "foreign exchange certificates" (FEC, also known as fake foreign currency) to the seller's account. The seller can either sell them to other traders in the import business, or use them to buy products from abroad. (In Burma, one can only import foreign commodities with FEC.)

16. Informants consistently said that jade mine bosses prefer to sell jade stones via auctions because intensive bidding guarantees a good price. The quantity of smuggled jade via border entrepôts like Ruili and Yingjiang is comparatively small. Moreover, the smuggled jade is mostly medium and low quality.

could not secure sufficient capital in the short term for reinvestment. In Mr. Duan's case, his mining business demands capital for buying fuel, payments to workers, and the payment of taxes at customs posts in the mining area. He had to seek financial support from relatives in different places. Since the change, he has had to bid on his own stones at the auctions if he wants to export them to Guangzhou for his business there.

Following rapid economic development in China and its increasing demand for jade products, most major jade companies in Burma have extended their business to Pingzhou. The extension has enhanced their competitive capacity in brokerage services. The bases in Burma take care of tax payments and shipment, while those in Pingzhou receive the goods, arrange tax payments there, and hand the goods to customers.[17] The jade companies in Pingzhou also organize alternating auctions, as mentioned earlier. They have developed clear rules regarding participation fees, the service charge rate, and the commission rate. The jade auctions, whether in Yangon, Naypyidaw, or Pingzhou, are distinctive sites where intensified circulations of commodities, capital, people, and information take place. Jade stones are brought from different sources and attract bidders from various countries. The bidding price for high-quality jade is often hundreds of thousands of euros, which usually attracts group bids backed by accumulated capital. Bidders use mobile phones to contact absent partners to discuss bid prices and exchange information. Each auction lasts several days to a week.

In 2006, I went to Yangmeicun in Jieyang County, four hours by bus from Guangzhou, to observe the jade trade there. By Mr. Duan's arrangement, I met a local dealer, Mr. Xia, who took me around to visit the jade market and an auction that was taking place (Figure 7–6). The auctions of jade stones in Jieyang or Pingzhou resemble those in Yangon: they are silent; bidders place their statements of offered prices in boxes, and at the end, the boxes are opened and those who have offered the highest amounts win the bids. The process of opening the boxes and checking the price statements is filmed and shown simultaneously on a big screen, where bidders can watch the proceedings.

---

17. For shipment, a jade company contacts a shipping service company like Mr. Peng's.

Figure 7–6. A jade stone auction in Jieyang

The Jieyang traders are mostly from Yangmeicun, originally a small village. The residents are Chaozhou, and over 80 percent of them are involved in the jade trade. Since the mid-1980s, when jade stones were smuggled from Burma to Yunnan, Jieyang people have gone to Yunnan to buy them for making products. Informants from Yangmeicun recalled that their ancestors during the Qing period had already been involved in this economic activity.[18] Each family house is like a small factory, where family members work on cutting and carving jade stones. The village has become well known for the sale of high-grade jade products since 2000. Moreover, the villagers are known for their bidding on high-priced jade stones in

---

18. Historically, from the time of the Ming period, the jade stones from upper Burma were transported to Yunnan by means of mule caravans, and then farther north to the Chinese court in Beijing (Chen 1966, 86; Sun 2000, 134–54; Xia 1948, 77–78). At the end of the Qing dynasty, sea transportation of jade stones to China was also undertaken because of the easing of restrictions on coastal trade; most of the high-quality precious stones made their way from Yangon to Hong Kong, Guangzhou, and Shanghai. The medium-quality stones were still transported by land to Yunnan (TCXZ 1995, 413; Xia 1948, 107). The Yangmeicun villagers may have been involved in working on jade stones as a result of this sea transportation.

Yangon and Naypyidaw auctions. Whereas dealers from Hong Kong and Taiwan were the primary jade stone buyers prior to the mid-1990s, those from Yangmeicun in Jieyang have become the new leading group of buyers with their superior number of participants and amount of capital.[19]

Seeing Jieyang people play the leading role in the jade product business, I asked several Yunnanese merchants in Guangzhou if the former would overtake the Yunnanese in the jade trade. They said that the economic force of the traders from China is superior to that of the Yunnanese from Burma, and they have thus predominated in buying jade stones at auctions and making and selling jade products in China. However, on account of their local status and intra-group connections, the mining business and brokerage are still controlled by the Yunnanese traders of Burma. In comparison, the Yunnanese traders of Thailand are no longer as active as their counterparts in Burma. This is partly due to the shift of the jade market as analyzed above, and partly because Thai society offers more diverse career opportunities to the younger generation of Yunnanese migrants, unlike in Burma, where career choices are limited and the jade trade remains an attractive business for young people.

Nevertheless, as the social, political, and economic situation in Burma is unstable, the continuity of the trade—as well as other economic activities in Burma—is uncertain. The government occasionally announces sudden halts to the export of jade stones, sometimes due to political considerations, at other times simply because it does not have enough staff to administer the exports, normally after auctions.[20] Also, the government changes trading policies and regulations every now and then without warning. This compels traders to continually adopt new strategies or make structural shifts. Furthermore, the international economic sanctions on Burma have had a negative impact. The gem trade is criticized as being a major

---

19. In 2002, more than fifty Yangmeicun villagers collaborated to bid for a jade stone with the price of about seventy million RMB in a Yangon auction. There are about four thousand traders from China at each jade stone auction. Since 2012, Jieyang traders have taken chartered airplanes from Jieyang to Naypyidaw to participate in bidding at the auctions.

20. In October 2004, after the arrest of the former prime minister Khin Nyunt on charges of corruption, the government halted the export for three months. In May 2012, because of continuous fighting between the Burmese army and the KIA, the government announced a halt to jade mining, and so far has not lifted the ban. In 2012 (March) and 2013 (July), there was only one auction each year in Naypyidaw.

source of foreign currency for the Burmese government (Cho 2008; Saw Yan Naing and Echo Hui 2014; 8088 for Burma 2008).[21] In response to international appeals, the banks in Hong Kong, which formerly helped transfer money to the Burmese government's account for the jade trade, stopped the service in August 2006. Traders were pressured to look for alternatives to cope with the situation. Based on his knowledge of transnational trade and his numerous connections, Mr. Peng embarked on the business of money transfer. He found a particular bank in Singapore that was willing to help. Neither he nor his daughter revealed how this is done, but they emphasized that their new involvement is meant to help fellow traders carry on the trade. In their view, the legality of the practice may be decided by different national or international political entities, but these external power structures do not have the ability to stop this regional trade, which has been undertaken by their predecessors for many centuries.

Circulation

The stories of the Duans and the Pengs highlight the economic agency of the Yunnanese traders in Burma in combating subjugation by the state. Their mobility connects them with external markets and keeps them conscious of new developments. Concretely, their venture to the jade mines and extension of the jade trade to Chiang Mai, Yunnan, and Guangzhou have resulted in the circulation of people, commodities, capital, information, techniques, and trade knowledge. In terms of human circulation, we learn of traders' extensive travels and recruitment of their family members and close kin. Yunnanese merchants commonly acknowledge the connection between traveling and the accumulation of knowledge of the jade trade. Before receiving mining and trading permission from the KIA, many Yunnanese traders like Mr. Peng and Mr. Duan had already risked visits to the mining area. They stayed there for a few months or longer and shopped around the mines for ideal stones. They called this search "roaming the holes" (*guang dongzi*). The process of visiting the jade mines

---

21. Western governments have removed most economic and political sanctions on Burma following the Burmese government's democratic reforms since 2011, but the US government still maintains its ban on gem imports from Burma (Eckert 2013).

is important as it provides chances to learn the distinctions among jade stones according to their mines of origin. Informants confided that skilled traders are able to tell which mine a stone is from by looking at its surface and feeling the texture of the crust. The surface evaluation relates to further appraisal of the quality contained within. When the jade trade was extended to Yunnan in the mid-1980s, local buyers were not able to make good evaluations because of their initial lack of trade knowledge, even when stones were cut.

With respect to circulation of commodities, the outflow of jade stones was accompanied by the inflow of contraband merchandise from Thailand and China. Before the opening of the jade trade in Burma, many jade traders, especially those with smaller capital, had to run both import and export trafficking in order to maximize profits. After selling their stones in Thailand or China, they purchased local goods for the trip back to Burma, as shown in chapter 5. In addition, if we treat labor as a type of commodity (McKeown 2011), jade mining in Kachin State has driven waves of migrant workers from the south to the north, especially before the use of machinery was popularly applied. (Of course, we can also treat this phenomenon as the circulation of people.)

Closely related to the flow of goods and human beings is the circulation of capital. Both mining and trading jade stones require investments of money. There were different ways to activate this circulation prior to the establishment of Inwa Bank in Hpakant in 1999. The simplest one was that traders or mining bosses carried money with them to the jade mines. However, the stay took at least several months to half a year. After the money was used up, traders or mining bosses had to borrow money from local peddlers, shop owners, or money creditors. This money-lending business was mostly run by women, as exemplified by Qiu Dajie and Zhou Dajie in chapter 6. After lending money to traders or mining bosses, the creditors left the mines and went to the borrowers' homes to collect debts plus interest with written acknowledgments of indebtedness. This was a risky undertaking, as the lenders could have been robbed on the way. Moreover, some debtors refused to pay their debts or disappeared altogether, as Qiu Dajie's story reveals. Informants remarked that it was comparatively safer for women to take up this job because their traveling attracted less attention. This may have been because traditionally, most petty traders in the country had been women; their movement with traded goods was regarded as common. Yet, a male jade trader confided to me that while all men wanted to make fortunes from jade deals, they despised engagement in money lending.

Since the establishment of the Inwa Bank in Hpakant, people have turned to its service for money transference, which is said to be safer and the service charge lower than previous underground transfers. However, the opening of jade mining by the government and the increasing need for greater amounts of capital investment have limited investment possibilities. Prior to 1992, anyone with a small amount of capital could participate in a mining venture secretly. After choosing a site that was not being worked by other people, the investor could begin mining. He usually hired a team of three to four people to dig one pit. Unavoidable costs included taxes to the KIA and food and board for the miners. Mining tools were primitive, limited to hoes, spades, shovels, and drills. The mining boss tried his luck until his capital was used up. By comparison, since 1992, only those with large amounts of capital are able to enter the mining enterprise and meet the requirements of both bidding for jade mines and buying machines.

In terms of the circulation of information, the movement of caravans between Thailand and Burma functioned as the primary carrier for both oral and written messages (as referred to by Zhang Dage in chapter 5). News from different places was disseminated in this way. As Mrs. Duan noted, there would occasionally be news about traders being kidnapped or killed along the way. In addition, there is the circulation of techniques, such as importation of machinery. Daqing mentioned to me that a Japanese delegation from an excavator company came to Burma in 2010 because Burma had become the company's biggest client.

In an essay investigating the circulation of copper and cotton between Southwest China, upper mainland Southeast Asia, and Southeast China from the seventeenth to the nineteenth centuries, Giersch (2011) stresses the need to place regional history in a larger global framework in order to build a dynamic picture of the circulatory regimes. The research leads him to conclude that human institutions, networks, and historical events were the major factors in shaping the fluid economic geography of the trades in question. In line with his viewpoint, this chapter also attests to the fact that the circulation of the jade trade has no fixed geographical space or territorial boundaries. The circulatory regime is affected by ethno-social, political, economic, and technological forces, and it has the potential for constant shifting and expansion. Each set of forces may be further divided into different levels—local, national, transnational, and international. In response to these various factors, the Yunnanese traders resort to personal networks, grounded on kinship ties, as well as institutional connections supported by the jade companies, to facilitate the operation of the trade. In other words, the pattern of their business organization is predicated both on horizontal relationships among traders themselves and hierarchical affiliation among the traders and the jade companies. Before the opening of trade in Burma, the latter aspect was especially distinct.

From the socialist period to the present, the social life of the jade trade has undergone a series of changes. Modern conveyance by vehicle, ship, and air that guarantees speedy and larger-quantity delivery has replaced the mule caravans for transportation of jade stones. Nevertheless, beneath the veneer of modern technology, unsettling undercurrents infiltrate political confrontation, economic conflicts, and environmental disputes. These multifarious tensions have complicated the "totality of circulations" of the jade trade. Strident condemnations against Yunnanese economic dominance and clientral relationship with the military junta from time to time appear in the media and reinforce xenophobic sentiments among the indigenous, especially in cities. This antagonistic tendency parallels the former anti-Chinese trends in Burma as well as in other Southeast Asian countries (Coppel 1983; Purcell 1960; Skinner 1957; Wickberg 1965) and creates an air of uncertainty in Burma. Digging increasingly deeper into the ground to procure the gradually diminishing quantities of jade stones seems to bring to the surface ever more intricate problems.

Epilogue

From Mules to Vehicles

> In those days living in the mountains, mules and horses were the best companions to human beings, as they shouldered the responsibility for transportation.
> —Zhang Dage, 2002

Throughout history, the migration culture of diasporic Yunnanese has largely been characterized by political instability and a peripatetic tradition, which have pushed them to keep moving and often take up itinerant professions. Their economic possibilities have ranged from being muleteers, soldiers, miners, rotating-market traders, or migrant laborers, to caravan traders or jade stone dealers. One may try multiple undertakings during one's lifetime. The transition from one profession to another, however, does not guarantee upward mobility. In reality, one's fortune may fluctuate, as shown in the narrators' stories. Despite this fact, travel has been a prevailing means among migrant Yunnanese for searching out opportunities and success, one that has contributed to their frequent border crossing, geographically and figuratively.

While illuminating a range of diasporic modes (as victim, military, labor, and trade), the narrators' accounts also outline different patterns of movement in relation to their home places in Burma. Some are not able to return; some continually leave and come back; some choose to return after leaving for a long time; and some return occasionally. No matter what patterns they have followed, travel opens their horizons, enriches their life experiences, and entails a comparative perspective for them to assess multiple lifestyles, places, and peoples. Moreover, it inspires their imaginations for different possible futures. Their departure, whether owing to a need to flee or a desire to pursue ambitions, compels them to say good-bye to their original lifestyle, family members, close friends, and things dear to them. Their migratory stories thus always intertwine complex emotions that project their subjective liminality.

Travel predicates fluidity of time and space. It helps shape travelers' lives and nurtures stories in their memory that in turn stimulate their narrativity. Among themselves, Yunnanese migrants frequently exchange stories of traveling or memories of the past. The writing of this ethnography is also grounded on their narrativity. In this epilogue I would first like to present a dialogue focused on the subject of mules and horses, which epitomizes the temperament of Yunnanese mobility and mirrors an intimate relationship between humans and their animals (from male perspectives in this case).

On August 25, 2008, I met Zhang Dage (the narrator of chapter 1) and Li Dage[1] at a well-known Thai restaurant in Taichung, central Taiwan, characterized by its exquisite cuisine and spacious, luminous structure styled in Thai exoticism. Li Dage is the owner. Like Zhang Dage, he grew up in a mountain village in Shan State and then moved with his family to Xincun in northern Thailand. He came to Taiwan for further education and afterward settled here. Whenever Zhang Dage and Li Dage meet, they have much to talk about—their memories of life in Burma and Thailand, their common friends, and developments in Taiwan.

I clearly remember that day. Classic Thai music filled the air. A montage of fieldwork images from Burma and Thailand flashed through my mind. It was lunchtime, and Zhang Dage ordered an array of splendid dishes—seafood salad, deep-fried shrimp cake, steamed sea bass in lemon sauce, stir-fried pork with Yunnanese pickles, Thai-style fried noodles, tamarind glazed crispy chicken, stir-fried water spinach in Thai bean paste, shrimp vermicelli pot, and sago coconut milk. These Thai and Yunnanese delicacies guaranteed good afternoon talk.

---

1. Li Dage, the fifth younger brother of Mr. Li (the father in chapter 3), had helped contact his brother about my visit to Taunggyi first in 2006 and again in 2007, although the latter seemed not to have heard about me.

Li Dage told me he had heard much about me and my research from Zhang Dage and was very willing to share his life stories with me. I briefly asked about his biographical information, but quickly he and Zhang Dage took over the conversation, beginning with childhood reminiscences. A major part of their discussion was about mules and horses. I recorded their conversion that day and extracted a part as follows:

Li Dage: "When we lived in Changqingshan, every household had a stable of horses and mules. In the morning, a muleteer would beat a gong—*dong, dong, dong*—and on hearing it, we would release our livestock and let the muleteer chase them to the higher part of the mountain to graze. That muleteer helped look after all the livestock of the whole village. Villagers had no problem identifying their own animals later in the day. . . .

"Much of Changqingshan was grassland. There was a very tall banyan tree, which we called the 'tree of grand green' [*daqingshu*]. We could see it from afar. It was the only tree on a large piece of grassland where the muleteer took the animals to graze during the day. In the evening, he chased them back to the village. On hearing his beating the gong, villagers would go to bring their animals home."

Zhang Dage: "Our village didn't have a common muleteer. Yours was more organized. Perhaps you had more horses and mules. Every region had its way of doing things. Bianliang was a valley, and the nearby mountain was covered with poppy farms. Each house released its own mules to graze in the morning and went to look for them in the evening. When we saw our neighbors' animals, we also helped chase them back home."

Li Dage: "Well, our place was more organized. . . . There was a large playground with a big pond, and the livestock were kept away from the pond because the water was for humans. The animals were led to a ditch on their way back to the village."

Zhang Dage: "Was the muleteer a kid?"

Li Dage: "No, he was an adult. . . . Our place had another type of horse and mule, which we called *fangsheng ma* [released horse or mule]. They were horses and mules that were too old to carry things. We released them to the mountain and let them die naturally. There was a hierarchy among the livestock. Only those which engaged in transportation were given feed."

Zhang Dage: "Yes, those that participated in the long-distance caravan trade ate the best—they were fed with yellow beans."

Li Dage: "That's right! If a mule took part in transportation that day, it would be rewarded with feed put in a bag."

Zhang Dage: "*Maliao dai* [feedbag]."

Li Dage: "Exactly. It was hung under its mouth, and the mule munched the feed while walking. After the mule returned to the stable, it was again given fodder mixed with feed."

Zhang Dage took my notebook and started to draw a mule (Figure E–1) and explained to me the harness placed on it:

"Wen-Chin, I've mentioned to you that I went to Thailand with an armed caravan. You know at the end of the first day after riding a mule for so long, I couldn't walk. I could hardly stand. I had been given a *jiatou ma*, a mule with no proper saddle but just a wooden frame on its back, which was meant for transporting goods. I had to squat on the framework with one leg braced on the collar [*panxiong*]. When going upward, I could still manage to stay on its back, but when going downward, I kept sliding off the mule. It was dreadful."

Li Dage: "You were lucky to ride a *jiatou ma*. You know what mule I rode from Mong Nai to Thailand? There was neither a saddle, nor a wooden frame, but simply a small piece of tree trunk tied on the back. A piece of quilt was placed under the trunk. Whenever we were moving downward, I slid."

Zhang Dage: "I know what you mean. A piece of bark was made concave, and you put your butt on it. It was very uncomfortable."

Li Dage: "It was. I would rather have walked than ride that mule. Adults kept scolding me: 'You chicken. You dare not ride.' I didn't know how to explain to them."

Zhang Dage: "I had the same experience. We were still kids with short legs, but adults gave us big horses to ride. The structure didn't fit us. There's still another kind of horse and mule—*huama*, with no harness at all. You can only grab its mane while riding. Some people are very good at riding bareback simply by pressing their legs tightly against the horse's sides."

Zhang Dage and Li Dage continued to share funny experiences of riding these types of mules and horses during their childhood, a golden time with unforgettable adventures and joy.

Undoubtedly, horses and mules played a significant role for a great number of migrant Yunnanese in Burma, as they were the major means of transportation for going beyond their villages and engaging in economic pursuits before the mid-1980s.[2] Not only did these animals fulfill many

---

2. In some places mule, horse, and ox transportation (in small numbers) is still seen.

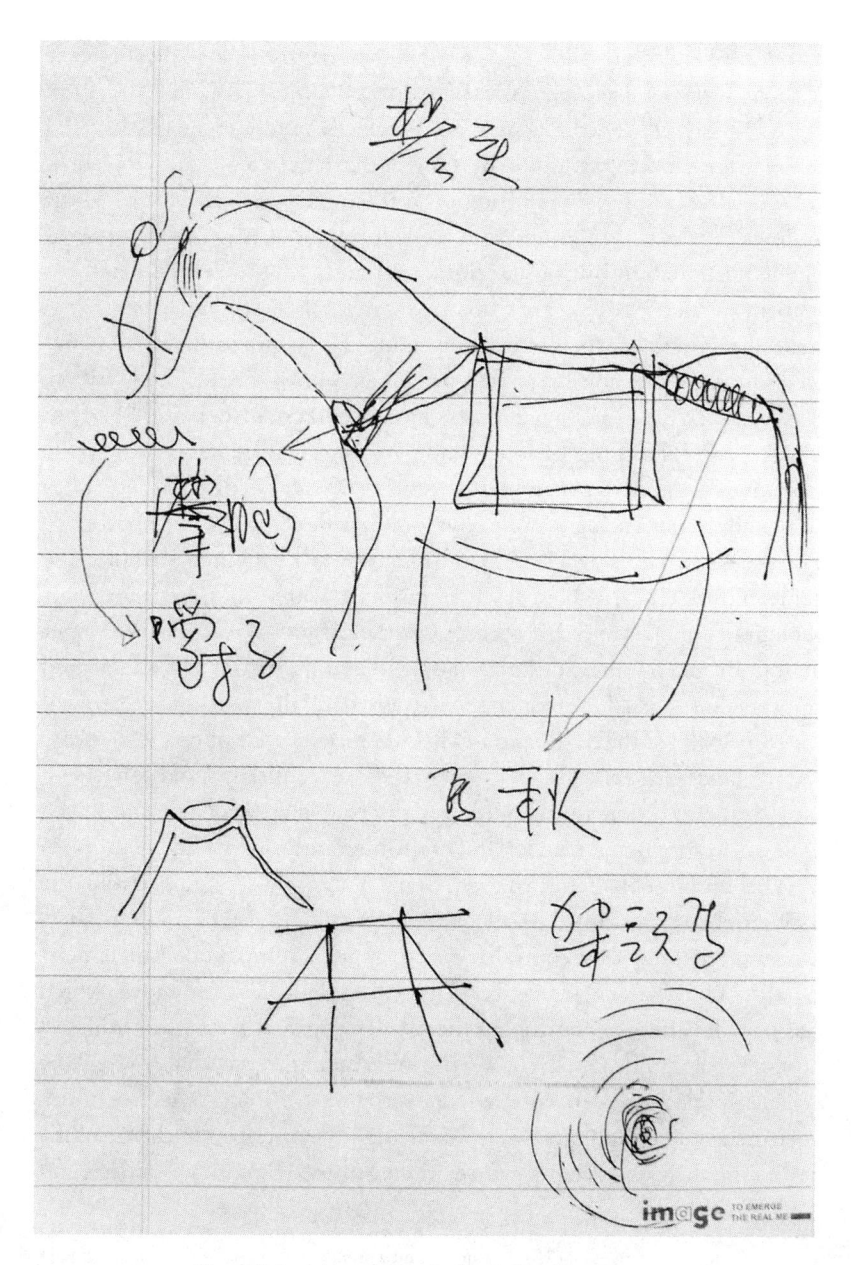

Figure E–1. A harnessed mule sketched by Zhang Dage

Yunnanese ambitions and quests for livelihood; those who had experience of them nurtured these memories with affection. Mules frequently recur in the narratives of the older generation, especially of those who participated in the mule caravan trade, and of those in the generation that followed, as we see in the childhood reminiscences of Zhang Dage and Li Dage. These animals' tracks covered numerous trails throughout the rugged topography in northeastern Burma and the borderlands of northern Thailand.

Being an outsider who grew up in a different place, and not having experienced repeated overland movement under harsh circumstances, I struggled for a long time to envision informants' accounts, both oral and written, and stumbled again and again upon objects I had not seen, places I had not been to, painful feelings I had not endured, as well as inconsistencies in the narratives. To a small extent I became familiar with their descriptions after personally experiencing some of the locations described in their accounts. For the most part, however, I had to manage with my imagination. The caravan trade I heard about so often in stories, with its hundreds or even a thousand or more mules, has become history. Large mule caravans no longer exist in Burma or other countries of upland Southeast Asia.[3] To understand this traveling trade, I came as close as I could to firsthand experience, traveling some parts of the trading routes by car or motorcycle or on foot, observing the landscape and sites that remain there, encountering and conversing with former muleteers and traders. I wish I could take a time machine back through history to the wonderland of the migrant Yunnanese.

The movement of the contemporary Yunnanese migrants from the 1950s to the 1970s was primarily involuntary. Their refugee status, borderland resettlement, and contraband involvement compounded their marginality. However, their livelihood as borderlanders on the move, which has had the effect of connecting them to an expansive outside world and sustaining a significant part of the Burmese economy, especially during the socialist period (though not officially recognized), compels us to rethink their marginality and other peripheral attributes ascribed to them. While reviewing their experiences, which are constrained by national policies and

---

3. Van Schendel mentions Chinese and Burmese mule caravans near the border with Bangladesh that transport contraband, but he does not provide further details about a caravan's organization or who these "Chinese and Burmese" traders are (2005, 165–66). Judging from a picture of a caravan shown in the book (p. 166; the picture was taken in 2000), its size is small, and the simple organization looks quite different from the ones engaging in long-distance trade that Yunnanese informants described.

regulations, we also witness their dynamism, their power, as well as their struggles to survive, and apprehend what Anna Tsing has tried to do by illuminating the "margins." She says: "I use the term [margins] to indicate an analytic placement that makes evident both the constraining, oppressive quality of cultural exclusion, and the creative potential of rearticulating, enlivening, and rearranging the very social categories that peripherize a group's existence" (1994, 279).

Lifestyle in Shan State has changed much. Given the shift to a market-oriented economy since the end of 1988, Burma (or Myanmar) has been experiencing profound transformations, compounded by numerous ecological, social, and political ruptures. The government has opened several border towns for trade with neighboring countries. They include Muse, Loije, Laiza, Chinshweshaw, and Kambaitti adjacent to China; Tachileik, Myawaddy, and Kawthaung connecting Thailand; and Tamu and Reed bordering India (Maung Chan 2005). Among them, Muse, which adjoins Ruili in Yunnan Province, has been the busiest point since the mid-1990s, owing to the rapid growth of the Sino-Burmese trade. The Ruili-Muse connection has channeled the largest amount of bilateral trade.[4]

Several times, I traveled from Mandalay to Lashio on the "new" Burma Road, and in October 2013 I made my way to Muse and Namkham.[5] This historic route, which witnessed the plying of mule caravans for centuries, is now completely dominated by overloaded trucks, buses, and motorcycles. Yunnanese migrants in Burma, using their familiarity with the route and expertise in the long-distance trade, have assumed a substantial role in transportation ventures and the import-export trade. Some of them have also launched investments in Ruili, Kunming, Guangzhou, and other Chinese cities, especially in the jade and gem trade. In addition, many Yunnanese migrants have expanded to other fields of investment inside Burma,

---

4. In 2011 China overtook Thailand as Burma's largest trading partner, with trade amounting to US$6.5 billion, according to International Monetary Fund figures (Aye Thidar Kyaw 2012; Kurtenbach 2012). Its investment is concentrated in gas, oil, mining, plantation, and hydroelectric dam projects. For the Chinese side, Ruili/Jiegao handles 70 percent of Yunnanese-Burmese trade, or 34 percent of Sino-Burmese trade (Meng and Si 2009, 16); for the Burmese side, Muse channels 70 percent of the nation's total trading amount with China (Wikipedia, http://en.wikipedia.org/wiki/Muse,_Burma).

5. The original Burma Road was constructed during the Second World War and ran between Kunming and Lashio, for transporting the Allies' supplies from Burma to China via the Wanding–Kyukok connection at the Sino-Burmese border. The new Burma Road follows by and large the old route via the Ruili–Muse gateway at the border and has been extended from Lashio to Yangon via Mandalay. It has been a primary transportation line in Burma since the 1990s.

including logging, land speculation, construction, crop transactions, fish farming, chicken farming, and running hotels and restaurants.

From the socialist period to the current regime, the economic structure has changed from a highly state-controlled system to a more open but still controlled market-oriented economy (Taylor 2001; Turnell 2009). Corruption remains, or has even intensified (Steinberg 2010, 100–101; Chang 2013). Ethnic conflicts have eased in some areas, but politically, the country remains divided (Chin 2009; Skidmore 2004; Smith 1993; South 2008; Steinberg 2006; Thawnghmung 2012; Wilson 2006). Parallel to the situation in Kalimantan described by Tsing (2005), the arrival of international corporations in the last two years is accelerating Burmese economic explorations and also generating new frictions (Banyan 2013; TSYO 2011; Woods 2012). While exerting their economic agency in response to new economic flexibility, the Yunnanese migrants are also facing an acute backlash from local communities.[6] The display of wealth among some Yunnanese in Yangon and Mandalay—extravagant houses, expensive cars, and excessive wedding parties in particular—incites local discontent. This phenomenon, while pointing to serious unevenness of development in a third-world country, also disguises the fact that the majority of Yunnanese migrants in the country are small- and medium-level merchants.

Taking the perspective from below at the "interstices of transnational and transcultural processes," Thongchai Winichakul calls for traversing "the margins of national identity and national history, looking for the 'in-between' locations of encounters" (2003, 23), or writing "a history at interstices." By composing an ethnography of lives, of individualities, and of a migrant group beyond borders, I have attempted to answer his call and also to carry forth in the spirit of Tsing and other scholars working on the livelihoods of borderlanders. The migration history and economic transnationalism of the contemporary Yunnanese migrants of Burma have provided illuminating insight into the way in which their mercantile dynamism reflects the intricate politico-economic scenarios in Burma. The stories told here negate an essentialized understanding of center versus periphery, legality versus illegality, autochthons versus allochthons, and the absolute legitimacy attached to the nation-state.

---

6. While those with larger amounts of capital may be seeking collaboration with foreign investments, especially those from China, small merchants may be forced out of business owing to intensive competition. Further research is required to trace this new development.

Glossary

Selected people's names and place names, as well as verse passages, proverbs, and other sayings are included below.

Chinese Words

ai 愛   love

baba 粑粑   rice cakes, made especially for the Moon Festival in the eighth month of the lunar calendar and Chinese New Year

babasi 粑粑絲   Yunnanese cooked noodles

baitiandi 拜大地   to worship Heaven and Earth

baiyi shi zhuai zhe hanren shi cheng zhe 百夷是跩著漢人是撐著   Baiyi women, they would have abandoned their children; but we Han women have to endure the condition.

baozi 包子   steamed stuffed bun

beibei 伯伯   senior uncle

bianjiaoshi 邊角石   small sliced pieces of jade stones, "leftovers" from larger pieces that have been used for making bangles or other larger ornaments

biaohui 標會   loan-bidding association

Glossary

bie nian le 別念了　Stop reciting.

bielai zheli nao 別來這裡鬧　Do not create disturbances here.

buke paotouloumian 不可拋頭露面　confined to domestic life and restricted from the public sphere

buyecheng 不夜城　bustling town where the lights are never turned off even during the night

changkoushui 場口稅　tax at (jade) mines

Changqingshan 長青山　(place name)

changzi 腸子　sausage

Chiang Ching-kuo 蔣經國　(personal name)

Chiang Kai-shek 蔣介石　(personal name)

chuang 闖　to explore the world

chunlian 春聯　New Year's couplets

dachi dahe 大吃大喝　spending much money on food and drink

dadie 大爹　senior uncle

dage 大哥　senior brother

daguotou or ***maguotou*** 大鍋頭/馬鍋頭　big-pot head / pot head of a mule caravan

dajie 大姊　elder sister

Dajie huijia lei wangwang / Choumei kulian su dieniang / Younyu mojia heshunxiang / Shinian shougua banyueshuang 大姐回家淚汪汪, 愁眉苦臉訴爹娘。有女莫嫁和順鄉, 十年守寡半月雙　Eldest sister came home, tears in her eyes. / Sullenly she related her stories to her parents. / Do not marry your daughter to a man of Heshun. / During a period of ten years, the couple is together for half a month.

dalu gongzuochu 大陸工作處　the Intelligence Mainland Operation Bureau

dama 大媽　senior aunt

dan 擔　The act of carrying water by placing a carrying pole on the shoulders with one bucket hung on each end is called *danshui* (擔水), and one *dan* of water refers to two buckets of water.

dangguande 當官的　officials

dao waimian quchuang 到外面去闖　to explore the world

dapiao bian 大票變　demonetization of the Burmese kyat

daqingshu 大青樹　banyan tree

dashen 大嬸　junior aunt

Dashuitang 大水塘　(place name)

datianxia 打天下　to explore the world

ding tian li di 頂天立地　with feet planted on the ground and head supporting the sky

Dongmiu guanyinsi 洞謬觀音寺　a Chinese temple in Amarapura, eight miles south of Mandalay

douchi 豆豉　fermented soybeans

doufu 豆腐   soybean curd

Du Wenxiu 杜文秀   (personal name)

Duan Xiwen 段希文   (personal name)

duizhan 堆棧   places for storage

duli diertuan tuanzhang 獨立第二團團長   the commanding officer of the Second Independent Regiment

erfang 耳房   the side room

erjiangdao 二漿刀   the second incision

erjie 二姊   the second elder sister

erxiaojie 二小姐   the second young lady

fangsheng ma 放生馬   released horse/mule

feicui 翡翠   high-quality jadeite

fengshui 風水   geomancy

Fuguo xuechi shouchuang zhongzhen jiaoyu / xingbang tuqiang peiyang aiguo wenhua 復國血恥首創忠貞教育，興邦圖強培養愛國文化   Recover the motherland and wipe out national shame through the teaching and transmission of loyalty; regain and develop the nation with the cultivation of patriotic culture.

fujun rumian 夫君如面   a formal address to one's husband at the beginning of a letter

fuqin daren 父親大人   a formal address to one's father at the beginning of a letter

fushifei 副食費   fees for non-staple food

gai/jie 街   marketplace

gaoxiao 高校   middle school

Gengma 耿馬   (place name)

gonglu 公路   public roads

gongpan 公盤   public auction

gou weidao 夠味道   exciting (used figuratively)

guang dongzi 逛洞子   to roam the jade mines for purchase of jade stones

guanxi 關係   connections

gugu 姑姑   aunt; sister of one's father

guiqiao 歸僑   returned overseas Chinese

guiren 貴人   important person

Gui Wang 桂王   Prince Gui

guo 鍋   pot

guogan minzu wenhuahui 果敢民族文化會   Ethnic Kokang Cultural Association

guoganren 果敢人   Kokangs

hanchao huizi 漢朝回子   Muslims of the Han Empire

hanjiao 漢教   Han religion; believers of Han religion

hanzu huijiao 漢族回教   Muslims of Han nationality

he 和   peace

Heshun 和順 (place name)

hongqi baiqi 紅旗白旗 red flags versus white flags

hua yanbao 劃煙包 to incise poppy pods

huama 滑馬 horse with no harness

hui 會 rotating credit

huijiao 回教 Islam; believers of Islam

huiqian 會錢 money for participating in a loan-bidding association

huitou 會頭 organizer of a loan-bidding association

hunsang huzhuhui 婚喪互助會 Association of Mutual Help for Weddings and Funerals

huotou 伙頭 headman

huotui 火腿 ham

ji wang kai lai 繼往開來 to carry on the heritage so as to pave the way for future generations

Jiao yisheng wodeer / Xiting genyou / Feirongyi / Fuyangni / Shi qi ba jiu / Zong quyuan / yizhike / Sinian sanqiu 叫一聲我的兒, 細聽根由; 非容易, 扶養你, 十七八九; 縱去遠, 亦只可, 四年三秋 I call my son once again, / Listen to my words carefully. / It is hard to raise you; / Aged only seventeen, eighteen, or nineteen, / You are setting off on a long journey. / See you again perhaps in three or four years

jiaohua 教化 to civilize the barbarous people

jiatou ma 架頭馬 a mule with no proper saddle

Jieyang 揭陽 (place name)

Jin Yong 金庸 a popular Chinese martial-arts fiction writer based in Hong Kong

Jinduoyan tudici 金多堰土地祠 a Chinese temple in Mandalay

jinjina 金雞納 cinchona

juntun 軍屯 military settlement

kai sao 開燒 to cook outdoors

kaibazi 開壩子 to open the valley

Kanchai mokan putaoteng / Yangnyu mojia ganmaren / Sanshi wanshang zuoxifu / Chuyi zaoshang tichumen 砍柴莫砍葡萄藤, 養女莫嫁趕馬人; 三十晚上做媳婦, 初一早上提出門 Do not cut grape vines for firewood. / Do not marry off your daughter to a muleteer. / Bride [of a muleteer] on the 30th eve, / her husband leaves at dawn of the first [the next day].

kaojiu 烤酒 distillery

keyi duo bukeyi shao 可以多不可以少 It has to be more and not less.

kongduo/kongtuo 空馱 mules that carried kitchenware and food

kuajing minjian 跨境民間 transnational popular realm

Kuomintang or KMT 國民黨 the Chinese Nationalist Party

lantouche 藍頭車 bull-nosed Hino trucks from Japan

laoda 老大　big brother

laodun 老盾　old silver coins

laomian 老緬　old Burmans

laoshi 老師　teacher

laoxiang 老鄉　countrymen, preferably from one's home village

laoye 老爺　an old-fashioned way of addressing one's father

laoyinyuan 老銀元　old silver Chinese coins

leine zashilei 累呢絷實累　very tired

Li Wenhuan 李文煥　(personal name)

lianzhang 連長　company commander

Luo Xinghan 羅星漢　(personal name)

Ma Linyu 馬麟玉　(personal name)

mabang wenhua 馬幫文化　mule caravan culture

maliao dai 馬料袋　feedbag

malibaren 麻栗巴人　people of Maliba (Kokangs)

Meng Gen 孟艮　(place name)

miandian tongbao 緬甸同胞　compatriots from Burma

minggong buhe 命宮不合　incompatible destinies

minghuo 明貨　jade stones that have been cut through

minjian 民間　popular realm

mintun 民屯　civilian settlement

Mu Bang 木邦　(place name)

nande kuadekuai nyude zhangbudehao 男的垮的快女的漲不得好　Men may go bankrupt quickly, but women are only able to obtain petty profits.

Nanjing Yingtianfu 南京應天府　(place name)

neibing 內病　internal illness; sexual urge (used figuratively)

nianqing zhiqigao 年輕志氣高　young and ambitious

nibuzuo yao efan 你不做要餓飯　If you don't take risks, you starve.

nyuer bi erzi gujia 女兒比兒子顧家　Daughters look after the household better than sons.

Panlong 搬攏　(place name)

Panglong 邦隆　(place name)

Pannong 班弄　(place name)

panxiong 攀胸　horse collar

pao mabang 跑馬幫　to engage in the mule caravan trade

pao shengyi 跑生意　to conduct (transnational) trade (by vehicle)

ping 平　harmony

pu er cha 普耳茶　Pu-er tea

250   Glossary

Qiao Da 僑大   a college that offers preparatory courses to Chinese overseas students before they are assigned to universities in Taiwan

qingzhen 清真   Islamic concept, literally "purity and truth"

Qiong Yao 瓊瑤   a popular romance novelist based in Taiwan

qiong zou yifang ji zou chang (窮走夷方急走廠)   When one was in need of money, one joined the caravan trade and traveled to places inhabited by "barbarians" (other ethnic groups), or hoped to get lucky in the jade and other mineral mines (in Burma).

qiuqian 求籤   to seek divine guidance by drawing lots

quzhang 區長   division chief

rang ta daowaimian chuang yi chuang 讓他到外面闖一闖   Let him go and explore the outside world.

ren 仁   benevolence

Rensheng wugendi / Piaoru moshangchen / Fensan zhufengzhuan / Ciyi feichangshen / Luodi weixiongdi / Hebi qingurou / Dehuan dangzuole / Doujiu jubilin / Shengnian buzailai / Yiri nanzaichen / Jishi dangmianli / Suiyue budairen 人生無根蒂 / 飄如陌上塵 / 分散逐風轉 / 此已非常身 / 落地為兄弟 / 何必親骨肉 / 得歡當作樂 / 斗酒聚比鄰 / 盛年不再來 / 一日難再晨 / 及時當勉勵 / 歲月不待人   Life has no roots / Like dust floating on a footpath / Scattered by the wind without a destination / The physical body is not eternal / Having been born to this world / We are all brothers / There is no need for bloodshed / Enjoy life whenever possible / Drink with neighbors / This life will not come again / Just like a day passes by / Act now / Time never awaits you.

rensiluo 人死囉   already dead

Ruili 瑞麗   (place name)

sangai* /*sanjie 三街   three rotating markets

sanmin zhuyi 三民主義   the Three Principles of the People, created by Dr. Sun Yat-sen, the national father of the Republic of China

Sanzijing 三字經   an ancient Chinese text, used in children's education

shan shen 山神   mountain gods

Shangliuhu 上六戶   (place name)

shangtun 商屯   merchant settlement

shenghuo xiguan 生活習慣   lifestyles

shengji 生基   grave

shuiyantong 水煙筒   water pipe

side qiongbude 死得窮不得   You may die but you cannot be poor.

silaomian 死老緬   damn old Burman

sipolian de zheng 撕破臉的爭   to fight for one's domain without considering appearances

siwei bade 四維八德   four ethical principles and eight cardinal virtues *taiwan laijiang* 台灣來獎　a prize from Taiwan

tangge 堂哥　paternal cousin

Tengchong 騰衝　(place name)

ting xiaoxi 聽消息　to listen to news

tong jiamen 同家門　member of the same genealogy

tou 偷　to steal

toujiangdao 頭漿刀　the first incision

tudong 土洞　underground cave

tugong 土共　local Communists

tusi 土司　native official

wode gushi sanbenshu ye xiebuwan 我的故事三本書也寫不完　Even three books would not be enough to record my story.

wode gushi santian sanye ye shuo buwan 我的故事三天三夜也說不完　Three days and three nights would not exhaust my story.

wodeyisheng dou aihu renmin chile henduoku women shi buaiqian ai mingyi 我的一生都愛護人民，吃了很多苦，我們是不愛錢，愛名義　I have cared for my people my whole life. I have suffered a great deal. I do not aim for money but for name.

women shi tong guokou 我們是同鍋口　We are from the same pot.

wuxia xiaoshuo 武俠小說　Chinese martial arts fiction

wuziqiang 五子槍　five-bullet gun

xia jiangbianpo 下江邊坡　to walk downwards to a river

xiang women miandianren daoqian 向我們緬甸人道歉　to apologize to us Burmese

Xianluo [Huaqiao] Ribao 暹羅華僑日報　a Chinese newspaper company in Bangkok

xiao 孝　filial piety

xidoufen 稀豆粉　gruel cooked from ground garden peas

xihuan jiu qu toulai 喜歡就去偷來　to steal a girl for marriage

xin 信　trust

Xishi xianwen 昔時賢文　an ancient Chinese text, used in children's education

yan tade sichu 醃她的私處　to stuff into a mistress's vagina

yancai 醃菜　pickled vegetable

Yangmeicun 揚美村　(place name)

yao zhuanqian jiuyou fengxian pafengxian jiu zhuanbuliaoqian 要賺錢就有風險，怕風險就賺不了錢　If you are afraid of risks, you can't make profits.

yaqiang tiruo 壓強提弱　to suppress the bully and assist the weak

yi 義　justice

yi sao lu 一燒路　a journey that requires cooking one meal

yiba 一把　a small unit of a mule caravan

yiben zhengjing 一本正經　serious manner

yibian zou yibian tanlu 一邊走一邊探路　to ask for information while walking *yidanbang/yixiaobang* 一單幫/一小幫   a small mule caravan

yige chufang rongbuxia liangge nyuren 一個廚房容不下兩個女人   A kitchen does not accommodate two women.

yiren zhaizi 夷人寨子   village of barbarous people

yishan burong erhu 一山不容二虎   A mountain cannot accommodate two tigers.

youtiao 油條   deep-fried breadstick

yuqi jie 玉器街   jade market

zhangqi 瘴氣   pestilential vapors in forests that cause illnesses

zhao poniang 找婆娘   to look for mistresses

Zhenkang 鎮康   (place name)

zhenzhi 針織   machine knitting

zhenzhu 真主   the True Lord

zheshi sheme 這是什麼   What is this?

zhiqi 志氣   ambition

zhong 忠   loyalty

zhong di 種地   farming

zhong yuanzi 種園子   cultivating gardens

zhonghua wenhua 中華文化   Chinese culture

zhuan gai/jie 轉街   rotating market

zidibing 子弟兵   younger dependent troops

zitie 字帖   copybooks for practicing Chinese calligraphy

zongjuede gegeburu 總覺得格格不入   do not fit together well

zongzi 粽子   glutinous rice dumplings prepared especially for the Duanwu Festival during the fifth month of the lunar calendar

zuixiyimin 罪徙移民   exiles

zuo huishui 做匯水   to conduct business that involves transferring money (of different currencies)

Burmese Words

byo ပျော်   happy

daba khawlei ဒါဘာခေါ်လဲ   What is this?

danpauk ဒန်ပေါက်/ဒံပေါက်   Indian *biriyani*

dikaung ဒီကောင်   kid

hmatpontin မှတ်ပုံတင်   identification card

hmaungkho မှောင်ခိုဈေး   black market

kapya ကပြား   mixed blood

lanma လမ်းမ   main road

longyi လုံချည်   a sarong-like skirt commonly worn by both men and women in Burma

lukyi လူကြီး   big men; officials

monhinkha မုန့်ဟင်းခါး:   rice vermicelli in fish soup

Mo-ywa-yin mo-ye-cho-meh / Me-Me la-yin no-so-meh / Pe-Pe la-yin oun-thi kweh-sa-meh မိုးရွာရင် မိုးရေချိုးမယ်။ မေမေလာရင် နို့စို့မယ်။ ဖေဖေလာရင် အုန်းသီးခွဲစားမယ်။   When rain comes, we take a shower in the rain. / When mama comes, we drink milk from her. / When daddy comes, we eat the coconut he cuts for us.

saikka ဆိုက်ကား:   trishaw

tayoke soe တရုတ်ဆိုး:   damned Chinese

References

Abu-Lughod, Lila. 1993. *Writing Women's Worlds: Bedouin Stories*. Berkeley: University of California Press.

Akanle, Olayinka. 2013. *Kinship Networks and International Migration in Nigeria*. Newcastle: Cambridge Scholars Publishing.

Andaya, Barbara Watson. 2006. *The Flaming Womb: Repositioning Women in Early Modern Southeast Asia*. Honolulu: University of Hawai'i Press.

Anzaldúa, Gloria. 1987. *Borderlands / La Frontera: The New Mestiza*. San Francisco: Aunt Lute Books.

Appadurai, Arjun. 1986. "Introduction: Commodities and the Politics of Value." In *The Social Life of Things: Commodities in Cultural Perspective*, edited by Arjun Appadurai. 3–63. Cambridge: Cambridge University Press.

Archer, W. J. 1892. "Report on a Journey in the Me-kong Valley." In *Blue Books, Siam*, no. 1, vol. C-6558: 13. London: HMSO.

Atwill, David G. 2006. *The Chinese Sultanate: Islam, Ethnicity, and the Panthay Rebellion in Southwest China, 1856–1873*. Stanford, CA: Stanford University Press.

Aung Su Shin. 2003. "Muslims Flee Religious Persecution." *Irrawaddy*, November 11.

Aye Thidar Kyaw. 2012. "China Firms Trade Position in Myanmar." *Myanmar Times*, January 16.

Banyan. 2013. "Redeveloping Myanmar: Where There's a Will." *Economist*, December 18.

References

Bao Jiemin. 2005. *Marital Acts: Gender, Sexuality, and Identity among the Chinese Thai Diaspora*. Honolulu: University of Hawai'i Press.

Basch, Linda, Nina Glick Schiller, and Cristian Szanton Blanc. 1994. *Nations Unbound: Transnational Projects, Postcolonial Predicaments and Deterritorialized Nation-States*. Amsterdam: Gordon and Breach Publishers.

Baud, Michiel, and William van Schendel. 1997. "Toward a Comparative History of Borderlands." *Journal of World History* 8, no. 2: 211–42.

Behar, Ruth. 1993. *Translated Woman: Crossing the Border with Esperanza's Story*. Boston: Beacon Press.

Belsey, Catherine. 1991. "Constructing the Subject, Deconstructing the Text." In *Feminisms: An Anthology of Literary Theory and Criticism*, edited by Robyn Warhol and Diane Price Herndl, 593–609. New Brunswick, NJ: Rutgers University Press.

Berlie, J. A. 2008. *The Burmanization of Myanmar's Muslims*. Bangkok: White Lotus.

Bhabha, Homi K. 1994. *The Location of Culture*. London: Routledge.

———. 1996. "Culture's In-Between." In *Questions of Cultural Identity*, edited by Stuart Hall and Paul du Gay, 53–60. London: Sage Publications.

Biehl, João, Byron Good, and Arthur Kleinman. 2007. "Introduction: Rethinking Subjectivity." In *Subjectivity: Ethnographic Investigations*, edited by João Biehl, Byron Good, and Arthur Kleinman, 1–23. Berkeley: University of California Press.

———, eds. 2007. *Subjectivity: Ethnographic Investigations*. Berkeley: University of California Press.

Boucaud, André, and Louis Boucaud. 1992. *Burma's Golden Triangle: On the Trail of the Opium Warlords*. Bangkok: Asia Books.

Bouman, F. J. A. 1983. "Indigenous Savings and Credit Societies in the Developing World." In *Rural Financial Markets in Developing Countries*, edited by J. D. Von Pischke, Dale W. Adams, and Gordon Donald, 262–68. Baltimore: Johns Hopkins University Press.

Bruner, J. S. 1987. "Life as Narrative." *Social Research* 54:11–32.

Butler, Judith. 1990. *Gender Trouble: Feminism and the Subversion of Identity*. New York: Routledge.

Cai Shan. 1989. *Guogan* (Kokang). N.p.

Callahan, Mary P. 2003. *Making Enemies: War and State Building in Burma*. Ithaca, NY: Cornell University Press.

Cattell, Maria G., and Jacob J. Climo. 2002. "Introduction: Meaning in Social Memory and History: Anthropological Perspectives." In *Social Memory and History: Anthropological Perspectives*, edited by Jacob J. Climo and Maria G. Cattell, 1–36. Walnut Creek, CA: Altamira Press.

Chai Chen-hsiao. 2006. "Qianyi wenhua yu rentong—mianhua yimin de shequn jiangou yu kuaguo wangluo" (Migration, cultures, and identities: The social construction and transnational networks of Burmese-Chinese immigrant Communities in Yangon, Jhong-he, and Toronto). PhD dissertation, National Tsing Hua University, Hsinchu, Taiwan.

Chang, Wen-Chin. 1999. "Beyond the Military: The Complex Migration and Resettlement of the KMT Yunnanese Chinese in Northern Thailand." PhD dissertation, KU Leuven, Belgium.

———. 2001. "From War Refugees to Immigrants: The Case of the KMT Yunnanese Chinese in Northern Thailand." *International Migration Review* 35, no. 4: 1086–105.

———. 2002. "Identification of Leadership among the KMT Yunnanese Chinese in Northern Thailand." *Journal of Southeast Asian Studies* 33, no. 1: 123–46.

———. 2003. "Three Yunnanese Jade Traders from Tengchong." *Kolor: Journal on Moving Communities* 3, no. 1: 15–34.

———. 2004. "*Guanxi* and Regulation in Networks: The Yunnanese Jade Trade between Burma and Thailand, 1962–88." *Journal of Southeast Asian Studies* 35, no. 3: 479–501.

———. 2005. "Invisible Warriors: The Migrant Yunnanese Women in Northern Thailand." *Kolor: Journal on Moving Communities* 5, no. 2: 49–70.

———. 2006a. "Home away from Home: Migrant Yunnanese Chinese in Northern Thailand." *International Journal of Asian Studies* 3, no. 1: 49–76.

———. 2006b. "The Trading Culture of Jade Stones among the Yunnanese in Burma and Thailand, 1962–88." *Journal of Chinese Overseas* 2, no. 2: 107–31.

———. 2009. "Venturing into 'Barbarous' Regions: Transborder Trade among Migrant Yunnanese between Thailand and Burma, 1960–1980s." *Journal of Asian Studies* 68, no. 2: 543–72.

———. 2011. "From a *Shiji* Episode to the Forbidden Jade Trade during the Socialist Regime in Burma." In *Chinese Circulations: Capital, Commodities and Networks in Southeast Asia*, edited by Eric Tagliacozzo and Wen-Chin Chang, 455–79. Durham, NC: Duke University Press.

———. 2013. "The Everyday Politics of the Underground Trade by the Migrant Yunnanese Chinese in Burma since the Socialist Era." *Journal of Southeast Asian Studies* 44, no. 2: 292–314.

Chao Tzang Yawnghwe. 1990 [1987]. *The Shan of Burma: Memories of a Shan Exile*. Singapore: Institute of Southeast Asian Studies.

———. 1993. "The Politics and the Informal Economy of the Opium-Heroin Trade: Impact and Implications for Shan State of Burma." In *Religion, Culture and Political Economy in Burma*, edited by Bruce Matthews, 27–44. Proceedings of the Fifth Annual Conference of the Northwest Consortium for Southeast Asian Studies. Vancouver: University of British Columbia.

Charney, Michael W. 2009. *A History of Modern Burma*. Cambridge: Cambridge University Press.

Chen Ruxing. 1992. "Han tang zhi song yuan shiqi zai miandian de huaren" (Chinese in Burma during the Han, Tang, Song, and Yuan periods). *Haiwai huaren yanjiu*, no. 2: 41–57.

Chen Wen. 1996. *Kunsa jinsanjiao chuanqi* (Khun Sa: Stories of Golden Triangle). Taipei: Yunchen wenhua.

Chen Yi-Sein. 1966. "The Chinese in Upper Burma before A.D. 1700." *Journal of Southeast Asian Researches*, no. 2: 81–89.

Chin, Ko-lin. 2009. *The Golden Triangle: Inside Southeast Asia's Drug Trade*. Ithaca, NY: Cornell University Press.

Chiranan Prasertkul. 1990. "Yunnan Trade in the Nineteenth Century: Southwest China's Cross-Boundaries Functional System." Institute of Asian Studies, Chulalongkorn University, Asian Studies Monograph, no. 044.

Cho, Violet. 2008. "New Gem Auction Scheduled in Rangoon." *Irrawaddy*, January 14.
Chou, Cynthia. 2005. "Southeast Asia through an Inverted Telescope: Maritime Perspectives on a Borderless Region." In *Locating Southeast Asia: Geographies of Knowledge and Politics of Space*, edited by Paul H. Kratoska, Remco Raben, and Henk Schulte Nordholt, 234–49. Singapore: Singapore University Press and Ohio University Press.
———. 2010. *The Orang Suku Laut of Riau, Indonesia: The Inalienable Gift of Territory*. London: Routledge.
Clifford, James. 1992. "Traveling Cultures." In *Cultural Studies*, edited by Lawrence Crossberg, Cary Nelson, and Paula A. Treichler, 96–116. New York: Routledge.
———. 1994. "Diasporas." *Cultural Anthropology* 9, no. 3: 302–38.
Clifford, James, and George E. Marcus. 1986. "Introduction: Partial Truths." In *Writing Culture: The Poetics and Politics of Ethnography*. Berkeley: University of California Press.
Cochrane, Henry Park. 1904. *Among the Burmans: A Record of Fifteen Years of Work and Its Fruitage*. New York: Fleming H. Revell Co.
Cohen, Robin. 1997. *Global Diasporas: An Introduction*. Seattle: University of Washington Press.
Colquhoun, A. R. 1900. *Overland to China*. New York: Harper & Bros.
Conway, Susan. 2006. *The Shan: Culture, Art and Crafts*. Bangkok: River Books.
cooke, miriam, and Bruce B. Lawrence. 2005. Introduction to *Muslim Networks from Hajj to Hip Hop*, edited by miriam cooke and Bruce B. Lawrence, 1–28. Chapel Hill: University of North Carolina Press.
Coppel, Charles A. 1983. *Indonesian Chinese in Crisis*. New York: Oxford University Press.
Cornell, Vincent J. 2005. "The Networks and Loyalties of a Medieval Muslim Scholar." In *Muslim Networks from Hajj to Hip Hop*, edited by miriam cooke and Bruce B. Lawrence, 31–50. Chapel Hill: University of North Carolina Press.
Cowell, Adrian. 2005. "Opium Anarchy in the Shan State of Burma." In *Trouble in the Triangle: Opium and Conflict in Burma*, edited by Martin Jelsma et al., 1–21. Chiang Mai: Silkworm Books.
Crapanzano, Vincent. 1980. *Tuhami: Portrait of a Moroccan*. Chicago: University of Chicago Press.
Daniel, E. Valentine, and John Chr. Knudsen. 1995. Introduction to *Mistrusting Refugees*, edited by Valentine E. Daniel and John Chr. Knudsen, 1–12. Berkeley: University of California Press.
———, eds. 1995. *Mistrusting Refugees*. Berkeley: University of California Press.
Dawson, G. W. 1912. *Burma Gazetteer: The Bhamo District*. Rangoon: Office of the Superintendent, Government Printing.
Denzin, Norman K. 1991. "Presenting Lived Experiences in Ethnographic Texts." *Studies in Symbolic Interaction* 12:59–70.
Dong Ping. 2000. *Heshun fengyu liubai nian* (The six-hundred-year history of Heshun). Kunming: Yunnan Renmin chubanshe.
Donnan, Hastings, and Thomas M. Wilson. 1994. "An Anthropology of Frontiers." In *Border Approaches: Anthropological Perspectives on Frontiers*, edited by Hastings Donnan and Thomas M. Wilson, 1–14. Lanham, MD: University Press of America.

———. 1999. *Borders: Frontiers of Identity, Nation and State*. Oxford: Berg.

Duan Ying. 2009. "Miandian huaren: Zuqunxing gongmin guishu yu wenhua zhengzhi" (Being Chinese in Burma: Ethnicity and cultural citizenship). PhD dissertation, Chinese University of Hong Kong.

Eckert, Paul. 2013. "U.S. Updates Myanmar Sanctions to Maintain Gem Import Ban." *Reuters*, August 7.

Egreteau, Renaud. 2011. "The Burmese Jade Trail: Transnational Networks, China and the (Relative) Impact of International Sanctions on Myanmar's Gems." In *Myanmar's Transition: Openings, Obstacles and Opportunities*, edited by Nick Cheesman, Monique Skidmore, and Trevor Wilson, 89–116. Singapore: Institute of Southeast Asian Studies.

8808 for Burma. 2008. "Blood Jade: Burmese Gemstones and the Beijing Games." www.8808forburma.org.

Ellis, C., and M. G. Flaherty. 1992. "An Agenda for the Interpretation of Lived Experience." In *Investigating Subjectivity: Research on Lived Experience*, edited by C. Ellis and M. G. Flaherty, 1–13. Newbury Park, CA: Sage Publications.

Fadiman, Anne. 1998. *The Spirit Catches You and You Fall Down: A Hmong Child, Her American Doctors, and the Collision of Two Cultures*. New York: Farrar, Straus and Giroux.

Fan, Hongwei. 2012. "1967 Anti-Chinese Riots in Burma and Sino-Burmese Relations." *Journal of Southeast Asian Studies* 43, no. 2: 234–56.

Fang Guoyu. 1982. *Dianshi luncong*, no. 1 (A study of Yunnanese history, vol. 1). Shanghai: Shanghai renmin chubanshe.

Fang Shiduo. 2002. *Fang shiduo xiansheng quanji yi zhi xianhua dianbian ji tian nan tan* (The complete works of Mr. Fang Shiduo, vol. 1, essays on Yunnan and its southern countries). N.p.

Fang Tie and Fang Hui. 1997. *Zhongguo xinan bianjiang kaifashi* (History of southwestern China). Kunming: Yunnan minzu chubanshe.

Fang Yijie. 2003. "Dijing fengshui yu rushang wenhua: Yunnan Heshun qiaoxiang de minjian wenhua yu guojia xiangzheng shijian" (Landscape geometry and the culture of gentry businessmen: The folk culture and practices of state symbolism in Heshun Township of Yunnan). Master's thesis, National Tsing Hua University, Hsinchu, Taiwan.

Fei, Hsiao-Tung (Fei Xiaotong) and Chang Chih-I. 1948. *Earthbound China: A Study of Rural Economy in Yunnan*. Chicago: University of Chicago Press.

Fischer, Michael. 2003. *Emergent Forms of Life and the Anthropological Voice*. Durham, NC: Duke University Press.

FitzGerald, C. P. 1972. *The Southern Expansion of the Chinese People*. New York: Praeger.

Forbes, Andrew D. W. 1986. "The 'Panthay' (Yunnanese Chinese) Muslims of Burma." *Journal of Muslim Minority Affairs* 7, no. 2: 384–94.

———. 1987. "The 'Cin-ho' (Yunnanese Chinese) Caravan Trade with North Thailand during the Late Nineteenth and Early Twentieth Centuries." *Journal of Asian History* 21, no. 1: 1–47.

———. 1988. "History of Panglong, 1875–1900: A 'Panthay' (Chinese Muslim) Settlement in the Burmese Wa States." *Muslim World* 78, no. 1: 38–50.

Forbes, Andrew [D.W.], and David Henley. 1997. *The Haw: Traders of the Golden Triangle*. Chiang Mai: Asia Film House.
Freedman, Estelle B. 2003. *The History of Feminism and the Future of Women*. London: Ballantine Books.
Giersch, C. Patterson. 2006. *Asian Borderlands: The Transformation of Qing China's Yunnan Frontier*. Cambridge, MA: Harvard University Press.
———. 2011. "Cotton, Copper, and Caravans: Trade and the Transformation of Southwest China." In *Chinese Circulations: Capital, Commodities and Networks in Southeast Asia*, edited by Eric Tagliacozzo and Wen-Chin Chang, 37–61. Durham, NC: Duke University Press.
Gillette, Maris Boyd. 2000. *Between Mecca and Beijing: Modernization and Consumption among Urban Chinese Muslims*. Stanford, CA: Stanford University Press.
Gilmartin, David. 2005. "A Networked Civilization?" In *Muslim Networks from Hajj to Hip Hop*, edited by miriam cooke and Bruce B. Lawrence, 51–68. Chapel Hill: University of North Carolina Press.
Gilroy, Paul. 1993. *The Black Atlantic: Modernity and Double Consciousness*. London: Verso.
Gladney, Dru C. 1996 [1991]. *Muslim Chinese: Ethnic Nationalism in the People's Republic*. Cambridge, MA: Harvard East Asian Monographs 149.
———. 2004. *Dislocating China: Muslims, Minorities, and Other Subaltern Subjects*. Chicago: University of Chicago Press.
Gold, Steven J. 1992. *Refugee Communities: A Comparative Field Study*. Newbury Park, CA: Sage Publications.
Hall, Donald E. 2004. *Subjectivity*. New York: Routledge.
Hall, Stuart, and Paul Du Gay, eds. 1996. *Questions of Cultural Identity*. London: Sage Publications.
Hanna, A. C. 1931. "The Panthays of Yunnan." *Moslem World*, no. 21: 69–74.
Hansen, Art, and Anthony Oliver-Smith, eds. 1982. *Involuntary Migration and Resettlement: The Problems and Responses of Dislocated People*. Boulder, CO: Westview Press.
Hao Zhengzhi. 1998. *Hanzu yimin rudian shihua—nanjing liushuwan gaoshikan* (The history of Han immigration into Yunnan). Kunming: Yunnan daxue chubanshe.
Harriden, Jessica. 2012. *The Authority of Influence: Women and Power in Burmese History*. Copenhagen: NIAS Press.
Harvey, G. E. 1933. *1932 Wa Precis*. Rangoon: Government Printers.
Hayami, Yoko. 2007. "Traversing Invisible Borders: Narratives of Women between Hills and the City." In *Southeast Asian Lives: Personal Narratives and Historical Experience*, edited by Roxana Waterson, 253–77. Singapore: NUS Press.
Hemrich, Gerald I. 1996. *The Handbook of Jade*. Mentone, CA: Gembooks.
Herzfeld, Michael. 1996. *Cultural Intimacy: Social Poetics in the Nation-State*. New York: Routledge.
High, Holly. 2009. "Dreaming beyond Borders: The Thai/Lao Borderlands and the Mobility of the Marginal." In *On the Borders of State Power: Frontiers in the Greater Mekong Sub-Regions*, edited by Martin Gainsborough, 75–100. London: Routledge.
Hill, Ann Maxwell. 1998. *Merchants and Migrants: Ethnicity and Trade among Yunnanese Chinese in Southeast Asia*. New Haven, CT: Yale Southeast Asia Studies.

Hirschman, Albert O. 1995. *A Propensity to Self-Subversion*. Cambridge, MA: Harvard University Press.
Ho, Engseng. 2006. *The Graves of Tarim: Genealogy and Mobility across the Indian Ocean*. Berkeley: University of California Press.
Hondagneu-Sotelo, Pierrette. 1994. *Gendered Transitions: Mexican Experiences of Immigration*. Berkeley: University of California Press.
Horstmann, Alexander, and Reed L. Wadley. 2006. "Introduction: Centering the Margin in Southeast Asia." In *Centering the Margin: Agency and Narrative in Southeast Asian Borderlands*, edited by Alexander Horstmann and Reed L. Wadley, 1–24. New York: Berghahn Books.
Hsieh, Shih-chung. 1995. "On the Dynamics of Tai/Dai-Lue Ethnicity: An Ethnohistorical Analysis." In *Cultural Encounters on China's Ethnic Frontiers*, edited by Steven Harrell, 301–28. Seattle: University of Washington Press.
Hsu, Francis L.K. 1967 [1948]. *Under the Ancestors' Shadow*. Garden City, NY: Anchor Books.
Hu Qingrong [Ding Zuoshao]. 1974 [1967]. *Dianbian youjishihua* (History of guerrilla wars along the border between Yunnan and Burma). Tainan (Taiwan): Zhongguo shiji zazhishe.
Huang Chia-mu. 1976. "Dianxi huimin zhengquan de lianying waijiao" ("British Relations with the Panthay Regime of Western Yunnan, 1868–1874"). Monograph Series no. 37, Institute of Modern History, Academia Sinica, Taipei.
Huang, Shu-min. 2010. *Reproducing Chinese Culture in Diaspora: Sustainable Agriculture and Petrified Culture in Northern Thailand*. Lanham, MD: Lexington Books.
Irrawaddy. 2013. "'Political Opportunists' and 'Religious Extremists' behind Riots: Thein Sein." March 28.
Jagan, Larry. 2009. "Closer Ties between Burma and China's Southwestern Province Raise Concerns in Beijing." *Irrawaddy* 17, no. 6: 20.
Jarnigan, Laura. 2008. *A Confluence of Transatlantic Networks: Elites, Capitalism, and Confederate Migration to Brazil*. Tuscaloosa: University of Alabama Press.
Jiang Junzhang. 1944. *Miandian dili* (Geography of Burma). Chongqing: Jianshe chubanshe.
Jing Dexin. 1991. *Du Wenxiu qiyi* (The uprising led by Du Wenxiu). Kunming: Yunnan minzu chubanshe.
Johnson, David E., and Scott Michaelsen. 1997. "Border Secrets: An Introduction." In *Border Theory: The Limits of Cultural Politics*, edited by Scott Michaelsen and David E. Johnson, 1–39. Minneapolis: University of Minnesota Press.
Johnson, Elizabeth. 1975. "Women and Childbearing in Kwan Mun Hau Village: A Study of Social Change." In *Women in Chinese Society*, edited by Margery Wolf and Roxane Witke, 215–41. Stanford, CA: Stanford University Press.
Jonsson, Hjorleidur. 2005. *Mien Relations: Mountain People and State Control in Thailand*. Ithaca, NY: Cornell University Press.
Kaplan, Caren. 1996. *Questions of Travel: Postmodern Discourses of Displacement*. Durham, NC: Duke University Press.
Keyes, Charles F. 1984. "Mother or Mistress but Never a Monk: Buddhist Notions of Female Gender in Rural Thailand." *American Ethnologist* 11, no. 2: 223–41.

Khoo Thwe, Pascal. 2002. *From the Land of Green Ghosts: A Burmese Odyssey*. New York: HarperCollins.
Kimura, Mizuka. 2006. "Unnan Kaimin no Ijū to Toransunasyonarizumu ni kansuru Bunkajinruigakuteki Kenkyū" (Cultural anthropological study on the migration and transnationalism among the Yunnanese Muslims). PhD dissertation, Osaka University.
King, Nicola. 2000. *Memory, Narrative, Identity: Remembering the Self*. Edinburgh: Edinburgh University Press.
Kratoska, Paul H. 2002. "Between China and the Japanese: Wartime Affairs in Kokang State and the Failure of the Spiers Mission." In *Southeast Asian Minorities in the Wartime Japanese Empire*, edited by Paul H. Kratoska, 39–54. New York: RoutledgeCurzon.
Krulfeld, Ruth M., and Linda A. Camino. 1999 [1994]. *Reconstructing Lives, Recapturing Meaning: Refugee Identity, Gender, and Culture Change*. Singapore: Gordon and Breach Publishers.
Kuhn, Philip A. 2008. *Chinese among Others: Emigration in Modern Times*. Lanham, MD: Rowman & Littlefield.
Kuo Tsung-fei. 1941. "A Brief History of Trade Routes between Burma, Indochina and Yunnan." *T'ien Hsia* 12, no. 1: 9–32.
Kurtenbach, Elaine. 2012. "Boomtown Ruili Faces Backlash." *Irrawaddy*, June 1.
Kyaw Yin Hlaing. 2001. "The Politics of State-Business Relations in Post-Colonial Burma." PhD dissertation, Cornell University.
Kyle, David. 2003. *Transnational Peasants: Migrations, Networks, and Ethnicity in Andean Ecuador*. Baltimore: Johns Hopkins University Press.
Langness, L. L., and Gelya Frank. 1981. *Lives: An Anthropological Approach to Biography*. Novato, CA: Chandler and Sharp Publishers.
Launay, Robert. 1992. *Beyond the Stream: Islam and Society in a West African Town*. Berkeley: University of California Press.
Leach, E. R. 1993 [1954]. *Political Systems of Highland Burma: A Study of Kachin Social Structure*. London: Athlone Press.
Leider, Jacques P. 2012. "'Rohingya,' Rakhaing and the Recent Outbreak of Violence—a Note." *Bulletin of the Burma Studies Group*, Spring/Fall 2012, 8–11.
Lemere, Maggie, and Zoë West, comp. and eds. 2011. *Nowhere to Be Home: Narratives from Survivors of Burma's Military Regime*. San Francisco: McSweeneys Books.
Lessinger, Johanna. 2001. "Inside, Outside, and Selling on the Road: Women's Market Trading in South India." In *Women Traders in Cross-Cultural Perspective: Mediating Identities, Marketing Wares*, edited by Linda J. Seligmann, 73–100. Stanford, CA: Stanford University Press.
Li Fuyi. 2003 [1979]. "Monggen tusi" (Monggen chieftain). In *Manhuang neiwai* (Savage land in and out). Taipei: Furen Shuwu.
Li Xuehua. 2008. *Zouguo jinshanjiao* (Traveling through the Golden Triangle). Taipei: Xiuwei zixunkeji gufenyouxiangongsi.
Li, Yi. 2011. "Local and Transnational Institutions in the Formation of Chinese Migrant Communities in Colonial Burma." PhD dissertation, School of Oriental and African Studies, University of London.

Lintner, Bertil. 1988. "All the Wrong Moves: Only the Black Economy Is Keeping Burma Afloat." *Far Eastern Economic Review*, October 27.

———. 1994. *Burma in Revolt: Opium and Insurgency since 1948*. Bangkok: White Lotus.

Lipman, Jonathan N. 1997. *Familiar Strangers: A History of Muslims in Northwest China*. Seattle: University of Washington Press.

Liu Xiaobing. 1991. *Dian wenhuashi* (Cultural history of Yunnan). Kunming: Yunnan remin chubanshe.

Lorente, Beatriz P., Nicola Piper, Shen Hsin-Hua, and Brenda S. A. Yeoh, eds. 2005. *Asian Migrations: Sojourning, Displacement, Homecoming and Other Travels*. Singapore: Asia Research Institute, National University of Singapore.

Lu, Hsin-Chun. 2011. "Public Soundscapes and Performing Nostalgia among Burmese Chinese in Central Rangoon." *Asian Music* 42, no. 2: 19–55.

Lu Ren. 2001. *Bianqian yu jiaorong mingdai yunnan hanzu yimin yanjiu* (Transformation and incorporation: A study on the Han migration in Yunnan in the Ming dynasty). Kunming: Yunnan jiaoyu chubanshe.

Lugo, Alejandro. 1997. "Reflections on Border Theory, Culture and the Nation." In *Border Theory: The Limits of Cultural Politics*, edited by Scott Michaelsen and David E. Johnson, 43–67. Minneapolis: University of Minnesota Press.

Luo Xinghan. 2006. "Kanke guohou shi tantu" (In the wake of adversity). In *Miandian shanbang guoganminzu wenhuazonghui chengli sanshi zhounian jiniantekan* (A special edition on the 30th anniversary of the Ethnic Kokang Cultural Association in the Shan State of Burma), edited by Ethnic Kokang Cultural Association, 19–23. N.p.

Ma, Laurence J. C., ed. 2003. *The Chinese Diaspora: Space, Place, Mobility, and Identity*. Lanham, MD: Rowman & Littlefield.

———. 2003. "Space, Place, and Transnationalism in the Chinese Diaspora." In *The Chinese Diaspora: Space, Place, Mobility, and Identity*, edited by Laurence J. C. Ma and Carolyn Cartier, 1–49. Lanham, MD: Rowman & Littlefield.

Ma Hsin. 2011. "Longgang qingzhensi shequn de xingcheng han qi quanqiuhua mailuoxia de fazhan" (Formation, development, and globalization of the Longgang mosque community). Master's thesis, National Chiao Tung University, Hsinchu, Taiwan.

Ma Shitu. 1985. "Yunnan mabang qushi" (Episodes of Yunnanese caravan trade). *Yunnan wenxian*, no. 15: 152–55.

Mahler, Sarah J., and Patricia R. Pessar. 2001. "Gendered Geographies of Power: Analyzing Gender across Transnational Spaces." *Identities. Global Studies in Culture and Power* 7, no. 4: 441–59.

Mahmood, Saba. 2001. "Feminist Theory, Embodiment, and the Docile Agent: Some Reflections on the Egyptian Islamic Revival." *Cultural Anthropology* 16, no. 2: 202–36.

Malkki, Liisa H. 1995. *Purity and Exile: Violence, Memory, and National Cosmology among Hutu Refugees in Tanzania*. Chicago: University of Chicago Press.

Mandaville, Peter. 2001. *Transnational Muslim Politics: Reimagining the Umma*. New York: Routledge.

Marcus, George E., and Michael M. J. Fischer. 1986. *Anthropology as Cultural Critique: An Experimental Moment in the Human Sciences*. Chicago: University of Chicago Press.

Markovits, Claude, Jacques Pouchepadass, and Sanjay Subrahmanyam. 2003. "Introduction: Circulation and Society under Colonial Rule." In *Society and Circulation: Mobile People and Itinerant Cultures in South Asia, 1750–1950*, edited by Claude Markovits, Jacques Pouchepadass, and Sanjay Subrahmanyam, 1–22. Delhi: Permanent Black.

Mattson, Kevin. 2002. *Intellectuals in Action: The Origins of the New Left and Radical Liberalism, 1945-1970*. University Park, PA: Pennsylvania State University Press.

Massey, Doreen B. 1994. *Space, Place, and Gender*. Minneapolis: University of Minnesota Press.

Massey, Douglas S., et al. 1993. "Theories of International Migration: A Review and Appraisal." *Population and Development Review* 19:431–66.

Maule, Robert B. 1992. "The Opium Question in the Federated Shan States, 1931–36: British Policy Discussions and Scandal." *Journal of Southeast Asian Studies* 23, no. 1: 14–36.

Maung Chan. 2005. "Miandian junzhengfu de caiyuan yu bianjing maoyi" (The economic sources of the Burmese military junta and its border trade). *Dajiyuan*, February 2, 2005.

Maung Maung Lay. 1999. "The Emergence of the Panthay Community at Mandalay." In *Studies in Myanmar History*, 1:91–106. Yangon: Innwa Publishing House.

McAdam, Doug. 1982. *Political Process and the Development of Black Insurgency, 1930–1970*. Chicago: University of Chicago Press.

McCoy, Alfred W. 1991. *The Politics of Heroin: CIA Complicity in the Global Drug Trade*. Brooklyn, NY: Lawrence Hill Books.

McKeown, Adam. 2001. *Chinese Migrant Networks and Cultural Change: Peru, Chicago, Hawaii, 1900–1936*. Chicago: University of Chicago Press.

———. 2011. "The Social Life of Chinese Labor." In *Chinese Circulations: Capital, Commodities and Networks in Southeast Asia*, edited by Eric Tagliacozzo and Wen-Chin Chang, 62–83. Durham, NC: Duke University Press.

Meng Biguang and Si Lizhang. 2009. "You yige meili de difang" (A beautiful place). In *Ruili gaige kaifang sanshinian* (Thirty years of reform in Ruili). Edited by Ruili gaige kaifang sanshinian bianweihui, 14–19. Luxi, Yunnan: Dehong minzu chubanshe.

Min Zin. 2012. "Burmese Attitude toward Chinese: Portrayal of the Chinese in Contemporary Cultural and Media Works." *Journal of Current Southeast Asian Affairs* 31, no. 1: 115–131.

Ming Guangxi. 1998. *Dianmian bianjing: Panglong huijiao bainian cangsang jianwenlu* (Panglong booklet). N.p.

Ministry of Information, the Union of Burma. 1953. *The Kuomintang Aggression against Burma*. Rangoon: Ministry of Information.

Mya Maung. 1994. "On the Road to Mandalay: A Case Study of the Sinonization of Upper Burma." *Asian Survey*, 34, no. 5: 447–59.

Mya Than. 1996 [1992]. *Myanmar's External Trade: An Overview in the Southeast Asian Context*. Singapore: ASEAN Economic Research Unit, Institute of Southeast Asian Studies.

———. 1997. "Ethnic Chinese in Myanmar and Their Identity." In *Ethnic Chinese as Southeast Asians*, edited by Leo Suryadinata, 115–46. Singapore: Institute of Southeast Asian Studies.

Nasr, Seyyed Hossein. 2002. *Islam: Religion, History, and Civilization*. New York: Harper San Francisco.
Natanson, Maurice. 1973. "Phenomenology and the Social Sciences." In *Phenomenology and the Social Sciences*, vol. 1, edited by Maurice Natanson, 3–44. Evanston, IL: Northwestern University Press.
Nations, Richard. 1977. "Politics and the Poppy." *Far Eastern Economic Review*, April 15, pp. 24–25.
Neisser, Ulric, and Robyn Fivush. 1993. *The Remembering Self: Construction and Accuracy in Self Narrative*, edited by Sarah Nuttall and Carli Coetzee. Cambridge: Cambridge University Press.
Nguyen, Nathalie Huynh Chau. 2009. *Memory Is Another Country: Women of the Vietnamese Diaspora*. Santa Barbara, CA: Praeger.
Nin Chao. 1987. "Guijia minjia ji qi yu Qianlong nianjian de zhongmian zhi zhan" (The history of the Guis and the Mins in Burma and the Sino-Burma war during the Qianlong era). In *Dongnanyashi lunwenji* (History of Southeast Asia), edited by Zhongguo dongnanya yanjiuhui, 318–40. Henan: Henan renmin chubanshe.
Ochs, Elinor, and Lisa Capps. 1996. "Narrating the Self." *Annual Review of Anthropology* 25:19–43.
Ong, Aihwa. 1999. *Flexible Citizenship*. Durham, NC: Duke University Press.
Ong, Aihwa, and Donald M. Nonini, eds. 1997. *Ungrounded Empires: The Cultural Politics of Modern Chinese Transnationalism*. New York: Routledge.
Ortner, Sherry B. 1996. *Making Gender: The Politics and Erotics of Culture*. Boston: Beacon Press.
Pan, Lynn. 1994 [1990]. *Song of the Yellow Emperor: A History of the Chinese Diaspora*. New York: Kodansha International.
Pessar, Patricia R., and Sarah J. Mahler. 2003. "Transnational Migration: Bringing Gender In." *International Migration Review* 37, no. 3: 812–46.
Portelli, Alessandro. 1997. *The Battle of Valle Giulia: Oral History and the Art of Dialogue*. Madison: University of Wisconsin Press.
Priestley, Harry. 2006. "The Outsiders." *Irrawaddy* 14, no. 1.
Purcell, Victor. 1960. *The Chinese in Modern Malaya*. Singapore: Eastern University Press.
Qin Yihui. 2009. *Jinsanjiao guojun xieleishi* (The tragic history of the KMT troops in the Golden Triangle, 1950–1981). Taipei: Zhongyang yanjiuyuan and Lianjing chubanshe.
Reid, Anthony. 1988. *Southeast Asia in the Age of Commerce, 1450–1680*, vol. 1, *The Lands below the Winds*. New Heaven, CT: Yale University Press.
———, ed. 1996. *Sojourners and Settlers: Histories of Southeast Asia and the Chinese*. Honolulu: University of Hawai'i Press.
Riessman, Catherine Kohler. 1993. *Narrative Analysis*. Newbury Park, CA: Sage Publications.
Roberts, Jayde Lin. 2011. "Tracing the Ethos of the Sino-Burmese in the Urban Fabric of Yangon, Burma (Myanmar)." PhD dissertation, University of Washington.
Robinne, François, and Mandy Sadan. 2007. *Social Dynamics in the Highlands of Southeast Asia: Reconsidering Political Systems of Highland Burma*. Leiden: Brill.

Rosaldo, Renato. 1993 [1989]. *Culture and Truth: The Remaking of Social Analysis*. Boston: Beacon Press.
Rouse, Roger. 1991. "Mexican Migration and the Social Space of Postmodernism." *Diaspora* 1, no. 1: 8–23.
Sadan, Mandy. 2014. "The Extra-ordinariness of Ordinary Lives." In *Burmese Lives: Ordinary Life Stories under the Burmese Regime*, edited by Wen-Chin Chang and Eric Tagliacozzo, 25–52. New York: Oxford University Press.
Sai Aung Tun. 2009. *History of the Shan State: From Its Origins to 1962*. Chiang Mai: Silkworm Book.
Sai Kham Mong. 2005. *Kokang and Kachin in the Shan State, 1945–1960*. Bangkok: Institute of Asian Studies, Chulalongkorn University.
———. 2007. "The Shan in Myanmar." In *Myanmar: State, Society and Ethnicity*, edited by N. Ganesan and Kyaw Yin Hlaing, 256–77. Singapore: Institute of Southeast Asian Studies.
Said, Abdul Aziz, and Meena Sharify-Funk, eds. 2003. *Cultural Diversity and Islam*. Lanham, MD: University Press of America.
Said, Edward. 1999. *Out of Place: A Memoir*. New York: Alfred A. Knopf.
Sao Saimong Mangrai. 1965. *The Shan States and the British Annexation*. Ithaca, NY: Southeast Asia Program, Department of Asian Studies, Cornell University.
Saw Yan Naing and Echo Hui. 2014. "Hong Kong Jade Prices Soar from Fear of Burmese Jade Shortage." *Irrawaddy*, January 7.
Scott, J. G. 1901. *Gazetteer of Upper Burma and the Shan States*. Part 2, vol. 2. Assisted by J. P. Hardiman. Rangoon: Government Printing.
Scott, James C. 2009. *The Art of Not Being Governed: An Anarchist History of Upland Southeast Asia*. New Haven, CT: Yale University Press.
Scudder, Thayer, and Elizabeth Colson. 1982. "From Welfare to Development: A Conceptual Framework for the Analysis of Dislocated People." In *Involuntary Migration and Resettlement: The Problems and Responses of Dislocated People*, edited by Art Hansen and Anthony Oliver-Smith, 267–87. Boulder, CO: Westview Press.
Seligmann, Linda J. 2001. "Introduction: Mediating Identities and Marketing Wares." In *Women Traders in Cross-Cultural Perspective: Mediating Identities, Marketing Wares*, edited by Linda J. Seligmann, 1–24. Stanford, CA: Stanford University Press.
Selth, Andrew. 2003. "Burma's Muslims: Caught in the Crossfire." *Irrawaddy* 11, no. 7.
Shami, Seteney. 1993. "The Social Implications of Population Displacement and Resettlement: An Overview with a Focus on the Arab Middle East." *International Migration Review* 22, no. 1: 4–33.
Shen Xu. 1994. "Lishishang yunnan han taiguo zhijian de jiaotong maoyi" (The traffic and trade between Yunnan and Thailand in history). *Sixiang zhanxian*, no. 1: 62–68.
Shore, David Harrison. 1976. "Last Court of Ming China: The Reign of the Yung-Li Emperor in the South." PhD dissertation, Princeton University.
Sima Qian. 1988. *Shiji zhuyi* (The annotated *Shiji*). Xian: Sanqian chubanshe.
Skidmore, Monique. 2004. *Karaoke Fascism: Burma and the Politics of Fear*. Philadelphia: University of Pennsylvania Press.
Skinner, G. William. 1957. *Chinese Society in Thailand: An Analytical History*. Ithaca, NY: Cornell University Press.

———. 1964. "Marketing and Social Structure in Rural China, Part I." *Journal of Asian Studies* 24, no. 1: 3–43.

Sladen, E. B. 1870. *Official Narrative of the Expedition to Explore the Trade Routes to China via Bhamo, under the Guidance of Major E. B. Sladen*. Calcutta: Office of Superintendent of Government Printing.

Smith, Martin J. 1993 [1991]. *Burma: Insurgency and the Politics of Ethnicity*. London: Zed Books.

South, Ashley. 2008. *Ethnic Politics in Burma: States of Conflict*. London: Routledge.

Stargardt, Janice. 1971. "Burma's Economic and Diplomatic Relations with India and China from Early Medieval Sources." *Journal of the Economic and Social History of the Orient* 14, no. 1: 38–62.

Steinberg, David I. 2006. *Turmoil in Burma: Contested Legitimacies in Myanmar*. Norwalk, CT: EastBridge.

———. 2010. *Burma/Myanmar: What Everyone Needs to Know*. Oxford: Oxford University Press.

Sturgeon, Janet C. 2005. *Border Landscapes: The Politics of Akha Land Use in China and Thailand*. Seattle: University of Washington Press.

Suchart Settamalinee. 2010. "The Transformation of Chinese Muslim Identities in Northern Thailand." PhD dissertation, University of Hawai'i at Manoa.

Sun, Laichen. 2000. "Ming-Southeast Asian Overland Interactions, 1368–1644." PhD dissertation, University of Michigan.

———. 2011. "From *Baoshi* to *Feicui*: Qing-Burmese Gem Trade (ca. 1644–1800)." In *Chinese Circulations: Capital, Commodities, and Networks in Southeast Asia*, edited by Eric Tagliacozzo and Wen-Chin Chang, 23–220. Durham, NC: Duke University Press.

Suryadinata, Leo, ed. 2006. *Southeast Asia's Chinese Businesses in an Era of Globalization: Coping with the Rise of China*. Singapore: Institute of Southeast Asian Studies.

Tagliacozzo, Eric. 2005. *Secret Trades, Porous Borders: Smuggling and States along a Southeast Asian Frontier, 1865–1915*. New Haven, CT: Yale University Press.

———. 2013. *The Longest Journey: Southeast Asians and the Pilgrimage to Mecca*. Oxford: Oxford University Press.

———. 2014. "Burmese and Muslim: Islam and the Hajj in the Sangha State." In *Burmese Lives: Ordinary Life Stories under the Burmese Regime*, edited by Wen-Chin Chang and Eric Tagliacozzo, 83–106. New York: Oxford University Press.

Tan Chee Beng. 1988. *The Baba of Melaka: Culture and Identity of a Chinese Peranakan Community in Malaysia*. Petaling Jaya: Pelanduk Publication.

Tarrow, Sidney G. 1998. *Power in Movement: Social Movements and Contentious Politics*. Cambridge: Cambridge University Press.

Taylor, Robert H. 1973. "Foreign and Domestic Consequences of the KMT Intervention in Burma." Data paper no. 93, Southeast Asia Program, Department of Asian Studies, Cornell University.

———, ed. 2001. *Burma: Political Economy under Military Rule*. London: Hurst & Co.

TCXZ. 1995. *Tengchong xianzhi* (Gazetteer of Tengchong county). Beijing: Zhonghua shuju chuban.

Thant Myint-U. 2006. *The River of Lost Footsteps: A Personal History of Burma*. New York: Farrar, Straus and Giroux.

———. 2011. *Where China Meets India: Burma and the New Crossroads of Asia*. London: Faber and Faber.
Thawnghmung, Ardeth Maung. 2012. *The "Other" Karen in Myanmar: Ethnic Minorities and the Struggle without Arms*. Lanham, MD: Lexington Books.
Thompson, Paul. 1988. *The Voice of the Past: Oral History*. Oxford: Oxford University Press.
Thongchai Winichakul. 1994. *Siam Mapped: A History of the Geo-body of a Nation*. Honolulu: University of Hawai'i Press.
———. 2003. "Writing at the Interstices: Southeast Asian Historians and Postnational Histories in Southeast Asia." In *New Terrains in Southeast Asian History*, edited by Abu Talib Ahmad and Tan Liok Ee, 3–29. Athens: Ohio University Press; Singapore University Press.
Topley, Marjorie. 1975. "Marriage Resistance in Rural Kwangtung." In *Women in Chinese Society*, edited by Margery Wolf and Roxane Witke, 67–88. Stanford, CA: Stanford University Press.
Tsing, Anna Lowenhaupt. 1993. *In the Realm of the Diamond Queen: Marginality in an Out-of-the Way Place*. Princeton, NJ: Princeton University Press.
———. 1994. "From the Margins." *Cultural Anthropology* 9, no. 3: 279–97.
———. 2005. *Friction: An Ethnography of Global Connection*. Princeton, NJ: Princeton University Press.
TSYO. 2011. "Shweli under Siege: Dams Proceed amid War in Burma." Ta'ang Students and Youth Organization. http://www.palaungland.org/media/Report/Shweli_under_sieges/Sheweli%20Under%20Siege%20report%20in%20English.pdf (January 20, 2014).
Turnell, Sean. 2009. *Fiery Dragons: Banks, Moneylenders and Microfinance in Burma*. Copenhagen: NIAS Press.
Ty, Eleanor, and Donald C. Goellnicht, eds. 2004. Introduction to *Asian North American Identities: Beyond the Hyphen*. Bloomington: Indiana University Press.
van Schendel, Willem. 2005. *The Bengal Borderland: Beyond State and Nation in South Asia*. London: Anthem Press.
Wade, Geoff. 2000. "The Southern Chinese Borders in History." In *Where China Meets Southeast Asia: Social and Cultural Change in the Border Regions*, edited by Grant Evans, Christopher Hutton, and Kuah Khun Eng, 28–50. Bangkok: White Lotus.
Walker, Andrew. 1999. *The Legend of the Golden Boat: Regulation, Trade and Traders in the Borderlands of Laos, Thailand, China and Burma*. Honolulu: University of Hawai'i Press.
Wang Gungwu. 1991. *China and the Chinese Overseas*. Singapore: Times Academic Press.
———. 2001. *Don't Leave Home: Migration and the Chinese*. Singapore: Times Academic Press.
Wang Mingda and Zhang Xilu. 1993. *Mabang wenhua* (Culture of caravan trade). Kunming: Yunnan renmin chubanshe.
Wang Yingpeng. 1993. "Mingguo shiqi dali fengyi de mabang" (The caravan trade from Dali and Fengyi during the Republic period). In *Yunnan wenshi ziliao xuanji no. 42* (Anthology of Yunnanese history), edited by Zhongguo renmin zhengzhi xieshanghuiyi yunnanshen weiyuanhui wenshiziliao yanjiu weiyuanhui, 309–17. Kunming: Yunnan renmin chubanshe.

Wang Yizhi. 1997. "Lun Yunnan gudai hanzu lutian gaiyao" (A brief history of early Han immigration into Yunnan). In *South-west China Cultural Studies* 2, edited by Institute of History, Yunnan Academy of Social Sciences, 87–103. Kunming: Yunnan minzu chubanshe.

Warren, James Francis. 2007. *Pirates, Prostitutes and Pullers: Explorations in the Ethnohistory and Social History of Southeast Asia*. Quezon City: New Day Publishers.

Waterson, Roxana. 2007. "Introduction: Analyzing Personal Narratives." In *Southeast Asian Lives: Personal Narratives and Historical Experience*, edited by Roxana Waterson, 1–37. Singapore: NUS Press.

Watson, Lawrence C., and Maria-Barbara Watson-Franke. 1985. *Interpreting Life Histories*. New Brunswick, NJ: Rutgers University Press.

Wickberg, Edgar. 1965. *The Chinese in Philippine Life, 1850–1898*. New Haven, CT: Yale University Press.

Wiens, Herold J. 1954. *China's March toward the Tropics: A Discussion of the Southward Penetration of China's Culture, Peoples, and Political Control in Relation to the Non-Han-Chinese Peoples of South China and in the Perspective of Historical and Cultural Geography*. Hamden, CT: Shoe Strings Press.

Wilson, Tamar Diana. 2009. *Women's Migration Networks in Mexico and Beyond*. Albuquerque: University of New Mexico Press.

Wilson, Trevor, ed. 2006. *Myanmar's Long Road to National Reconciliation*. Singapore: Institute of Southeast Asian Studies.

Woods, Kevin. 2011. "Rubber Planting and Military-State Making: Military-Private Partnerships in Northern Burma." New Mandala. http://asiapacific.anu.edu.au/newmandala/2011/02/04/rubber-planting-and-military-state-making-military-private-partnerships-in-northern-burma/.

———. 2012. "Ceasefire Capitalism: Military–Private Partnerships, Resource Concessions and Military-State Building in the Burma-China Borderlands." *Journal of Peasant Studies* 38, no. 4: 747–70.

Wu Xingnan. 2002. *Yunnan duiwai maoyishi* (External trading history of Yunnan). Kunming: Yunnan daxue chubanshe.

Wu Zheliang and Cun Zhenhua. 2007a. "Dierci shijie dazhanqian de yunnan huiguan shilyue" (A brief history of the Yunnanese Association before the Second World War). In *Miandian mandele wacheng yunnan huiguan shilyue* (History of the Yunnanese Association in Mandalay), edited by Yunnan wacheng tongxianghui, 65–68. Mandalay: Wacheng yunnan tongxianghui.

———. 2007b. "Dongmiu guanyinsi shilyu" (A brief history of the Dongmiu Guanyin Temple). In *Miandian mandele wacheng yunnan huiguan shilyue* (History of the Yunnanese Association in Mandalay), edited by Yunnan wacheng tongxianghui, 41–53. Mandalay: Wacheng yunnan tongxianhui.

Xia Guangnan. 1948. *Zhong yin mian dao jiaotong shi* (History of traffic between China, India, and Burma). Shanghai: Zhonghua shuju.

Yang, Bin. 2008. *Between Winds and Clouds: The Making of Yunnan (Second Century BCE–Twentieth Century CE)*. New York: Columbia University Press.

Yang, C. K. 1994. *Religion in Chinese Society: A Study of Contemporary Social Functions of Religion and Some of Their Historical Factors*. Taipei: SMC Publishing.

Yang, Li. 1997. *The House of Yang: Guardians of an Unknown Frontier*. Sydney: Bookpress.
Yang, Mayfair Mei-hui. 1994. *Gifts, Favors, and Banquets: The Art of Social Relationships in China*. Ithaca, NY: Cornell University Press.
Yang Zhaojun et al., eds. 1994. *Yunnan huizushi* (History of the Yunnanese Muslims). Kunming: Yunnan renmin chubanshe.
Yegar, Moshe. 1966. "The Panthay (Chinese Muslims) of Burma and Yunnan." *Journal of Southeast Asian History* 7, no. 1: 73–85.
———. 1982. "The Muslims of Burma." In *The Crescent in the East: Islam in Asia Major*, edited by Raphael Israeli, 102–39. London: Curzon Press.
Yeni. 2009. "When Good News Goes Bad." *Irrawaddy*, April 27.
Yin Wenhe. 1984. "Yunnan han heshun qiaoxiangshi gaishu" (A general migration history of Heshun). *Yunnansheng lishi yanjiusuo jikan*, no. 2: 273–301.
You Zhong. 1994. *Yunnan minzushi* (History of Yunnan). Kunming: Yunnan daxue chubanshe.
Young, Kenneth Ray. 1970. "Nationalist Chinese Troops in Burma: Obstacle in Burma's Foreign Relations, 1949–1961." PhD dissertation, New York University.
Yu Dingbang. 2000. *Zhongmian guanxishi* (Sino-Burmese diplomatic history). Beijing: Guangming ribao chubanshe.
Zaman, Muhammad Qasim. 2005. "The Scope and Limits of Islamic Cosmopolitanism and the Discursive Language of the 'Ulama.'" In *Muslim Networks from Hajj to Hip Hop*, edited by miriam cooke and Bruce B. Lawrence, 84–104. Chapel Hill: University of North Carolina Press.
Zeng Yi (Ministry of Defense, Republic of China). 1964. *Dianmian bianqu youji zhanshi* (History of guerrilla wars in the Sino-Burmese border areas). 2 vols. Taipei: Guofangbu shizheng bianyinju.

Index

Locators in *italic* indicate figures.

Abu-Lughod, Lila, 47–48
Ae Maew (narrator), 46–48, 97, 107, 139n36, 188, 194, 195; Chinese education, 60–62; drug addiction in family, 71–72, 75; family history and conflicts, 51–55, 63–79, 164; family's flight to Burma, 54–55, 64–66; memories of mules and horses, 48–50; migration to Taiwan, 62, 74, 76, 112, 214; sentiments toward Burma, 58; subjectivity of, 47, 58; at Taunggyi University, 60–63; work experience, 59–60, 62
anticommunism, 31–32, 35, 43
Appadurai, Arjun, 215
Arab countries, 133–36
armed ethnic groups: alliances and power structures, 96, 108, 156; and civilians, 93–94, 98; as escorts for mule caravans, 89–90, 151–52, 155–56, 158–61, 163, 166, 218; ruby trade, 107–9. *See also* Khun Sa's army; KKY; KMT
ASEAN (Association of Southeast Asian Nations), 27
Association of Mutual Help, 130

Bangkok, 101–5
Baud, Michiel, 175
Behar, Ruth, 77
Bhabha, Homi, 138
Bianliang, 30–31, 151
Bianliang Revival Elementary School, 28–31, 37
birth control and abortion, 193–94
black market, 98, 150, 153, 160–62, 167, 169, 173–74, 181. *See also* smuggling; underground trade
Bogyoke Aung San, 41n15

Index

borderlands, 12–15; as barbarous, 5, 16, 55, 84, 173
bribery, 160, 169, 190–91, 202–4
British colonial rule, 4, 6, 83n9, 116, 124, 127
Buddhism, 68–69, 114
Burma: ban on Chinese education, 85n12, 92; ban on transnational trade, 151, 156; bribery and corruption of government officials, 160, 169, 190–91, 202–4, 232n20, 244; economic policies, 7, 209, 244; ethnic groups, 38, 57, 118, 244; international economic sanctions on, 232–33; military junta, 7, 9, 209, 221–22; natural resources, 167, 184; socialist period, 6–7, 150, 171–72, 175. *See also* Communist Party of Burma (CPB); Ne Win regime
Burma Road, 178, 243n5
Burmese army, 91, 155, 161, 163, 232n20
Burmese Muslims, 114

Cantonese migrants. *See* Guangdong (Cantonese) migrants
center and periphery, 12–15, 174–75, 244
Changqingshan, 82, 85–86, 88, 91–92, 95, 108
Chao Tzang Yawnghwe, 89
Chaozhou (Teochiu), 231
Chiang Ching-kuo, 85
Chiang Kai-shek, 31, 85, 141n41
Chiang Mai, 103, 105, 167, 170, 224, 227, 233
Chinese, overseas/maritime, 8, 17, 56–57
Chinese Communism, 5, 24, 31–32, 35, 64, 84, 200, 216
Chinese culture, maintenance of, 27–28, 31–32, 56–57
Chinese education, 24, 28–30, 32, 37–39, 60–62, 66–69, 85, 85n12, 92
Chinese merchandise, 167, 184, 191
Chinese Muslims, 115, 125. *See also* Muslims, Yunnanese
Chinese Nationalist Party, 68n, 85, 122. *See also* KMT
Chinese New Year celebrations, 72–74
Christianity, 66, 71, 73–74
circulation, 210, 233–36
Clifford, James, 16, 175
Cold War period, 2, 31, 85n11, 97
Colson, Elizabeth, 27

Communist Party of Burma (CPB), 33–34, 38, 90–91, 93–96, 156
confiscated goods, 114, 160, 167, 190–92
Confucianism, 31–32, 56, 68–69, 124, 125n19, 134–35
cross-border trade: history of, 4–5; Sino-Burmese, 8n10, 179, 184, 243; Thai-Burmese, 6, 16–17, 31, 35, 70, 126n, 150, 166, 172–75, 216, 218, 220; water routes between Burma and Thailand, 168–72; Yunnan-Burmese, 22, 70, 150, 167, 220. *See also* mule caravans
Cultural Revolution, 32

Dagudi (Ban Arunotai), 99–100
Dajie (narrator), 189–93
Dali Sultanate, 120n8
Dashuitang, 82, 86
Dayaks in Kalimantan, 12, 32, 97, 173, 244
demonetization of Burmese kyat, 60, 70, 167, 210
distilleries, 197, 202–4
drug addiction, 70, 71–72, 75, 101, 179, 181
drug trafficking, 31, 89, 94, 103; international pressure against, 91n18, 156. *See also* opium trade
Duan family: in jade trade, 210–23, 225, 229, 233; kinship ties, 207–8, 225; Mr. Duan, 216–18, 229; Mrs. Duan, 220–22, 235; in Taiwan, 211, 214
Duan Xiwen, General, 30, 89, 94n
Du Wenxiu, 120

education. *See* Chinese education; Muslim education
elopement, 181, 187, 195, 196
Erjie (narrator), 189–93
ethnic groups and conflicts, 38, 57, 92–93, 97, 118, 244. *See also* armed ethnic groups
Ethnic Kokang Cultural Association, 83, 84–85, 87–88, 98

food: businesses, 190, 193, 200–201; cultural aspects, 102, 135–36, 140–42; in mule caravans, 151–52, 154; at traditional festivals, 26, 28; Yunnanese cooking, 179–81
Forbes, Andrew D. W., 124, 126
frictions, 12, 32, 44, 48, 76, 97, 138, 143, 173–74, 178, 244

Fujianese migrants, 56–57, 71, 101, 154n, 171–72, 186, 217

gambling, 52, 71, 144, 167, 198; on value of jade stones, 218–19, 227–28
gem trade, 109, 126, 131, 197, 214, 232, 233n, 243. *See also* jade trade; ruby trade
gender: in business and trade, 16–17, 178, 192–93; and division of labor, 194; and familial devotion and economic involvement, 26–28, 197–99, 205–6; inequality, 52, 77, 188, 193, 198; and migration, 185–88; role in fieldwork, 10–11. *See also* men; patriarchy; women
Gengma, 82–83
Giersch, C. Patterson, 14, 126n, 235
gold bars, trade of, 155
Guangdong (Cantonese) migrants, 56–57, 138n, 186, 217–18, 220
Guangzhou, 17, 207–8, 212–14, 229, 232–33
Guoguang (narrator), 80, 102, 111–12; on ethnic conflicts, 92–93; family life, 86–87, 111; on fighting in Shan State, 92–94; friendships and kinship bonds, 101, 105–7; journey to Thailand, 98–100; migration to Taiwan, 87, 105, 110–11, 139; work experiences, 86–87, 100–105, 110–11
Guowen Chinese School, 37–39

Hajj pilgrimage, 115, 124
Hanafi school of Sunni Islam, 117
Han Chinese identity, 84, 125–26
heroin, 101, 103
Heshun, 176n2
Hill, Ann Maxwell, 2–3, 126n
hmaungko market. *See* black market
Hong Kong: Chinese textbooks from, 85n12; jade trade, 17, 207–8, 213, 233
Hpakant, 183–84, 202, 209n2, 210, 212, 217–18, 224n, 234–35
Hsu, Francis L. K., 205n
hui (rotating credit), 184–85
Hui Muslims, 115, 117, 121–26. *See also* Muslims, Yunnanese

Imam Bao (narrator), 134, 136–38
Imam Liu (narrator), 134–36
Imam Ma (narrator), 134, 136–37
Imam Shan (narrator), 134–38

Indian Muslims. *See* Kala
Inle Lake, 76–78
interstitial states, 44, 58, 138
intersubjectivity, 10
Inwa Bank, 184, 234–35

jadeite, 167n21
jade markets: in Guangzhou, 208; in Mandalay, 47, 224–27; in Ruili, 209
jade mining, 70, 192, 212; environmental impact of, 223–24; excavators, 223, 235; government concessions, sale of, 110, 189, 222–23; by Kachins and Shans, 217–18; Yunnanese bosses, 223
jade stones: demand for, 207; export of, 229; products of, 212–14, 231–32; quality of, 218–19, 223, 227–29, 234; sale to foreign buyers, 229; "social lives" of, 215; taxes on, 216–17, 223–25, 229–30, 235
jade trade, 17, 86, 129, 151, 162–63, 167–68, 197, 217, 232; auctions, 227, 230; brokerage services, 224–25, 230; Burmese government ban on, 219–20, 224, 227–28, 232; in Chiang Mai, 224, 227, 233; circulation in, 210, 230, 233–36; companies, 215, 224–27; Duan and Peng families, 210–23, 225, 229, 233; foreign exchange certificates (FEC), 229n15; in Guangzhou, 17, 207–8, 212–14, 229, 232–33; Karen porters, 171–72; kinship networks, 214–15, 236; local links, 215; nationalized, 210, 216; overview of, 207–10; risks of, 210, 219; routes, 156, 159; smuggling, 219–20, 229, 231; women in, 220–22
Japan: invasion of Burma, 122, 129; tourist visas, 139–41; Yunnanese Muslim guest workers, 138–44
Jieyang jade traders, 230–32
Jin Yong, 60, 157

Kachin Independence Army (KIA), 216–17, 219, 232n20, 233
Kachin Independence Organization (KIO), 222
Kachin State: jade mines, 209, 212; military groups, 155
Kala (Indian Muslims), 97, 114, 118n4, 123, 124, 130, 132, 163
Karenni insurgents, 168–71

Kengtung, 39, 116, 118, 122, 158
Keyes, Charles F., 187
Khoo Thwe, Pascal, 28, 44–45
Khun Sa's army, 93–94, 96, 156, 163, 166, 172
kinship ties, 101, 105–7, 188, 207–8, 214–15, 225, 236
KKY (Ka Kwe Ye) (People's Volunteer Force), 80, 86, 90–95, 108, 155–56, 160
KMT (Kuomintang), 26, 55, 62, 64, 68, 94; anticommunism, 31, 216; disbanding of, 5n7, 30–31; Fifth Army, 30–31, 90, 96; fighting with Communist Party of Burma (CPB), 33–34; history of, 5–6; mule caravan trade, 26, 155–56, 158–61, 166; support for businesses, 199, 204; Taiwan Nationalist government support of, 5, 30; between Thailand and Burma, 6, 160; villages on Thai border, 166–67
KMT (Kuomintang) Third Army, 24, 30–31, 64, 85–86, 89–92, 96, 122; collaboration in jade trade, 217; escort of caravans, 89–90, 151–52, 155; in northern Thailand, 21, 168; smuggled arms, 94; solidarity in, 106; trading post in Bianliang, 30–31
Kokang (Guogan): history of, 82–85, 88–89; male subjectivity, 112–13; migration from, 220; military forces, 90–92, 155; opium production, 152–53; population in Burma, 83n5
Kunming, 122, 208
Kutkai, 35, 64, 91, 196–98
Kyawdalon, 160–61

Laikha, 46, 48, 51, 55, 59–60, 65, 71
Lashio, 22, 37–39, 43, 85, 96, 160, 178–79, 181–82
Leach, E. R., 13–14, 156
Lessinger, Johanna, 187
Li, Mr. (narrator), 169; family history, 82–85, 108–9; family migrations, 96–97; involvement in trade, 94–97; in KKY (Ka Kwe Ye) force, 80, 86, 94–96, 108; leadership and accomplishments, 81, 86, 95–96, 108, 112–13; military life, 88–92, 107–8, 156; mining businesses, 107–10; social connections, 87–88; in Taunggyi, 109

Li Dage (narrator), 238–42
Li Mi, 5
Li Wenhuan, 30, 89–90, 94, 122, 172
loan-bidding associations, 184–85
Loikaw, 168–71
Loilin, 40–41, 93, 97, 98
long-distance trade, 2–4, 43, 113, 175, 243; women in, 177, 186, 188; Yunnanese Muslims in, 116, 126. *See also* cross-border trade; mule caravans; underground trade
Longling, 24, 64
Lunggang Mosque, Chungli, 137
Luo Xinghan, 83, 95–96, 108

Mae Hongson, 168–71
Mae Sai, 65, 71, 103–4, 158
mahjong, 179, 182, 184, 204, 227
Mahler, Sarah J., 185–86
Mahmood, Saba, 206
Maliba, 83n9, 84. *See also* Kokang
Mandalay: black market trade, 160, 162; jade market, 212, 224–25; population of, 196; underground banking, 183; Yunnanese immigration, 46–47
Mandaville, Peter, 137–38
marginality, 9, 16, 114–15, 138, 143–44, 173, 242
Markovits, Claude, 210
marriage, 142–44, 181, 187, 195–96; women "stolen" for, 99, 196; Yunnanese Muslims, 123–24, 126, 132, 142–44
Massey, Douglas B., 150
Ma Yeye (narrator), 118–24, 133
Maymyo. *See* Pyin U Lwin
men: cross-border migration as rite of passage, 113, 150; exploring the world, 24, 112, 205; as migrant workers, 139–40; mistresses of, 198–99; subjectivity, 112–13
migrants. *See* Yunnanese migrants in Burma
migration, risks of illegal, 105n
militia groups. *See* armed ethnic groups
Ming dynasty, 3–4, 82, 83, 84, 231n
mobility, 2, 17, 157, 174, 233, 237–38, 242
Mogaung, 216–17
Mogok, 132
Mohnyin, 162
money lending businesses. *See* underground banking

money transfers, international, 233
Mong Hsu, 60, 107–9, 182, 202
Mong Nai, 91, 93
Mongols, 3, 116, 125
Mongton, 99–100
Mong Zhang, 33–34
monosodium glutamate, 70, 170, 181, 191
mother-daughter identification, 205
Mount Loijie, 159–60
Mu Dadie (narrator), 127–33
mule caravans, 149–67, 238–42; armed ethnic group escorts, 89–90, 151–52, 155–56, 158–61, 163, 166, 218; difficulties of, 42–43; distance, metaphors for, 154–55; female roles in, 50; history of, 3–5, 149–50, 175; and KKY forces, 155–56, 160; and KMT forces, 26, 155–56, 158–61, 166; leaders, responsibilities of, 153–54; mountain routes, 149, 154, 161, 166; "mule caravan culture," 149; organizational structure, 153–54; overstaying in communities, 163–64; in rainy season, 166, 170; risks of, 161–64; river crossings, 159; size of, 152; sociocultural meaning of, 151–52, 157; trade routes, 156, 158–62, 243; use of public roads, 161; worship of mountain gods, 154–55. *See also* cross-border trade; smuggling; underground trade
mules: riding on, 240–41, *241*; villagers' care of, 48–50, 155, 239–42
muleteers, 151–54, 158–62, 176n1
Muse, 178, 243
Muslim education, 129–32
Muslim Rebellion (1856–1873), 5n5, 116, 118, 120–21, 125n18, 145
Muslims, Yunnanese: and Chinese culture, 124, 126, 133–34; discrimination against in Burma, 132–33, 139–40, 145; as guest workers, 138–42; history of, 116–18; identity, 143–44; intermarriage, 123–24, 126, 142–44; intra-group marriage, 132, 144; Islamic communities in Taiwan, 136–38; Islamic culture and cohesiveness, 126, 130–33, 144–45; Islamic transnationalism, 115, 133–38, 144–45; in long-distance trade, 116, 126; marginality of, 114–15, 138, 143; migration history, 16, 115, 145; mosques, 116n, *117*, 118, *119*, 129–30; in Panglong, 120–26, 129; in Pyin U Lwin, 127–33, 139–40, 142; *qingzhen* (halal food), 140, 142; studies in the Middle East, 132–36. *See also* Chinese Muslims; Hui Muslims; Kala (Indian Muslims)
Myawaddy-Mae Sot, 171

Nakhan, 92, 96–97
Nanjing Yingtianfu, 82, 84
nation-state, political ideology of, 12, 175, 244
Nawan, 160, 161n13
Naypyidaw, 227, 230, 232
nephrite, 167n21
Ne Win regime, 6, 89, 116, 123, 138n, 178, 216

opium: harvesting, 189; production, 26, 83, 90–91, 152–53
opium trade, 5n5, 31, 151, 155, 162; military participation in, 89–91, 94–95, 97–98

Panghsang, 159
Panglong, 120–26, 129
Panthay, use of term, 115, 123, 125. *See also* Muslims, Yunnanese
Pa-O (Taungthu/Dongsu), 57, 160
pao mabang (border trade by mule caravans), 190. *See also* mule caravans
pao shengyi (border trade by vehicle), 190. *See also* vehicles
patriarchy, 77, 188, 198–99, 205–6, 222
Payathonsu-Sangkhla Buri, 171
Peng family: in jade trade, 210–22, 210–23, 225, 229, 233; kinship ties, 207–8, 225; move to Taiwan, 211; Mr. Peng, 218–20, 229; Mrs. Peng, 220–22
Peng Jiasheng, 108
Pengxian, 218
periphery, 114–15, 194, 242–44; center and, 12–15, 174–75, 244
personal narrative approach to research, 9–12, 18, 88
Pessar, Patricia R., 185–86
phenomenology, 48
Piang Luang, 159–60
Pingzhou, 213–14, 230
Pinlong, 41, 51, 55, 161n12, 165
poppy farming, 189. *See also* opium

Index

popular realm *(minjian)*, 174–75
Portelli, Alessandro, 18
positionality in ethnographies, 47
Pouchepadass, Jacques, 210
propaganda, 32, 68n
Pyin U Lwin, 127–33, 139–40, 142

Qing period, 4, 120n8, 231
qingzhen (halal food), 140, 142
Qiong Yao, 60, 157
Qiu Dajie (narrator), 178–88

refugees: flight of, 22–23, 54–55, 64–66, 93–94; self-identity, 28
Republic of China, national flag of, 29, 31
Reshuitang Xincun. *See* Xincun
robbery, 109, 166, 182, 191, 200, 219, 234
Rohingyas, 114
Rosaldo, Renato, 13
rotating markets, 164–65
Rouse, Roger, 174
routes: jade trade, 156, 209; mountainous, 149, 154, 161, 166; mule caravans, 156, 158–62, 243; between Taunggyi and Loilin, 98; Thai-Burmese trade by water, 168–72; of Yunnanese refugees to Shan State, 22–23
ruby mines, 30n10, 60, 107–9, 203
ruby trade, 71, 107, 196; women in, 60, 182–83, 188
Ruili, 167, 182, 184, 191, 208, 217n8, 243

"sacrificial motherhood," 187, 193, 197
Saffron Revolution (2007), 9
Sai Kham Mong, 91n19, 93
Salween River, 152, 158, 170; caravan crossings, 159
Scudder, Thayer, 27
Seligman, Linda J., 177–78, 187
Shans: language, 169, 217; perceptions of, 57, 163, 195n18
Shan State: fighting between military forces, 89–96; history of, 81, 243; military groups, 155, 163
Shan United Revolutionary Army, 81n3, 94n, 161n12
short-distance trade, 158, 164–65
Shuli (narrator), 138–44; family, 140; subjectivity and marginality, 143–44

Sinocentrism, 37, 43, 84
smuggling, 6, 42, 98, 150, 160, 165–67, 169, 172, 174, 184, 190; jade, 219–20, 229, 231
social connections *(guanxi)*, 25, 87–88, 107, 112–13, 174
Sturgeon, Janet C., 14
subjectivity, 11, 13, 16, 47–48, 58, 112–13, 143–44, 199
Subrahmanyam, Sanjay, 210
Sun, Laichen, 83n6, 126n
Sun Yat-sen, 29, 31, 68n
Syria, 131, 134–35, 137

taboos, observance of, 154–55
Tachileik, 158, 182–83, 190
Tai Khoen, 116
Tai Lue, 116
Tai principalities and kingdoms, 116
Taiwan: citizenship, 62, 111, 139, 140n39; guest workers, 139; Intelligence Mainland Operation Bureau (Division 1920), 30, 200; Islamic communities in, 136–38; jade consumption, 211; migration to, 24, 39, 43, 62, 74, 76, 87, 105, 110–12, 138–39, 179, 211, 214; Muslim Association, 131; Nationalist government support of KMT, 5, 30; prejudice against Burmese, 141; textbooks from, 85
Tangge (narrator): family, 66; in jade trade, 167–68, 220; migration to Burma, 64; in mule caravan trade, 166–67; trade in rotating markets, 164–65; trade to Yunnan, 220
Tangyan, 23, 122, 129, 132, 152, 158; as center of black market trade, 160
Tao Yuanming, 44
Tarmoenye, 196
Taunggyi, 35, 36–37, 39, 43, 50–57, 54, 60, 109, 189; black market trade, 98, 160–61, 162; stores in, 165–66, 202
Taunggyi University, 60–63
taxes, underground, 192; on jade mining, 216; for smuggled commodities, 155, 160
Tengchong, 54–55, 64, 120, 158, 164, 167, 176n2
textiles, 155, 166, 167, 216
Thai Border Patrol Police (BPP), 166–67

Thailand: border villages, 65; commodities, 70, 153, 155, 165–66, 171; and KMT, 6, 21, 160, 168; legal status, 217; nation-building, 14; passports, 105, 110, 140; textiles, 155, 166, 216; water trade routes to Burma, 168–72; Yunnanese migrants in, 6, 39–43, 98–100, 105
Thein Sein government, 115n
Thongchai Winichakul, 14, 174, 244
Three Pagodas Pass, 172
Three Principles of the People, 68
trade. *See* cross-border trade; jade trade; mule caravans; routes; ruby trade; underground trade
transborder/transnational perspective of analysis, 12–15
"transmigrants," 25
transportation, 17, 72, 100n, 105n32, 116, 129, 171, 214–15, 237, 243. *See also* mule caravans; mules; vehicles
travel: importance of, 2–3. *See also* mobility
trucks, Burmese government, 39–40, 190
Tsing, Anna, 12, 32, 38, 76, 97, 173, 178, 243–44

underground banking, 183–84, 202, 234–35
underground trade, 94–95, 150, 160, 169, 190–92. *See also* black market; smuggling
Union of Myanmar Economic Holding Company Ltd., 228
United Nations resolution on KMT, 5n7
United States: opposition to narcotics trade, 156n6; sanctions on Burma, 228n, 232, 233n; support of KMT, 5
Uru River, 209n2, 224n

van Schendel, Willem, 12, 13, 175, 242n
vehicles: transport of civilians, 39–40; used in caravan trade, 159; used in trade, 171, 190–91

Walker, Andrew, 14
Wa region, 120–21, 126, 156, 163, 199, 204
water trade routes between Burma and Thailand, 168–72
weapons, 33–34, 43, 94, 121, 155

women, economic activities of, 177–79, 181–95, 197–205; and autonomy, 177, 184, 188, 195; in border trade by trucks/cars, 190–91; and emotional support, 194; entrepreneurship, 200–204; familial obligations and sacrificial motherhood, 26–27, 77, 177, 179, 186–87, 192–93, 195, 197–200, 205–6, 222; indigenous participation in trade, 194; in jade trade, 220–22; in long-distance trade, 177, 186, 188; in money-carrying business, 183–84, 234; in restaurant business, 200–201; risk-taking by, 183–84, 186; in rotating markets, 200; and self-fulfillment, 186, 195; selling at markets, 181, 190, 193; as transgression of borders, 194; work in Japan, 139
World War II, 122, 124, 129

Xincun (Reshuitang Xincun; Ban Mai Nongbour), 21, 41, 92, 158, 167
Xue Dashen (narrator), 195–99
Xunding, 41, 161, 166

Yang, Mayfair, 174–75
Yangmeicun, 230–32
Yangon, jade trade in, 212, 227–30, *228*, 232
Yaowarat (Chinatown in Bangkok), 102
Yegar, Moshe, 124, 126
Yongli, Emperor, 83, 84
Yuan dynasty, 3–4
Yue Dashu (narrator), 158–64
Yunnan: Chinese conquest of, 3, 84; cross-border trade with Burma, 22, 70, 150, 167, 220, 223; ethnic groups in, 4; Han Chinese immigration, 3–4, 84, 120n8; history of overland migration, 3–8, 15–18; Muslim immigration, 3–4
Yunnanese Association, 47, 178, 196, 201
Yunnanese migrants in Burma: after 1949 Chinese Communist takeover, 5, 8, 24, 64, 84, 216; economic agency of, 164, 173–75, 237; external instability, responses to, 32, 173; kinship, social networks, and territorial bonds, 105–7, 188, 236; marginality of, 9, 16, 114–15, 138, 143–44, 173, 242; personal narratives of, 1–2, 9–12, 15–16; religion, 56, 154–55;

Yunnanese migrants in Burma *(continued)* risk-taking in illegal business, 57, 164, 173; rural to urban migration, 5; sentiments toward Burma, 58; social status and class, fluidity of, 17; transnational popular realm, 173–75; xenophobic backlash against, 7, 244

Yunnanese Muslims. *See* Muslims, Yunnanese

Yunnanese villages, Thai names of, 23n

Yunnanese women. *See* women, economic activities of

Zhang Dage (narrator), 9, 80, 97, 235, 237; ambivalence as diasporan, 43–45; Burmese education, 37–38; childhood experiences, 24, 27–36; Chinese education, 24, 28–30, 37–39; Facebook page for migrant Yunnanese, 25; family burial plot, 22–23; family migration to Taunggyi, 36–37, 39, 43; family photograph, 29; friendships and Yunnanese intra-group bonds, 105–6; home, question of, 25–26, 43–45; migrations, 21, 24, 35–36, 37–39, 43; migration to Taiwan, 24, 39, 43, 112; migration to Thailand, 39–43; on mule caravan trade, 151–58, 238–42; nostalgia for Burma, 34–36, 45; pursuit of a better life, 43; in Taiwan, 214

Zhang Qian, 3

Zhao Dashu (narrator), 168–72, 217

Zhen Guang Arabic School, 130–32

Zhenkang, 82–83

Zhou Dajie (narrator), 157, 199–205